TOXIC RELATIONSHIPS
AND
HOW TO CHANGE THEM

TOXIC RELATIONSHIPS
AND
HOW TO CHANGE THEM

Health and Holiness in Everyday Life

Clinton W. McLemore, Ph.D.

JOSSEY-BASS
A Wiley Imprint
www.josseybass.com

Published by Jossey-Bass
A Wiley Imprint
989 Market Street, San Francisco, CA 94103-1741   www.josseybass.com

Jossey-Bass books and products are available through most bookstores. To contact Jossey-Bass directly call our Customer Care Department within the U.S. at 800-956-7739, outside the U.S. at 317-572-3986, or fax 317-572-4002.

Jossey-Bass also publishes its books in a variety of electronic formats. Some content that appears in print may not be available in electronic books.

Library of Congress Cataloging-in-Publication Data

McLemore, Clinton W., date.
  Toxic relationships and how to change them : health and holiness in everyday life / Clinton McLemore, foreword by Les Parrott.—1st ed.
      p.   cm.
Includes bibliographical references and index.
    ISBN 0-7879-6877-3 (alk. paper)
    1. Interpersonal relations—Religious aspects—Christianity.   I. Title.
    BV4597.52.M43   2003
    248.4—dc21   2003008454

Printed in the United States of America
FIRST EDITION
HB Printing   10 9 8 7 6 5 4 3 2 1

To my son Gregory C. McLemore

of whom I am extremely proud

CONTENTS

List of Illustrations   xi
Foreword by Les Parrott, Ph.D.   xiii
Matters of the Heart   xv
Introduction   1

PART ONE
Relationships as God Intends

1. The Spiritual Significance of Everyday Life: A Brief Theology
   of Relationships   5
2. Foundations of Health and Holiness   18

PART TWO
How People Train Each Other

3. Making Sense of Everyday Behavior   35
4. Modes and Styles of Ordinary Interaction   52
5. The Hidden Rules of Human Relationships   67
6. Overview of Interpersonal Toxicity   82

PART THREE
Eight Ways of Disappointing the Father

7. Controlling: Bossing and Ordering   103
   "Beware the leaven of the Pharisees" (Matthew 16:5)
8. Drifting: Obeying and Conforming   119
   "Solomon, whose heart had strayed, turned toward other gods"(1 Kings 11:4)

9. Intruding: Crowding and Smothering   136
   *"God was harsh with Job's advisors, whose advice had been
   false" (Job 42:7)*
10. Freeloading: Clinging and Depleting   155
   "Those who will not work shall not eat" (2 Thessalonians 3:10)
11. Humiliating: Demeaning and Belittling   172
   *"When Hagar became pregnant, she despised her mistress
   Sarai" (Genesis 16:4)*
12. Scurrying: Whining and Appeasing   190
   *"'Woman,' anxiously protested Peter, 'I do not know the
   man'" (Luke 22:57)*
13. Victimizing: Injuring and Exploiting   208
   *"His brothers spotted Joseph a long way off and conspired
   to kill him" (Genesis 37:18)*
14. Avoiding: Withdrawing and Rebelling   225
   *"But instead of going to confront Nineveh, Jonah decided
   to run away"(Jonah 1:3)*

PART FOUR
Toward Relational Health and Holiness

15. Three Myths About Behavior Change   245
16. Getting Out of Your Own Way   251
17. Some Final Thoughts on Changing Others   262

Sources and Recommended Reading   265
The Author   267
Index   269

LIST OF ILLUSTRATIONS

Figure 3.1. Two Primary Features ("Dimensions") of Interpersonal
Behavior   40

Table 3.1. Behavioral Combinations Implied by Figure 3.1   46

Figure 3.2. Behavioral Implications of Different Interpersonal
Postures   41

Figure 4.1. Four Conventional Modes of Relating to Other People   54

Figure 4.2. Interpersonal Strategies Corresponding to the
Four Conventional Modes of Relating   55

Figure 4.3. Eight Conventional Styles of Relating to Other People   57

Figure 4.4. Tactics Associated with Each of the Eight Conventional
Styles of Relating to Others   61

Figure 4.5. Conventional Modes, Strategies, Styles, and Tactics   65

Figure 5.1. How the Four Conventional Modes of Relating Invite
and Reinforce Each Other   77

Figure 5.2. How the Eight Conventional Styles Invite and Reinforce
Each Other   78

Figure 5.3. How the Tactics of Conventional Styles Invite and
Reinforce Each Other   79

Figure 6.1. Four Toxic Modes of Relating to Other People   86

Figure 6.2. Interpersonal Strategies Corresponding to the Four
Toxic Modes of Relating   89

Figure 6.3. Eight Toxic Styles of Relating to Other People   89

Figure 6.4. Tactics Associated with Each of the Eight Toxic Styles
of Relating to Others   90

Figure 6.5. Toxic Modes, Strategies, Styles, and Tactics   91

Figure 6.6. How the Four Toxic Modes of Relating Invite and
Reinforce Each Other   92

Figure 6.7. How the Eight Toxic Styles Invite and Reinforce
Each Other   92

Figure 6.8. How the Tactics of Toxic Styles Invite and Reinforce
Each Other   93

Figure 6.9. Conventional (Inner) and Toxic (Outer) Styles of
Relating to Other People   96

Figure 6.10. Personality Types Corresponding to the Eight Toxic
    Default Styles   99
Exhibit 7.1. Profile of the Controller   104
Exhibit 8.1. Profile of the Drifter   120
Exhibit 9.1. Profile of the Intruder   137
Exhibit 10.1. Profile of the Freeloader   156
Exhibit 11.1. Profile of the Humiliator   174
Exhibit 12.1. Profile of the Scurrier   192
Exhibit 13.1. Profile of the Victimizer   210
Exhibit 14.1. Profile of the Avoider   227

FOREWORD

NOTHING REACHES SO DEEPLY into the human personality or tugs so tightly as relationship. Why? For one reason, it is only in the context of connection with others that our deepest needs can be met. Whether we like it or not, each of us has an unshakable dependence on others. It's what philosopher John Donne was getting at when he said so succinctly, "No man is an island." We need camaraderie, affection, love. These are not options in life, or sentimental trimmings; they are part of our species' survival kit. We *need* to belong.

Social scientists call our longing for belonging assimilation, affiliation, or social webbing. Others call it fellowship, connecting, or relating. Whatever it's called, everyone agrees that we are born with an insatiable inner need for meaningful interaction with others. And everyone also agrees that this drive holds the potential to breed unhealthy relationships that are downright toxic.

While some relationships run smoothly, only hitting temporary turbulence from time to time, others aren't as easy. They require an inordinate amount of effort, and they can eat up extraordinary amounts of time. These toxic relationships make life more difficult than it needs to be. Whether it be through over-control, freeloading, humiliation, or victimizing, they can cause even the strongest among us to consider fleeing from people altogether. In those tumultuous times we may fantasize about the life of Daniel Defoe's Robinson Crusoe living alone on a desert island away from toxic people. Paradise? Only in fantasy. Consider the reality check Defoe offers in another of his writings: "I won't sink the ship. In fact, in time of storm I'll do my best to save it. You see, we are all in this craft and must sink or swim together."

That's the rub. We *are* all in this together. Our emotional and spiritual health depends, in great part, on how well we relate to even the most difficult people around us. We sink or swim depending upon how well we develop our relational acumen and skill. That's why it brings me great joy to see *Toxic Relationships and How to Change Them*. In these pages, Clinton McLemore has given us the navigational charts to cross even the most tumultuous relational waters. He means business. This is not a cute, pop-psych book trying to pass along snappy slogans as solutions. No. Clinton has plunged the depths for a thorough understanding of how we can find health and holiness in our everyday relationships. His thoughtful model of interpersonal understanding is rooted deeply in scripture. It is perhaps the first theology of relationships ever articulated with such sophistication. You hold in your hands a book that is conceptually sound, immensely applicable, and extremely rewarding.

I recently had dinner with a man I respect and asked him if he had read any good books lately. "I don't have time for good books," he replied, "only great ones." Of course I asked the obvious question: *What makes a book great?* He said that a great book is normally not an author's early work but rather one he has been writing and rewriting, tuning and tweaking for decades. *Toxic Relationships and How to Change Them* is such a book. It represents a life's work. This book was not an idea out of the blue that the author had one day while talking with a publisher. It has been in development for decades. How do I know? Because I first heard some of Dr. McLemore's thinking on the subject nearly twenty years ago as a graduate student in one of his classes. It was powerful then and even more powerful today.

You don't have to let toxic personalities take control of your life. You don't have to feel that your only option is a hasty exit. This book will show you a different way. Read it for all it's worth. You and your relationships will never be the same.

July 2003   Les Parrott, Ph.D.
                                               Seattle Pacific University

MATTERS OF THE HEART

IT IS MY EARNEST DESIRE that if you are already a Christian, this book will draw you even closer to God by strengthening your moment-by-moment awareness of Him in your relationships.

I also hope that if you have not yet established a living connection with God through the resurrected Christ, what I have written will inspire you to explore more thoroughly the truth-claims of Christianity. According to these claims, the beginning of wisdom for us, as mortals, is to reckon with our utter inability, apart from God, to triumph over death, successfully vanquish evil, or perfect human character.

Medicine and other forms of technology may prolong life and enhance its quality; laws and policies may promote the public good and, by implication, limit evil in its ever-mutating forms; and both education and humanitarian aid may help spread the values of civilization and, along the way, incline the masses toward benevolence as opposed to hatred. But according to Christian theology, humankind on its own will never conquer death, ensure world peace, or rid itself completely of malevolence. There is no *utopia*, a word that, literally translated, means "no place." Without God, there can be no lasting paradise, now or in the eons to come.

May the Lord of the Universe grant you life abundant and relationships infused with joy.

Acknowledgments

My wife, Anna, strongly encouraged me to return to my first professional love, which is writing, and for this I am grateful. She also read and offered excellent suggestions on each section of the manuscript as it emerged. So did our highly literate daughter, Anna-Marie, who despite her heavy academic workload at Deerfield Academy somehow found time to attend to the manuscript. Theresa Ortiz Martinez contributed valuable biblical research. And my close friend Willis B. Wood provided his usual encouragement and keen-minded insights.

Dr. J. Trevor Milliron had an indirect but important influence on the creation of this book because of a late-night conversation we had years ago, on the walkway in front of my home. My corporate consulting practice was thriving and we had just finished yet another high-intensity project. Trevor stopped abruptly, turned around, and said, "What you're doing is tragic. You should be writing your magnum opus." I have replayed that haunting conversation many times in my mind.

Mark Kerr, my editor at Jossey-Bass, was excited about this book from the beginning. His affirmation helped immensely during those long hours at the keyboard. Mark also made a number of helpful suggestions for improving the text. It has been a delight to work with two other eminently congenial and highly competent Jossey-Bass publishing professionals, Joanne Clapp Fullagar, Editorial Production Manager, and Sandra Siegle, Marketing Manager.

Pamela Harty of the Knight Literary Agency was also highly enthusiastic about this project. She is intelligent, conscientious, resourceful, energetic, proactive, and caring. What more could you ask for in an agent?

July 2003   Clinton W. McLemore

TOXIC RELATIONSHIPS
AND
HOW TO CHANGE THEM

INTRODUCTION

THIS BOOK IS FOR PEOPLE who want to understand relationships and how to improve them. It is also for those who desire to know if specific relationships are likely to change. Each of its chapters is intended to help you make better sense of what happens between human beings—often beneath the surface.

Over the past fifty years, psychologists have learned a great deal about how people act in relation to one another. In the pages to follow, I will summarize some of the most important findings to emerge from their studies. I will also strive to do this in a way that is easy to understand, practical, and perhaps, in places, entertaining. Throughout the text, you will find examples that bring the concepts to life. A good number of them are from the Bible, which is extraordinarily rich in source material. Anyone who wants to understand the nuances of interpersonal behavior is well advised to start with the book of Genesis.

Scripture, however, is more than a compendium of stories. For a Christian, it provides the ultimate standard against which all claims about relationships must be tested. While believers may differ, here and there, about certain points of interpretation, you do not need a seminary education to understand, in general, what God expects of us, not only in relation to Him, but also in relation to one another.

Yet, fallen creatures that we are, we have all sorts of ways of ignoring what scripture teaches. Or we so distort the biblical message that it is hardly recognizable. Nearly every Christian knows that we are to love God with all our hearts, minds, and souls and to love our neighbors as ourselves. Living this out—applying it in everyday life—is a lot harder than reciting it.

Loving our neighbors does not mean automatically allowing them to abuse, manipulate, or oppress us. There is a time to be soft and a time to be stern. Tough love is sometimes necessary. And so is insight. You have to know what other people are trying to do, *with* and *to* you, if you are going to enjoy life on earth to the fullest. Can you be a Christian without knowing much about how relationships work, while remaining unaware of their subtleties? Sure. Can you be a person of great faith? Yes, definitely. The question is whether you can be optimally effective.

Advances in the study of relationships over the past half-century can help us live happier and more fulfilling lives, especially if we have a dynamic relationship with God through Christ.

The principal objectives of this book are to enable you to do three things well:

○ Understand the impact you have on others and the subtle impacts they can have on you

○ Recognize when someone else is maneuvering you in a way that is toxic, both spiritually and emotionally

○ Increase your effectiveness by applying a few simple but powerful principles to all your relationships

You might think of this book as a navigation guide, because that is precisely what it is. The information it contains will help you make your way in what can sometimes feel like a raging storm. This information will help you more fully appreciate those wonderful moments of magic with other people that God generously grants you, but it will also minimize your moments of misery as you work your way through the stormier seas of life in relation to other human beings.

Different readers have different interests, so I want to make a few comments that may assist you in getting the most out of this book. Part One focuses on theology. If you want to explore what scripture reveals about relationships, read Chapter One, and if you are interested in how psychological well-being and Christian holiness relate to each other, go to Chapter Two. The four chapters in Part Two present the rules of relational compatibility, with special emphasis on how, without realizing it, people continually teach each other how to act. Readers who are interested in predicting interpersonal behavior, from moment to moment, will find this material of particular interest. If you primarily want to understand the eight ways in which people behave toxically and what to do about them, you will find the chapters in Part Three most rewarding. And if you want some concise and hard-hitting advice about how to change behavior, in yourself and others, consult Part Four. You might want to begin by reading one of the chapters in Part Three and, having digested it, return to Part One for the theology it contains and then move on to Part Two for its psychology. I suggest leaving Part Four for last.

May God bless you richly as you read.

PART ONE

RELATIONSHIPS AS GOD INTENDS

THE TWO CHAPTERS with which we begin our discussion of interpersonal relationships present the theological underpinnings for everything else in this book. We are not coming to our subject without assumptions. In truth, we couldn't do that even if we tried, and neither could anyone else. We all have biases and opinions, religious and otherwise, and nowhere are these more important than in the realm of relational behavior. While I hope that people of any faith or persuasion will find value in the pages to follow, I have written them from an explicitly Christian point of view.

Chapter One, titled "The Spiritual Significance of Everyday Life," provides a concise theology of relationships. What does it mean that we have been created in the image of God? As Christian disciples, where do our duties lie—what are our obligations to others? What is the essence of fellowship? Does God intend us to lose our individual identities as we enter into communion with other believers? What is the role of self-disclosure in the life of a Christian? How does forgiveness really work? Why is there pathos to life without Christ? Are we doomed because of our past, or can we choose who and what we will become? And where does the concept of sin fit into a psychology of interpersonal relations?

The second chapter, "Foundations of Health and Holiness," addresses some difficult questions. What is the nature of psychological health? What does it mean to lead a holy life? And what do health and holiness have to do with each other? What's right and what's wrong with how mental health has traditionally been defined? When is psychology, as a discipline, beneficial, and when is it destructive? How about psychiatry? What about the relationship between sin and sickness—is the difference between the two always clear? What is the nature of intimacy, in its various forms, and what does intimacy have to do with emotional health and Christian fellowship? Why is it important to be able to put feelings into words? What happens when people become isolated and have no meaningful relationships? How do toxic interactions leave you feeling—how can you tell if a relationship is toxic? And finally, what role does anxiety play in the development of such relationships?

THE SPIRITUAL SIGNIFICANCE OF EVERYDAY LIFE

A BRIEF THEOLOGY OF RELATIONSHIPS

I appeal to you therefore, brothers and sisters, by the mercies of God, to present your bodies as a living sacrifice, holy and acceptable to God, which is your spiritual [reasonable] worship. Do not be conformed to this world [age], but be transformed by the renewing of your minds, so that you may discern what is the will of God—what is good and acceptable and perfect.

—Romans 12:1–2 [NRSV]

THIS PASSAGE FROM PAUL'S letter to the Christians at Rome captures what it means to live in dynamic communion with God through Christ. Rome was the center of power for a vast empire, so the Christians to whom Paul is writing inhabit a thriving metropolis with a large cosmopolitan population. He is imploring them, and by implication us, to turn their very selves—their entire existence—into offerings. These holy offerings are to be living and ongoing, rather than one-time acts, and to take the form of moment-to-moment worship. Paul emphasizes that Christians must resist internalizing the values and thought-forms of the world around them. By having the mind of Christ (1 Corinthians 2:16), they are to live on a new plane of consciousness, which puts them in a better position to know God's will.

I begin with this radiant passage from Paul because, in the chapters ahead, we are going to consider some of the nastier sides of human nature. We will explore interpersonal toxicity in detail and thus stare long and hard into the face of relational sin. Doing this is not always easy. When you venture into the quagmires of evil, it can be difficult to keep your eyes on Christ and to remember why you even exist—to love God with all your heart, mind, soul, and strength, and to love your neighbor as yourself (Mark 12:28–31; Luke 10:25–28). Sin can get you down. It can also prompt you to blur the distinction between sin and sinner and, so, fail to keep in mind that we should hate the one but love the other. When you come up against interpersonal sin in all its ugliness, the natural tendency is to condemn and, in the process, to forget that as sinners, we are all cut from the same cloth. There is very little in this book that you, and I, have not been guilty of from time to time.

This does not mean that you should subject yourself to any more relational toxicity than is necessary. You have a stewardship responsibility for your life, which means that how you *feel* is tremendously important. For what *is* life aside from states of consciousness and the biological processes that sustain them? Reverence, gratitude, happiness, satisfaction, ecstasy, affection, and peace are all states of consciousness. So are arrogance, selfishness, anger, loathing, depression, tension, and humiliation. God cares intensely about our states of mind. It is our job, therefore, to pay them special attention. What we think and feel in relation to others, including God, matters more than anything else in creation. God not only expects but commands us to cherish our minds (hearts) as precious possessions. We are *not* to allow others to ruin our joy.

In this chapter, we will take a careful look at what Christian theology has to say about relationships. For us as Christians, the starting point for any inquiry into human nature must be scripture. What does the Bible say about the human heart and what God intends for us in relation to Him and our fellow creatures?

Relationality and the Image of God

Scripture indicates, first, that we have been made in God's image, and theologians have long debated what this means. Everyone agrees that it does *not* mean that we physically look like God, since God has no bodily form.

Having been created in God's image means that we can think and plan, and hence formulate long-range intentions. We can make conscious choices and, through these choices, define who and what we are. And we are *self-conscious*. We have the ability to reflect on ourselves, to look in a kind of psychological mirror, and also to view life through the lenses of morality—we can tell right from wrong. Most important of all, we are *spiritual* beings. Understanding the significance of this is pivotal to everything else we will discuss in this book.

God made us *like* Him. Spiritual beings have the capacity to commune with other spiritual beings and to define (structure) the nature of these relationships. No other creature can do this, which is precisely why we are said to be the pinnacle of creation. We are capable of complex mental (intellectual-emotional) states and therefore of genuine *interpersonal* dealings. Human beings have been designed for *fellowship,* which goes far beyond even the most affectionate relations to be found in the animal kingdom.

In his second letter to the Christians at Corinth, Paul writes that if anyone is in Christ, he or she is a new creation (2 Corinthians 5:17). Everything becomes new when we come to Christ, including how we view people. They are no longer just minds and bodies. We now see them for what they are, eternal spiritual entities. We perceive them, as it were, with supernatural eyes, which means that we can relate to them as we never could before.

Relationships as the Purpose of Creation

God is a relational being, an eternal fellowship of Father, Son, and Holy Spirit. We, too, are by nature relational. This similarity we bear to God is of supreme importance, because it embodies the very reason that we exist. God made us like Him so that we could relate to Him, and each other, in specific ways. There is an important clue to our true nature in the second chapter of Genesis, a passage to which we will return in Chapter Three.

What, we may ask, is God up to when he gives Adam the job of naming the animals? One answer is that, in doing this, Adam discovers something important about himself. The animals are unable to relate to Adam as spiritual beings. While they can amuse Adam, and perhaps return to him a certain measure of affection, they are not able to interact with him as peers. Animals cannot provide Adam with the communion he has been made for. So in response to Adam's abject loneliness, God creates a second person.

Without another human being to commune with, Adam would have remained sadly incomplete. "Then the LORD God said, 'It is not good that the man should be alone; I will make him a helper as his partner . . . [because] for the man there was [still] not found a helper as his partner'" (Genesis 2:18–20, NRSV).

As spiritual beings, we will *never* be full persons without relationships with other spiritual beings, including both the Creator-Provider-Sustainer and our fellow creatures. We may go through the motions and, for all outward appearances, seem to be full persons. But there will always be something missing. Without vertical *and* horizontal person-to-person relationships, we will be but caricatures of our true selves. It was to participate in relationships that God created us in the first place. And it was certainly not to relate toxically.

Discipleship and Awareness

Some of the nuances of the word *disciple* are traveling with, lining up behind, agreeing with, and comprehending and embracing the attitudes, views, and opinions of another. But the word *disciple* has a deeper significance. Because Jesus Christ is God, to become his disciple is also to become a disciple of God, the Creator and Sustainer of the universe. This, in turn, means to align oneself with the Word, *logos* (see John 1), the essence of all rationality. Or, as we might say today, of sanity.

Discipleship involves a number of things that are alien to secular culture. There is, first, humility: "At that time the disciples came to Jesus and asked, 'Who is the greatest in the kingdom of heaven?' He called a child, whom he put among them, and said, 'Truly I tell you, unless you change and become like children, you will never enter the kingdom of heaven'" (Matthew 18:1–3, NRSV). There is also the repudiation of what the world values: "They do all their deeds to be seen by others. . . . They love to have the place of honor at banquets and the best seats . . . and to be greeted with respect in the marketplaces" (Matthew 23:5–7, NRSV). And there is sometimes suffering: "In the world ye shall have tribulation" (John 16:33, KJV) and "See, I am sending you out like sheep. . . . They will hand you over to councils and flog you" (Matthew 10:16–17, NRSV). In relating to other people, then, we are to do so with humility, not expect that this will always lead to public acclaim, and realize that we may suffer.

It is important to note, however, that right after Jesus tells the disciples that he is sending them forth as sheep among wolves, he exhorts them to be "wise as serpents and innocent as doves" (Matthew 10:16, NRSV). We may have to pay a steep price for relating to others as God desires. This does not mean that we should be oblivious to what this price is. Jesus, in laying down his life for sinners, knew full well what he was doing. There are times when particular Christians are called by God to endure massive relational toxicity, in the full knowledge of what is happening to them at the hands of others.

Relational Obligations

As Christians, we have a duty to care, sincerely and deeply, about the well-being of others. This is the core of the love that we are to have for all persons. It is also the foundation for the fellowship we can enjoy with other persons of faith. It is our holy duty to preserve the dignity of all human beings, whether saint or sinner, criminal or humanitarian, rich or poor, culturally and ethnically like us or not. All of this is relatively easy to state, and agree with, in the abstract. It is harder actually to do.

Think of the people you most detest. You are to respect them. Think of the qualities in others that most upset you. You are nevertheless to be kind to those who have these characteristics. Think of the cultures or subcultures, if any, that make you uncomfortable and the ethnic or political groups, if any, that you find most alien. You are to embrace the people from all of these. Think also of the personalities you find obnoxious. And so on.

Just as God chose—actively embraced—ancient Israel as His cherished people, we are to embrace our fellow Christians and give them special places of honor. We will begin Chapter Twelve ("Scurrying") with the account of Peter's denial of Christ. This denial amounted to a renunciation of the relationship Peter had enjoyed with Jesus. Denial of Christ occurs whenever we treat other Christians with contempt or rudeness. It occurs also when we turn our backs on the needs of our neighbors (1 Timothy 5:8). None of this means condoning, much less encouraging, toxic conduct. It does imply that we should think long and hard before dismissing another human as irredeemably toxic.

But some human beings are, and probably will always be, toxic in this life. Prisons contain a good many of them, and there is no simple formula for how to relate to such people. Always, you have to balance duty to yourself with duty to others.

The Nature of Fellowship

If you look up the word *fellowship* in a standard dictionary, you will encounter such synonyms as *brotherhood, sisterhood, companionship, association, bond, camaraderie,* and *togetherness. Sharing* is also central to fellowship, which is by nature communal. You may also find the word *intimacy,* and this perhaps best conveys what the Bible means by *fellowship.*

As we will explore in Chapter Two, there are at least three kinds of intimacy, and we are not supposed to experience all of them with everybody.

Yet what often passes for fellowship in the local church is anything but. Just because people smile at each other on Sunday or sit side by side does not mean that they experience Christian intimacy, and without such intimacy there can be no fellowship.

The biblical word for fellowship implies communion. It is closely related to words that mean union with, connection to, bonding with, sharing with, partnering with, and joining oneself to something or someone. Fellowship, as we find it used in Paul's letters, is not mere companionship; it has an additional spiritual meaning, being unified in Christ (John 17:21).

Fostering genuine fellowship is not easy. Nor has it ever been. The Fall did more than disrupt our relationship with God. It also impaired our relationships with people, as demonstrated by what Cain, out of jealousy, did to Abel. Fellowship requires that we take emotional risks. These risks would be trivial were it not for human sin, but as things stand on earth they are anything but trivial.

When Paul writes of living according to the flesh, he means, in part, living for oneself. Life in the flesh is selfish. It involves an existence estranged and alienated from God's Spirit, a life that is the opposite of Christian fellowship. Such fleshly living is characterized not so much by sensuality as by a self-sufficient rejection of God and by setting oneself above other people. Note, for example, what Paul writes to the Christians in Corinth: "I fed you with milk, not solid food, for you were not ready for solid food. Even now you are still not ready, for you are still of the flesh. For as long as there is jealousy and quarreling among you, are you not of the flesh, and behaving according to human inclinations?" (1 Corinthians 3:2–4, NRSV).

Jesus calls the disciples friends (John 15:15) and has already said, "Love one another as I have loved you" (John 15:12). In the next verse, Jesus points to his own death by saying that there is no greater love than to lay down one's life for one's friends. Such fellowship is far more expensive than what we may be used to as we sip colas and devour pizza, all the while restricting conversation to everything except what sometimes matters most—what's going on inside of us.

Life in Christ and Individuality

As part of the church universal, a Christian is a member of a vast community that confers a special identity as an adopted child of the Father (Ephesians 1:4–6; Romans 8:15–17). Christians are the people of God (2 Corinthians 6:16–18; Hebrews 8:8–12; see also Romans 9–11). The New Testament repeatedly refers to Christians as a family.

Note that Jesus stressed spiritual over biological ties. Recall the incident of Jesus in the temple (Luke 2:41–51), his comments about who is and who is not a member of his true family (Mark 3:31–33), and his piercing words about how becoming his disciple may require making painful domestic choices (Luke 14:26).

In addition to their earthly citizenships, all Christians enjoy a common heavenly citizenship (Philippians 3:20) that is based on a new set of relationships, with God and other believers. These relationships offer a whole new realm of experience. Differences between Christians are no longer to divide them (Galatians 3:28). And they enjoy an expanded level of personal freedom and have been released from oppressive legalism or arbitrary social censure (Colossians 2:13–19).

Yet Christians are still part of secular society and retain their individual identities. They remain connected with the social order. Becoming a Christian does not cause a person to merge into some amorphous cosmic oneness and thus lose all sense of personal uniqueness. This implies that, with the added dimension of faith, relationships between Christians can be enormously rich and varied.

The Centrality of Self-Disclosure

Our relationship to God, while we remain on Earth, is one of faith. He has chosen to remain invisible and not to overwhelm or frighten us. God wants us, above all, to love Him, and as we will see in Part Three love is by nature voluntary. It cannot be forced or commanded, or it ceases to be love. We know of God *only* because He has chosen to reveal himself.

Our relationships with other people are a mixture of the seen and the unseen. While we can see each other's bodies, we cannot directly perceive each other's minds. What we know of others—their inner lives—is mostly what they have chosen to share with us. Although we may accurately conclude things about a person that he or she would prefer to hide, almost everything we know about another individual's mental life is what that person has elected to disclose.

Self-disclosure is therefore central to interpersonal relationships and hence to fellowship. Without sharing what is going on inside of us, there can be no true fellowship. How can we love those we do not know? This is a sobering reality. It implies that many relationships passing as Christian fellowship are unworthy of the name. Exchanging superficial pleasantries over a cup of coffee and a donut hardly qualify as Christian intimacy.

Just as our knowledge of God is to be intimate and personal, rather than abstract and theoretical, our knowledge of each other must be intimate and personal. There can be no deep knowledge of each other, and hence no fellowship, without genuine candor.

Cheap Forgiveness

Twenty years ago, the notion of forgiveness had little or no place in psychology, but today one hears the term used freely. This, of course, is a good thing.

Forgiveness in the New Testament is used in the sense of releasing, leaving behind, and allowing something to go unpunished. It is the core process or mechanism for restoring marred or broken relationships. Forgiveness means canceling another person's debt and thus letting go of resentment. It involves accepting rather than rejecting the person who has wronged us. Just as forgiveness was central to the work of Jesus (Mark 2:1–12, 10:45; Matthew 18:21–35), it is central to our work as Christ's representatives.

We should not view forgiveness as some unusually worthy act of righteousness, something we do for extra credit in God's grade book. It is, rather, a natural part of new life in Christ, of becoming new creations (2 Corinthians 5:17). "For if you forgive others their trespasses, your heavenly Father will also forgive you; but if you do not forgive others, neither will your Father forgive your trespasses" (Matthew 6:14–15, NRSV). Hard words. "Whenever you stand praying, forgive, if you have anything against anyone; so that your Father in heaven may also forgive you your trespasses" (Mark 11:25, NRSV). Hard words also. "Do not judge, and you will not be judged; do not condemn, and you will not be condemned" (Luke 6:37, NRSV). Perhaps the hardest words of all.

It is difficult, in our assertive world, to forgive or even to refrain from judging. I suspect it has always been. We simply cannot do it unless we are able to put whatever suffering we endure in proper perspective. And this can only be accomplished by living in *gratitude* for God's acceptance and forgiveness of us. "Bear with one another and, if anyone has a complaint against another, forgive each other; just as the Lord has forgiven you, so you must also forgive" (Colossians 3:13, NRSV; see also Ephesians 4:32 and Romans 12:19–21).

Genuine forgiveness is not easy and, when the injury is severe, forgiving may take years. As part of our instant-results society, we are largely oblivious to what forgiveness may require. If someone has gutted your entire emotional life, perhaps in a bad marriage, or inflicted on you grave and permanent physical damage, it is unlikely that you will be able to forgive right away. God does seem, now and then, to grant certain people the grace necessary to forgive in an extraordinary manner. You will occasionally see on television the father or mother of a child who has been brutally murdered express what appears to be authentic forgiveness, often in the name of Christ. There is no reason to doubt that such miracles occur. But they are just that, miracles. Few of us could do what Jesus did. Going through the outrageously unjust and agonizing death of suffocation on a cross, I doubt that we would say, "Father, forgive them; for they know not what they do" (Luke 23:34, KJV). We might say a lot of other things, but probably not that.

To forgive someone who has done us a terrible wrong, one of two things usually has to happen. Either the other person must express remorse and ask for our forgiveness, or God has to work in our hearts to bring us to the place where we can forgive, which in some cases may take the better part of a lifetime. Dietrich Bonhoeffer, a World War II German theologian martyred by the Nazis, renounced what he called "cheap grace." As he well knew, all grace is cheap since, by definition, it costs nothing. What he meant was that many people want the benefits of God's grace without having to pay the cost of discipleship.

Christians today want cheap forgiveness. They do not want to spend the time it sometimes takes, the months and years of praying on their knees, for God finally to give them the healing they need to let go of grievances. Worse, they refuse to admit, to themselves or their fellow believers, that they have *not* forgiven and go on acting as if they had. Just as there is no cheap grace, there is no cheap forgiveness.

Forgiveness does not mean allowing another person endlessly to injure you. There are times when God may call us to suffer and perhaps even to die. Absent such a call, we have a solemn duty to care for ourselves and to achieve a balance between how much we take care of others and how much we take care of us. There is a time to call a halt to abuse and, when there is no other way to put a stop to it, to end the relationship.

No sane theologian would seriously advocate that Christians put their families in jeopardy by giving away all their money. Only a psychopath might ask you to do something so imprudent. While economists are notorious for disagreements—"put them end to end and they couldn't reach an opinion"—they generally agree that a dollar is a unit of stored labor. We work in order to acquire these units so that we can purchase the fruits of other people's labor in the form of food, housing, medical care, such other necessities as gas, electricity, and water, and perhaps an occasional evening out. Allowing someone to injure you, seriously and repeatedly, is like giving away your bank account, something that only a fanatic or a freeloader would urge you to do (see Chapter Ten). Forgiveness is not the same as self-destruction.

The Pathos of Life Without Christ

When I was in college, a friend of mine said that he wanted, someday, to write a book titled *The Pathos of Life Without Christ*. I have never forgotten this phrase because it seems to summarize the predicament of countless people in the twenty-first century.

There are only three viable philosophical-religious options for an educated person in modern Western society. One can embrace Christianity and, making some form of what is usually called Pascal's wager, bet on God. Or one can place one's faith in some version of utopianism, such as improved education, better government, enhanced economic or technological systems, or a redistribution of wealth. A third option, which is selected more often than it might seem, is simply to live in silent cynicism, never knowing when life will end or if it has any ultimate meaning. There is little hope or consolation in such an existence. Without God, there is only background despair punctuated by fleeting moments of pleasure. Many people indeed lead lives of quiet desperation. They may look like they have it all together, but underneath they are often aware of how short life is and perhaps of how futile also. For most of us, there is the gnawing realization, which grows with every passing year, that we are mortal.

Because we are spiritual beings, as well as biological ones, we are social (interpersonal) creatures. We have been hard-wired for fellowship with other spiritual beings. But we die alone, every one of us. Even if we have wonderful relationships, without God even these will not remove the sense of foreboding that we have, in the knowledge that someday our life on earth will come to an end.

Freedom and Responsibility

This is not a book on philosophy, and so I am not going to attempt a detailed discussion here of freedom versus determinism. But I do want to point out that we always have at least some freedom of choice, even if it's just a choice of attitude. A serious problem with psychology as a discipline is that it tends to be both reductionistic and deterministic. Reductionism involves oversimplification. A common example is biochemical reductionism. Because life is sustained by chemical processes, it is "nothing but" such processes. Determinism is the belief that everything that happens, including what we think, is the necessary (inescapable) result of what preceded it. Prior conditioning makes it so that we have to think exactly the thoughts that we do.

If this is so, if everything we think is merely the result of prior conditioning, the very idea of truth becomes difficult to defend. If determinism is true, how can we trust our own reasoning processes? When different thinkers disagreed about something, there would be no trustworthy way to decide between their opinions. Each thinker, we would have to believe, has simply been conditioned to think as he or she does. And if we did decide, how could we be sure that our decision was not the mistaken result of conditioning?

For reason to make sense, we have to assume that we are able, somehow, to rise above conditioning. And for moral responsibility to make sense, we have to assume that we have at least limited freedom. How else could we be accountable for what we do? A god who was a fiend might hold us accountable anyway, but that is not the Christian God, who loves us unceasingly and without measure but who is also serious about what He expects of us.

We cannot cop out when it comes to how we relate to other people. Everything we do or say to them is of eternal significance and therefore of infinite importance. This is an idea that brings with it awesome responsibility, especially when you think about how often in life you should have done things differently. It is a wonderful thing that, as Christians, we enjoy a full pardon because, if we were held accountable for all of our sins, we'd be serving time forever.

Flawed Human Existence

Your parents failed you. So has everyone else in your life with whom you've had a close relationship. This is the nature of our fallen world. All parents fail their children, all husbands and wives fail their spouses, and all friends fail each other. I have failed, and you have failed.

The pervasiveness of sin makes it so that no relationship can endure without the parties failing each other endlessly. As a result, you and I, and everyone else we know, have emotional scars, which often show up in faulty patterns of interpersonal behavior.

We've all had experience with these scars. Everything seemed to be going well when, out of the blue, the other person did something to spoil things—launched into a hostile attack, provoked a stupid argument, or backed away from us without warning. There may have been an emotional explosion, and, in that moment, we discovered a side to the other person that we never knew existed. Or maybe it was just the quiet refusal to answer our telephone calls—a sure sign of rejection, if not desertion and abandonment. Because we didn't see it coming, we felt as though King Kong had punched us in the stomach. Life can indeed be toxic.

Most of us would also have to admit that, at least once or twice in our lives, we were the culprits. We did the spoiling, perhaps by making a critical comment we shouldn't have made, overreacting to a statement that we later realized was well intended, or snapping at someone who didn't deserve it. It dawned on us, eventually, that we had misperceived what was going on. We responded out of past experiences that had little to do with the present or took out our frustrations on someone who had nothing to do with causing them. Worse, we didn't know how to fix things, and the relationship was therefore never quite the same.

Such events are the raw stuff from which life is made: tragic misunderstandings, sudden disappointments, emotional injuries, inappropriate reactions, and devastating surprises. We suffer and cause others to suffer. An adequate theology of relationships has to address such events, which move the doctrine of forgiveness to center stage.

Sin and Interpersonal Behavior

Even among Christians, it is not always fashionable to talk about sin. Sin is an awkward concept for many people in our society, especially if they have no connection with a church, because it seems to smack of moralistic rigidity and intellectual narrow-mindedness. Yet the concept of sin is so central to Christian theology that you can remove it only at the price of eviscerating Christianity itself. While you may still *call* yourself a Christian, and perhaps celebrate Jesus as an admirable teacher, without taking sin seriously you will have no grasp of what it means to relate to God through Christ as Lord and Savior. And the sin that is most important to be aware of is one's own.

Evil is that which is *radically* opposed to good. It is not some minor slippage, the result of an incomplete education or an ailing economy. Unfortunately, when we examine specific relationships or the actions of particular people, it is not always clear where to draw the line between ordinary behavior and toxic, even malevolent, conduct. And many times, it is not our job to worry about this.

Human actions are so subtle and multilayered that it is not always possible even to distinguish sharply between what is holy and what is sinful. This may come as a shock to you because you may immediately think of the many times when the difference is clear. I am not suggesting that we blur the lines between good and evil, only that the subtlety of the human heart sometimes does this for us. "The heart is deceitful above all things, and desperately wicked: who can know it?" (Jeremiah 17:9, KJV). What sometimes looks like goodness can turn out to be badness. "Satan himself masquerades as an angel of light" (2 Corinthians 11:14, NIV). And as stories with surprise endings sometimes show us, what looks like badness may turn out, in the end, to be goodness.

Christians who prefer simplicity to truth do not like this. They would prefer to sort everything into two discrete categories, the totally good and the totally bad. Yet many things in life are ambiguous mixtures of good and bad, which is why we should pray earnestly for wisdom and fall continually on God's mercy, lest we make tragic mistakes about others and the meanings of what they do.

It can be hard to decide when leading turns into dominating, caring becomes smothering, or striving takes on the character of humiliating. When does the healthy instinct to compete transform itself into the jealous need to outshine, to climb on others' shoulders or heads, simply to get a better view of the sunset?

Looking Ahead

In Chapter Two, we are going to examine the nature of holiness. We will also explore what it means to be emotionally healthy. And we will consider how these two pivotally important concepts, health and holiness, relate to each other. Are they the same? Can you reduce one to the other? Are they completely unrelated?

2

FOUNDATIONS OF HEALTH AND HOLINESS

May he strengthen your hearts so that you will be blameless and holy in the presence of our God and Father when our Lord Jesus comes with all his holy ones.

—1 Thessalonians 3:13 [NIV]

WHEN IS A RELATIONSHIP TOXIC? What does it mean to lead a holy life? How has psychological health traditionally been defined? And what do health and holiness have to do with each other? These are a few of the more important questions that we will take up in this chapter.

We will also consider a number of other questions. Is there any value to psychotherapy and counseling? What happens when psychology takes on the character of a religion? When it comes to emotional problems, is there a clear difference between sin and sickness? How are fellowship and intimacy related? Are there different kinds of intimacy and, if so, how important is each one? How crucial is language in relationships—is it necessary to put thoughts and feelings into words? What happens to people psychologically when they become isolated or when closeness with other human beings becomes inherently unpleasant? And how does anxiety set the stage for toxic behavior?

The Nature of Relational Toxicity

Relationships can be wholesome (nourishing) or toxic (harmful). And they can change from moment to moment. At any given instant, what goes on between people will fall somewhere on the following continuum, which you can think of as a relational barometer:

TOXIC ◄─────────────────► WHOLESOME

There are actually two such scales operating at the same time, one for each person. What you experience as a wholesome exchange may strike the other person as a toxic one. This is what sometimes happens, for example, when fans crowd celebrities and try to engage them in personal conversations.

Toxic relationships leave you feeling gray inside and sometimes sick. They may prompt you to get down on yourself or become angry at the world. You may feel confused as you try to make sense of what's going on and conclude that you're in a no-win situation, that no matter what you do things will not turn out well. Such relationships pull you down rather than lift you up; they certainly don't help you move closer to God. They can also cause tremendous anxiety because of all the uncertainty involved. Most of all, when you're in a toxic relationship, or when an otherwise great relationship takes a toxic turn, you may sense—if you are spiritually sensitive—that you're caught in the grip of sin. And you will be right. Only the sin may not be yours, or at least not all of it.

Life is a lot more fulfilling when relationships are wholesome, but you will be unable to eliminate all relational toxicity from your life. Some of it is inevitable. There are times, for example, when it is our duty, and perhaps our privilege, to endure a certain amount of toxicity. A dying relative who needs our help may turn vicious because of pain or dementia. This does not mean that we should walk away. The same is true of friendships and marriages, both of which can have their toxic moments.

God, however, did not create us to self-destruct. There is nothing inherently noble about suffering at someone else's hands. We were made to relate joyfully to Him and other people, and it is difficult to do either if we are constantly feeling poisoned.

What It Means to Be Holy

Holy means "belonging to God." It is to be called (see Romans 1:7 and 1 Corinthians 1:2) and guided by the Spirit of God: "For all who are led by the Spirit of God are children of God" (Romans 8:14, NRSV). This, in turn, means loving other Christians (Ephesians 1:15), helping them when necessary (Romans 12:13) and, to the extent possible, not using secular powers against them (1 Corinthians 6:1–7). The common interpretation of *holy* as being set apart is therefore a good one. Christians are to live in two worlds at the same time, the visible one and the realm of the sacred. And as we saw in Chapter One, they are to *relate* to all people in a way that reflects and expresses God's love.

Being holy has a great deal to do, therefore, with the nature of relationships: "For anyone who does not love his brother, whom he has seen, cannot love God, whom he has not seen" (1 John 4:20b, NIV). Jesus said, "I give you a new commandment, that you love one another. Just as I have loved you, you also should love one another" (John 13:34, NRSV). Without love toward others, there *is* no intimate communion with God (see 1 John 3:10; 4:7–12).

Love, as Jesus meant it, is costly. And why should it be otherwise? Love cost God the death of His son. Jesus understood how hard it can be even to love one's friends, who at times may be irritating, demanding, and bothersome. Yet he went further: "You have heard that it was said, 'You shall love your neighbor and hate your enemy.' But I say to you, Love your enemies and pray for those who persecute you" (Matthew 5:43–44, NRSV). There is a parallel passage in Luke 6:27–28: "Love your enemies, do good to those who hate you, bless those who curse you, pray for those who abuse you." While God does not intend us to let toxic people ruin our lives, He does mean us to love others as much as possible, no matter what they may do to us. God loves us regardless of what we do or fail to do, and that is how we are to love our neighbor. Who, then, is our neighbor? As the parable of the Good Samaritan (Luke 10:25–37) suggests, anyone who can fog a mirror.

Loving people in this way is no small order. Without knowing God and living in the power of His Spirit, it cannot be done. Holiness is not something we achieve by doing this or that but something that grows, spontaneously, from a life of communion with the Father through the Son.

Traditional Definitions of Psychological Well-Being

It has been easier for psychologists and psychiatrists to define mental health negatively than positively, by the absence rather than the presence of something. This is a carryover from the nineteenth century, when significant emotional difficulties became a major concern of medicine and psychiatry emerged out of neurology as a distinct medical specialty. Overall, this was good for society, because it reduced the cruelty that was often inflicted on people who acted in strange ways. But what began as an outgrowth of social enlightenment resulted in the medicalization of almost all behavior. We speak of "treating" emotional "disorders" through "therapy" and of mental "health" and "disease." The quoted words are all medical terms.

Sometimes what actually gets treated is human sin. Yet saying so in our society can make one sound like an intellectual Neanderthal or a religious fanatic.

Most psychotherapists and counselors have on their shelves an impressive 943-page volume, published by the American Psychiatric Association, titled the *Diagnostic and Statistical Manual of Mental Disorders* (4th ed., Text Revision, known as the DSM-IV-TR). When I was a graduate student in the late 1960s, the DSM, in its second edition at the time, was a small plastic-bound guidebook that you could carry in a large pocket, which supports the claim I am making about the expansion of psychiatry and clinical psychology.

Much of what you will find in the DSM belongs there. Several hundred pages are devoted to problems that are caused by some form of organic pathology, such as a brain tumor or the ingestion of a mind-altering substance like LSD or PCP. You will also find detailed descriptions of disorders, such as childhood autism and adult schizophrenia, which experts agree are largely rooted in biology, even though we don't yet know precisely how. But the DSM also contains a host of problems that are medical only if you greatly stretch the term. These include fifty pages of "personality disorders," which is what Part Three of this book is about.

Mental health professionals tend to assume that if you *don't* have any of the disorders listed in the DSM, you are emotionally intact, which is not necessarily the case. There are plenty of people who, although they have no official mental disorder, are selfish and vindictive, which hardly qualifies them as paragons of emotional well-being. Psychiatry and psychology have done a wonderful job of cataloguing what emotional well-being is *not*. But they have done a terrible job of stating what it is.

Health Versus Holiness

Psychological health cannot be reduced to holiness. There are people in the world who appear to enjoy close relationships with God but nonetheless suffer from mental disorders. Their genes may have left them vulnerable to emotional problems, or other people in their lives, such as parents or siblings, may have mistreated them. It is simply not true that everyone who is holy is healthy.

Nor can holiness be defined as mental health. A person may be psychologically sound and still be a scoundrel, with no love for God or people. Because of the temptations embedded within earthly existence (Romans 6–8), it is unlikely that any Christian is ever going to be free of conflict. Perhaps the only kind of person who could possibly live without tension is one totally given over to evil. Good psychological adjustment, in the usual sense, is no sign of a holy heart. Thus if we define health and holiness in conventional ways, we simply cannot equate them or reduce one to the other.

Where Health and Holiness Intersect

There is nonetheless a connection between health and holiness, an area of life where the two overlap, and it is the domain of interpersonal relationships. How we relate to other spiritual beings, which by definition means God and people, is more important than *anything* else in life, including whatever we may achieve, what we own, where we went to school, or even our state of physical health.

Relationships are not just one among many topics in theology and psychology. Theology is the study of God and His ways with us, but its ultimate aim is to straighten out our ways with God, which means our relationship to the Creator. Psychology, like theology, is made up of many specialties, but nearly all of them are intended in some way to improve human life. Many psychiatrists and psychologists have repeatedly insisted that what is most central to the quality of life is the nature of one's relationships.

So whether we are coming at our subject from a theological or a psychological direction, the intersection of health and holiness at the crossroads of relationships is where the action is. It is the most important feature of our existence.

Psychology as Helpful but Insufficient

According to Christian theology, becoming whole requires allowing God to create you anew, to give you an existential makeover. New life in Christ implies repentance of sin, conscious and unconscious, and a new purpose in life that centers on the Gospel. Paul writes to the Christians at Philippi, "Forgetting what is behind and straining toward what is ahead, I press on toward the goal to win the prize for which God has called me" (Philippians 3:13–14, NIV). Paul never lost sight of his purpose.

By itself, psychology cannot provide us with such a purpose and so offers nothing to meet us at the point of our most pressing need. All attempts to become fully adjusted to this world through psychological counseling alone are folly. To what, after all, are we trying to adjust if not to reality? And if God exists and has disclosed Himself to us in Jesus Christ, what could be more central to reality than encountering the Risen Lord and putting Him at the core of our lives?

Scripture is certainly concerned with how we relate to our fellow human beings. But the Bible is not a textbook on interpersonal psychology, and it has been left largely to us to develop such a psychology. Parts Two through Four of this book do exactly that. Any psychology of human behavior will be incomplete, however, if it is not understood within the wider context of theology. To make adequate sense of human interaction, it is important to take sin seriously, for example, and not treat it as some minor blemish on the otherwise blissful landscape of the human heart. Interpersonal psychology is powerful but, by itself, inadequate. It will help you understand how people treat each other, but it will not save you from death, enable you self-sufficiently to triumph over evil, or bring you the kind of joy that results only from dynamic faith.

False Religion and Counterfeit Salvation

Psychology is destructive when it becomes a religion. It can take on the character of an imitation Christianity, in which people use pious words but mean entirely different things by them. Holiness becomes self-esteem, sin becomes dysfunction, growing in Christ becomes making therapeutic progress, repentance and conversion both become processing feelings and working on issues, and salvation is reduced to some version of improving mental health. All of this is false religion. The term *religion* comes from a root word that means "reconnected." True religion centers on getting reconnected to the one true God.

Counterfeit religion is, of course, not new. The Roman Empire had its fair share of people who looked wistfully back on Greece as the font of all wisdom. Why they did this is not hard to understand. Although the Romans were superb organizers of armies, competent governors of territories, and magnificent builders of roads, aqueducts, walls, and amphitheaters, their skills were primarily administrative and practical. Nothing emerged in first-century Rome to rival the intellectual contributions of the Greek philosophers, who in turn were likely influenced by earlier Hebrew thinkers.[1] At several points, Paul has to warn his fellow Christians not to go scampering after the latest in high-brow learning, as if this were a superior path to God:

---

[1]That ancient Jewish thought-forms probably helped shape Greek philosophical ideas may come as a surprise to some readers. For a variety of reasons, knowledge of such influence seems to have been suppressed from the late eighteenth century onward. See Popkin, R. H. (ed.). *Columbia History of Western Philosophy*. New York: MJF Books, 1999, pp. 3–5.

"Do not deceive yourselves. . . . The wisdom of this world is foolishness with God" (1 Corinthians 2:18–19, NRSV). And "Beware lest any man spoil you through philosophy and vain deceit, after the tradition of men . . . and not after Christ" (Colossians 2:8, KJV). And also, "We . . . speak a message of wisdom . . . but not the wisdom of this age. . . . We speak of God's secret wisdom . . . that has been hidden. . . . None of the rulers of this age understood it, for if they had, they would not have crucified the Lord of glory" (1 Corinthians 2:6–8, NIV).

If Paul were writing today, he'd probably be warning us about psychology. To many people, some of them professing to be Christians, psychology is the new Gnosticism. The Gnostics, who flourished in the first few centuries A.D., believed that they, and only they, had secret knowledge essential to salvation. In contrast to Paul, who proclaimed that Jesus openly revealed what had been hidden through the ages (Ephesians and Colossians), the Gnostics believed themselves to have spiritual insight that could only be understood by insiders.

Problems arise when psychologists make philosophical statements and pass them off as scientific ones or when psychology, as a discipline, promises more than it can deliver. Although the information I am going to share may help you understand interpersonal behavior a good deal better than you understand it now, nothing in psychology will reconcile you to God and thus repair what is most broken in the human soul.

Psychotherapy, Counseling, and Psychiatry

What I have just written does not in any way diminish the value of well-conducted psychological services. To the contrary, such services have been sources of enormous blessing to millions of people. Properly applied to an individual who is ready to benefit from them or to a couple or family willing to embrace constructive change, they can be life-changing.

People can be freed from oppressive guilt that has been built into them by others but has nothing to do with God. They can learn to express their feelings and longings to loved ones and so get close to them, perhaps for the first time. And they can rid themselves of symptoms, from anxiety attacks to eating disorders, which cripple or endanger their lives. The list of benefits derived from competent psychotherapy and counseling is long, and if you've seen people go from feeling like worms to floating like butterflies, you understand how powerful such services can be.

Nor do my earlier comments call into question advances in psychiatry, which is also changing lives, especially because of progress in pharmacology. People who sixty years ago would have "heard voices" are now free of such afflictions. Those who have been depressed and perhaps suicidal for years now live satisfying lives. And individuals who might have stayed indoors for the rest of their days are now able to venture forth and feel comfortable around people. I could go on.

Yet as stated earlier, none of this, by itself, will restore a person's relationship with God. While release from oppressive guilt or haunting hallucinations may *feel* like salvation, it is not. It has never saved a single soul from perdition and never will.

The Fuzzy Line Between Sin and Sickness

I have spent much of my adult life pondering the relationship between morality and psychiatry. Now in my late fifties, I'm still not sure that I, or anyone else, understand it very well. It is not hard to find books written by so-called experts who tell us exactly how to think about this issue. Such guidance usually assumes one of two forms. The first reminds me of Job's advisers and takes the form "It's all sin, and people with psychological problems should stop sniveling and repent." The second reminds me of the demented Emperor Nero, who presumably fiddled while Rome burned, and takes the form "It's all sickness, and those who want to further oppress the emotionally afflicted with discussions of sin should themselves repent." Both extremes are simple-minded. For reasons that I cannot go into here, God has *intentionally* built into our lives a tremendous amount of moral ambiguity, and arbitrary attempts to make this ambiguity disappear are arrogant, dim-witted, or authoritarian—and sometimes all three. As we discussed in Chapter One, it is not always easy to distinguish between goodness and badness. It is even harder, sometimes, to tell the difference between badness and illness.

In Part Three, we are going to look in detail at eight toxic ways of relating to other people. In each instance, the question of sin will be lurking just beneath the surface of our discussion. Is the person who detests all human beings, stubbornly fights them at every turn, and withdraws from society sick or immoral (see Chapter Fourteen)? Is the individual who refuses to pull his or her weight, preferring instead to leech off of others, psychologically impaired or just plain lazy (see Chapter Ten)? Is the one who constantly makes other people feel inferior suffering from a medical (psychiatric) disorder, or is this person merely self-centered and mean-spirited (see Chapter Eleven)?

Psychotherapists have long been regarded as secular priests, which reflects an insidious social problem. Turning over to therapists and counselors responsibility for spiritual and moral guidance is like handing a well-intentioned child a loaded gun. The child is bound, eventually, to pull the trigger, and when this happens someone is likely to get hurt. By remanding the question of sin versus sickness into the hands of mental health experts, society manages to sidestep a pivotal question and, in the process, stick its head in the sand. Having lost its moorings to God, it finds itself adrift and is more than ready to turn over the helm to any secular authority claiming to know how to find land.

The Nature of Intimacy

Fellowship, as discussed in Chapter One, is not optional for Christians. It is not an elective in the curriculum of existence, a sort of supplemental offering that we can take or leave, depending on our preferences, level of energy, or available free time. At the heart of genuine fellowship lies holy intimacy. Since the word *intimacy* is used in different ways, I want to describe its three major forms and, along the way, make clear what I mean by an intimacy that is holy.

Sexual Intimacy

When people speak of sexual intimacy, they usually mean intercourse, although the term is sometimes used to mean any kind of erotic contact. Although sexual relations between married Christians can be a form of worship (see Romans 12:1–2), sexual intimacy has nothing inherently to do with fellowship.

Sex does not always involve other forms of intimacy. Millions of people, for example, have sexual relations without experiencing personal closeness. Their contact is mechanical and, while it may provide pleasurable release from pent-up tension, the whole encounter is impersonal. The participants may even detest each other.

Emotional Intimacy

This is the intimacy that people experience when they share their inner worlds. Such intimacy often develops between people who have no physical relationship, such as between teacher and student, supervisor and subordinate, mentor and protégé, and of course friends. Emotional closeness is, however, the doorway to sexual involvement for people who are potentially attractive to each other, which has a number of implications. One is that the strongest bonds of fellowship should *not* be between persons married to different spouses.

We all enjoy the privacy of our own minds. As discussed in Chapter One, no one else has access to what we think and feel. This means that we can spend our days mentally alone, cut off from other people. Or we can think out loud. We can disclose what we feel to others and invite them to do the same. Such disclosure is the foundation for genuine fellowship, which must be based on trust.

Spiritual Intimacy

When two people are brimming with the love of God, have the mind of Christ, and commune with the Holy Spirit, they have the potential to develop still another kind of intimacy and, with it, a deep bond. They can talk about the things of the Spirit without lapsing into clichés, and they radiate the glow of the Lord on their faces. Such intimacy is not some vague sense of oceanic spirituality. Nor is it the dry sharing of doctrine. It is the powerful communion that emerges among those who know and love the Lord.

If I had to come up with a single definition of a psychologically *healthy* person, a positive as opposed to a negative definition, it would be having the capacity for emotional intimacy. If I had to come up with a definition of what it means to be a *complete* person, it would be having the capacity for spiritual intimacy. Spiritual intimacy is, in truth, emotional intimacy that is centered on Christ.

Why Intimacy Is Central to Human Existence

People are born with an innate need for human closeness. It is *not* simply that we have been conditioned by experience to associate such closeness with getting our biological needs met. We don't seek intimacy simply because, when we were infants, we discovered that having people around meant milk and a clean diaper. Human beings are programmed for it. God created us that way, and people who do not need intimacy are, in one way or another, warped.

Intimacy is the vehicle for emotional support between persons and, since we are spiritual-emotional creatures, it is also the vehicle for spiritual support. Close relationships with others remind us that we are not alone in the universe, that we are indeed significant. Intimacy involves *mutuality,* a kind of give and take and bonding together, without either person sacrificing his or her individuality. You may take care of and minister to another human being today, and tomorrow that same person may take care of and minister to you.

As we will discuss shortly, intimacy also allows us to correct our misperceptions. You may be familiar with what happens in sensory deprivation experiments, when people are immersed in water tanks for days and so cut off from ordinary stimulation. Eventually, they begin to hallucinate and can no longer distinguish between fantasy and reality. The same sort of thing happens when people have little or no emotional communion with others. Their ideas become peculiar, their beliefs strange, and their perspectives distorted. We need people to keep us anchored to reality.

We all have ideas and impulses inside of us that we would prefer *not* to acknowledge; this is part and parcel of being fallen creatures in a fallen world. Most of the time, we try to suppress such material and do our best to make sure that other people never suspect that it exists. People have secrets, which they indulge in the private screening rooms of their minds, where no one else can see. It is tragic when Christians spend time in what they call fellowship and yet never share any of their secrets. I am not suggesting, of course, that you suddenly disclose all of yours, since this would only shock and frighten others. Yet by gradually disclosing your inner being to them, you will learn better to live in the light (John 3:19; Romans 2:16; Hebrews 4:13).

Communing with other Christians allows us to practice communing with the Creator. Some Christians, when they pray, sound as if they are talking to a school principal. They are stiff and have difficulty opening up to a Father who knows what they need before they ask (Matthew 6:8). Because God does not interact tangibly with us and we see "through a glass darkly" (1 Corinthians 13:12, KJV), it is important to develop spiritual-emotional intimacy with other believers so that it becomes natural for us to enjoy intimacy with the Father. We can *practice* relating to those whom we can see, in order that we may better be able to relate to Him whom we cannot see (1 John 4:20).

There is an still another benefit to intimacy. Evidence is accumulating day by day for a close connection between the biological and the psychological. Your immune system, for example, is less able to fight off infection when you are stressed. Intimacy, and the social support that comes with it, is a form of protection from stress. When you feel like you're at the end of your rope, a long talk with a close friend may help you even more than a week's vacation in Hawaii.

Intimacy and Language

Intimacy rests on person-to-person communication that is accurate and complete, which means that words are important. The creation of intimacy requires the sharing of feelings, and you cannot share what you cannot express. Human emotions are so subtle that it is almost impossible to do a good job of expressing them without relying on speech.

Reading other people accurately almost always involves learning to decipher nonverbal behavior. People who lean toward you in a conversation, for example, are usually expressing involvement, while those who lean away may be expressing skepticism or disagreement. While such cues may reveal basic attitudes, they will never replace language. We human beings become intimate only when we are able to put complex emotional states into words.

The language of intimacy does not have to be Oxford English. Nor does it have to reflect advanced education. There are plenty of people who, though never having progressed past grade school, are well able to communicate their feelings. To be sure, some individuals seem naturally gifted at conveying what is going on inside, while others have trouble coming up with more than grunts and grimaces. Just as we can't all run the four-minute mile, earn a degree in nuclear physics, or have babies—only half the population can do this—we are not all equally skilled in the expression of emotion.

That some people find it easier and some harder to express themselves does not, however, alter the fact that verbal communication is essential to intimacy. This is an area where counseling professionals can be of enormous help, since any competent counselor is usually able to improve the expressive capacities of just about anyone.

Loneliness and the Trap of Isolation

People who lack intimacy in their lives are often profoundly lonely, which is a horrible state of existence. There is perhaps no better definition of hell than being cut off from contact with all other spiritual beings. As suggested earlier, when people do not communicate with others, they tend to become strange. Imagination takes the place of reality, and private mental conversations substitute for real ones. We all have beliefs and perceptions that are a little off and attitudes that are based on distorted views of the world. If we are fortunate enough to enjoy at least some intimacy with others, our ideas won't be too peculiar, and we will probably get on well in life. They will correct our thinking. "You're crazy," they may say good-heartedly when we say something that reflects a serious misperception. Intimates make such corrections for each other all the time. This is the stuff of which good friendships and satisfying marriages are made.

Isolated people never get to hear these sorts of corrections. They fall victim to a kind of perceptual drift and veer off course from reality. The result is that isolated people often behave in ways that others tend to punish.

Such punishment can range from ridicule to ostracism. The latter only intensifies the isolation, which in turn makes it all the more likely that the person will make social blunders. The whole thing becomes a vicious circle. Isolation leads to peculiarity (idiosyncrasy), which leads to even more social isolation, which in turn creates more peculiarity. Sometimes, however, the isolated person becomes the aggressor, predator rather than prey.

As I will elaborate later, moving away from people is often a form of moving *against* them. Isolation, therefore, is not simply a matter of deciding to be alone or to lead a private life; it can amount to making war on humanity. Such war is sometimes overt, as in the case of the Victimizer (Chapter Thirteen), and sometimes covert, as in the case of the Avoider (Chapter Fourteen). But overt or covert, it is war nonetheless, and it is damaging to everyone. We should, as much as possible, move *toward* people.

Love Versus Fear

Christians have a new life that allows them to relate to God as beloved children, and it is the knowledge of His love that provides the antidote to fear. Paul writes, "For you did not receive a spirit that makes you a slave again to fear, but you received the Spirit of sonship [adoption]" (Romans 8:15, NIV). And in 1 John 4:18, we read, "There is no fear in love. But perfect love drives out fear, because fear has to do with punishment" (NIV). We could also substitute the word *anxiety* for *fear* in these verses.

We will always be somewhat vulnerable to fear and anxiety. Just as we live in the tension between sin and holiness (Romans 6–8), we also live in the tension between faith and love, on one hand, and fear and anxiety, on the other. This tension lies at the core of human existence. It should be no surprise, then, that psychologists and psychiatrists have focused so much on anxiety. If there is any concept that is central to the work of therapists, and has been since the days of Sigmund Freud (1856–1939), it is this one.

Anxiety is closely related to fear but involves a diffuse sense of foreboding. Unlike fear, which is associated with a specific object, person, situation, or event, anxiety is by nature vague, amorphous, and generalized. It is akin to what we mean by insecurity and apprehension, only the source for it remains unclear.

It is this insecurity, this apprehension, that often prompts people to prevent or destroy intimacy. Anxiety is so unpleasant that we all develop strategies to reduce it. For some people, their anxiety reduction maneuvers make emotional closeness difficult if not impossible, and they repeatedly choose comfort over closeness. It is this choice that often sets the stage for toxic relationships.

Preview of Part Two

In Chapters Three through Five, we will examine how people typically behave toward each other. We will look at how they lead, nurture, bond, follow, compete, oppose, stonewall, and yield. Then, in Chapter Six, we will begin to see what happens when otherwise healthy behaviors become rigid or extreme.

HOW PEOPLE TRAIN EACH OTHER

THE FOUR CHAPTERS in Part Two contain an enormous amount of useful information in an accessible form. It is possible to skip these chapters and proceed immediately to those in Part Three that most interest you—the chapters that describe toxic behavior. I recommend, however, that you first work your way through these four chapters because together they provide an incredibly rich foundation for understanding what people do with, and to, each other. This foundation will allow you to make sense out of many interpersonal exchanges that you may have previously found baffling and confusing: Why in the world did he or she do *that*?

Chapter Three, titled "Making Sense of Everyday Behavior," presents an elegantly simple way to decode just about anything one person does in relation to another. The ideas and findings presented in the chapter are based on many years of research, and in my view every Christian should know something about them. Relationships are not optional. As can be seen throughout scripture, their quality matters enormously to the Father and should therefore matter enormously to us.

Chapter Four, "Modes and Styles of Ordinary Interaction," demonstrates how the information presented in Chapter Three can be used to categorize normal social behavior into one of four basic modes (Warm Assertion, Warm Subordination, Cold Assertion, Cold Subordination) and, on a more fine-grained level, into eight specific styles (Leading, Nurturing, Bonding, and so on). Each of the four modes expresses a fundamental strategic purpose (such as Caring or Attaching). And each of the eight styles brings with it specific tactics (Inspiring and Guiding, Protecting and Providing, Connecting and Appreciating, and the like).

Chapter Five, "The Hidden Rules of Human Relationships," begins to unveil the impressive power of interpersonal psychology, especially for the Christian who wants his or her relationships to reflect the presence of God. As you will see, we continually shape how others treat us, and they do the same in return. Understanding how this happens brings order out of chaos. It does this by enabling you to see how certain interpersonal acts invite and reinforce specific reactions from others. What may have seemed like random moves and countermoves on a chessboard suddenly become predictable steps in a dance. You can now understand the choreography.

Finally, Chapter Six, "Overview of Interpersonal Toxicity," provides an introduction to toxic behavior. The information in that chapter builds directly on concepts and principles presented in Chapters Three, Four, and Five.

3

MAKING SENSE
OF EVERYDAY BEHAVIOR

*Now the LORD God had formed out of the ground all the
beasts of the field and all the birds of the air. He brought them to
the man to see what he would name them; and whatever the man
called each living creature, that was its name.*

—Genesis 2:19 [NIV]

GOD GAVE US MINDS and expects us to use them. This is an important
implication of the second chapter of Genesis, in which God entrusts Adam
with the job of naming the animals. We have a moral duty to think.

Adam's assignment was not intended to be an exercise in random labeling. The sense of the passage is *not* that Adam was supposed to pull meaningless names out of the air and, without much in the way of thought,
haphazardly slap them onto whichever creatures wandered by. Implicit in
the passage is the notion that Adam was to bring order to the mind-
boggling diversity of nature, not for God's sake—God did not need Adam's
help—but for man's.

Adam is to devise what in modern scientific language we would call a
taxonomy, a systematic classification of the animals that accurately reflects
the relationships between and among them. No small undertaking!

The Challenge Before Us

The task we face today, in attempting to understand human behavior, is
no less daunting than Adam's, especially when the behavior we're trying

to get our minds around is what goes on *between* people, that is, inter-personal as opposed to individual behavior. Nor is our challenge any less noble. It is inconceivable that the God who breathed life into us as the pinnacle of creation wants us to bury our heads in the turf by refusing to use our intellect to comprehend what, as people, we do in relation to each other—and why.

Like the primeval science undertaken by the first man, this compre-hension has to start with classification. Our work begins with sorting behaviors into categories that reflect important similarities and differences. We have to figure out which features—characteristics—of interpersonal behavior best help us make sense of what people do with, and to, each other when they interact. In trying to understand person-to-person behav-ior, the fundamental question becomes this: Are there a few basic types of interpersonal transactions and, if so, what are they? Or, to put the ques-tion another way, what are the fundamental "moves" people make when they are in each other's presence?

Process Versus Content

We all learn from an early age to focus on what other people say. Parents tell us to "listen carefully," and teachers encourage us to "pay close atten-tion." The constant message is, "Make sure that you absorb the *content* of communication." An example of content would be Aunt Martha's instruction that we wash our hands before reaching for the candy in her cupboard.

Most of us quickly figure out that content is important. Failing to un-derstand it can prove costly. If we refuse to wash our hands, Aunt Martha withholds the candy. If we don't pay attention in math class, we flunk the exam. And if we ignore the motor vehicle code, we pay expensive fines and, eventually, forfeit the privilege of driving.

In many areas of life, content is pretty much all there is and therefore all you have to worry about. But when it comes to interpersonal relation-ships, *process* is just as significant as content and sometimes more so. What people intend by what they say, and how they say it, can be far more important than the words they use.

Process concerns how people position themselves in relation to each other and thus how they structure or define their interactions. It has largely to do with their social maneuvers.

While content is the domain of what's happening *explicitly* between people, process is the realm of what's going on *implicitly*. Content is more or less self-evident. Person A says "X" and Person B responds with "Y." No mystery to be found there. Process, by contrast, usually has to be decoded. Learning how to do such decoding, quickly and easily, is fundamental to understanding human interaction. Decoding means penetrating beneath the surface to discern the deeper meaning of what's transpiring. It requires posing and accurately answering this pivotal question, originally formulated by Harry Stack Sullivan (1892–1949): "What is this person trying to do with, or to, me (or others) in this situation?"

This is not the sort of question you learn to answer in school. You probably never took a course in the decoding of interpersonal messages. Nor is the ability to do this measured by conventional tests. Many otherwise gifted individuals attend only to content and, as a result, never comprehend what's happening around them. They are endlessly baffled by what other people say and do and are customarily the ones about whom we may say, "They just don't get it." Spend a minute or two reasoning your way through the following exercise.

○

Exercise 3.1

Two people are working together to decorate the large reception area adjoining a church. The following statements are made by one of them—let's call her Harriet. On the surface, they all communicate the same content, that Harriet wants help. This is the explicit message they have in common. Our interest lies in decoding their implicit messages. How would you describe the implicit message in each case?

1. "This is how I'd like you to assist me this afternoon."

2. "Would you possibly have time to help me later today?"

3. "Please make sure you get this done before you leave."

4. "If you can't help me, just forget it!—I'll do it myself."

○

What we can't determine from such printed sentences is tone of voice or body language, either of which could radically alter the meaning of what Harriet is communicating. If, for example, she sarcastically mutters the question in item 2, an otherwise gentle request for assistance may become a hostile attack. For the sake of this exercise, assume that no noteworthy nonverbal messages accompany each statement. While there are many potential answers to these questions, in a moment I will discuss an elegantly simple but powerful way to answer all such questions.

Bringing Order out of Confusion

Harvard psychologist Gordon W. Allport (1897–1967) once determined that there were over five thousand words in the English language having to do with behavior. Depending on how you count, the total may be closer to seven thousand. Spend even a few minutes thumbing through a dictionary and you will be impressed, if not astounded, by the number of nouns, adjectives, verbs, and adverbs that relate to how people think, feel, and act toward each other:

> "Harold is a terrible *grouch*." (noun)
>
> "The expression on Mary's face is always *friendly*." (adjective)
>
> "Susie *embraced* her husband when he returned home." (verb)
>
> "During the meeting, Tom spoke *sternly* to everyone." (adverb)

Is there a scientific way to distill such aspects of behavior into their basic qualities or components? Can we reduce the chaos and redundancy? How much of a real difference is there, for example, between *euphoric* and *elated*? While such nuances might matter to a novelist, do they make any significant difference in everyday life?

We could huddle around a conference table and debate what aspects of interpersonal behavior to regard as basic, but this would hardly qualify as science. There are, however, sound methods for answering such questions. During the past fifty years, they have yielded impressive results that bear directly on our subject. It is to these results that we now turn.

Two Primary Axes of Interpersonal Behavior

Long before there was any systematic research into human interaction, Karen Horney (1885–1952) suggested that there were three fundamental ways in which people "orient" themselves in relation to others: toward, against, and away. As we will see shortly, she correctly identified one of the two principal features of interpersonal behavior. She also contributed an insight that is worth mentioning early in our discussion.

While it is obvious that moving toward others is generally preferable to moving against them, Horney pointed out that moving against another person is, in many instances, better than moving away. This is because when you are arguing with someone else, for example, at least you remain engaged. The relationship is far more in danger of ending when one of the persons stops arguing. The ultimate form of relational power is to cut off all contact and communication with the other person, which is why suicide is such a horrendous act. Quite aside from what it does to the person committing it, self-destruction ends all communion. The conversation is over. As we will see in Chapter Six, there is a close connection between moving against people and moving away from them. Extreme forms of moving away can be just as toxic and devastating as overt combat.

The insights of early-twentieth-century clinicians like Sullivan and Horney paved the way for behavioral scientists to answer the fundamental question we posed earlier, which I will restate here in a slightly altered form: Are there a small number of interpersonal processes that explain much of what goes on between people and, if so, what are they and how do they work?

It became increasingly clear during the second half of the twentieth century that there are two principal characteristics of relational behavior (see Figure 3.1). The first has to do with whether Person A assumes an interpersonal posture that is *one-up* or *one-down* in relation to Person B and the second with whether A moves *toward* or *away* from B.

One-Up Versus One-Down

Moving "one-up" means acting assertively. Introduced into the English language sometime in the fifteenth century, *assert* comes from a Latin verb meaning "to lay claim to" or, more specifically, "to claim rights over something or someone else." Knowingly or not, a person who moves one-up is attempting to establish some correctness of opinion, accuracy of knowledge, legitimacy of attitudes, or some other form of superiority. The individual moving one-up is defining himself or herself as enjoying and perhaps deserving a higher level of power, control, and status.

It is important to remember that some people move one-up out of necessity, not because they have a personal need to assert themselves over other people. Someone who takes swift action to save others from life-threatening danger is, for a time, asserting superiority, assuming control, and wielding power. Yet posturing in this manner may be the furthest thing from that person's mind and certainly not his or her primary intention.

Moving one-down implies deferring to someone else. People who reflexively move one-down are often more comfortable when others take control, shoulder responsibility, and exercise power.

Toward Versus Away

Moving toward others implies warmth, the willingness to include them, and a desire to make interpersonal connections. This is usually what we mean by friendliness. Some psychologists use the term *affection* for moving toward.

**Figure 3.1. Two Primary Features ("Dimensions")
of Interpersonal Behavior.**

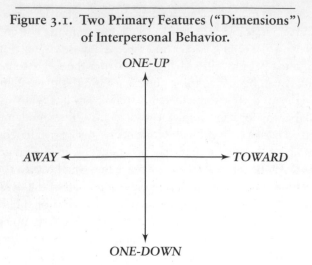

Source: © *Relational Dynamics Institute, Inc. Used by permission.*

Moving away, by contrast, reflects emotional coolness. If this coolness becomes pronounced, it turns into coldness and eventually aggression, which is active, or hostility, which is passive.

Actions that reflect high levels of moving toward tend to create pleasant relationships, at least for people not frightened by intimacy, while actions that involve moving away from others generally create unpleasant ones. Those who tend to move toward people prefer to remain on positive terms with them, while those who move away from people are more at home when relationships are distant or negatively toned.

Don't worry if you have trouble determining, right off, if someone you meet for the first time is trying to move toward or away from you. You will probably find out soon enough. And if you never do, it may not matter. But it could. In a potential romantic encounter, for example, neutrality could spell disaster. Nor would it work well for establishing a close friendship.

Figure 3.2 summarizes the behaviors that tend to go along with the different interpersonal stances.

Training Yourself to Think Relationally

Learning to think in these terms will take you a long way down the road toward understanding what's going on when people interact. It's like rapidly mastering a foreign language in that you quickly become able to

**Figure 3.2. Behavioral Implications
of Different Interpersonal Postures.**

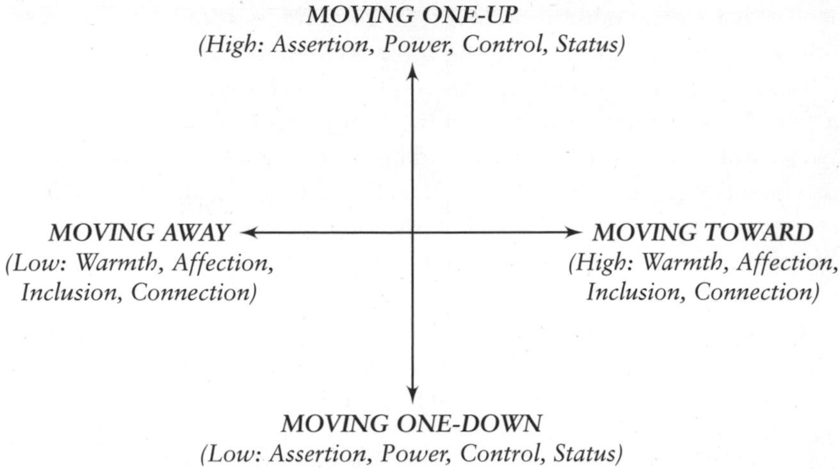

MOVING ONE-UP
(High: Assertion, Power, Control, Status)

MOVING AWAY ←——————————————→ *MOVING TOWARD*
(Low: Warmth, Affection,   *(High: Warmth, Affection,*
Inclusion, Connection)   *Inclusion, Connection)*

MOVING ONE-DOWN
(Low: Assertion, Power, Control, Status)

Source: © *Relational Dynamics Institute, Inc. Used by permission.*

translate (decode) just about anything another person says or does into its real (social) meaning. With a little practice, you will learn to make such translations almost instantly.

What sometimes makes the analysis of human relations difficult is that you have to think about what A and B are doing at the same time. If, for example, A attempts to move one-up while B tries to move up even further, there is likely to be conflict. But even this should eventually become second nature to you.

In learning to decode interpersonal behavior, you will inevitably make mistakes. But unless you intend to become a psychotherapist who specializes in personality disorders, it is not important to be able to detect every subtlety. You just have to be able to tell, more or less generally, how people are attempting to position themselves: what postures they are assuming and why they may be assuming them in the first place.

When Andrew speaks boisterously and never lets anyone else get a word in edgewise, what is he really doing, and what does he hope to accomplish? The short answer is that he is attempting to move one-up and away from others at the same time. He's attempting to exert aggressive control.

Examples of One-Up Versus One-Down and Toward Versus Away Behavior

Robert Bales spent most of his life trying to make sense of what people do when they interact, and some of his most important ideas are contained in *Personality and Interpersonal Behavior* (Holt, Rinehart and Winston, 1970). For what he called "interaction process analysis," he came up with twelve examples of behavior, arranged into four groups, and these turn out nicely to fit into our model (Figure 3.1). Recall that a model is a simplified representation that stands for and, in the ideal, captures the essence of real-life phenomena. It shows us how something looks or works, its structure or function.

For clarity, I have modified the name of each group so that it corresponds to one pole of either the "one-up *versus* one-down" or "toward *versus* away" axis (dimension). Here they are, with Bales's behavioral examples:

> *One-Up* (N): Gives suggestion, gives opinion, gives information
>
> *One-Down* (S): Asks for suggestion, asks for opinion, asks for information
>
> *Toward* (E): Seems friendly, dramatizes, agrees
>
> *Away* (W): Seems unfriendly, shows tension, disagrees

The letters in parentheses indicate the four cardinal points on a compass (north, south, east, west), as if Figure 3.1 were a map, and in a sense it is. The model it depicts is a kind of navigation guide to how human beings act with, and toward, each other. Try the following exercise.

○

Exercise 3.2

Using the information just given, classify the behavior of each of the following persons into one of the following categories: one-up, one-down, toward, or away.

1. Lillian solicits other people's opinions and suggestions and frequently asks questions.

2. Greg makes recommendations, freely expresses his views, and shares lots of facts.

3. Judy is warm and highly expressive and often says "Good idea!" when others contribute.

4. Steve seems distant, fidgets uncomfortably, and often takes exception to what other people say.

○

By comparing Lillian's behavior (item 1) with the behavioral examples provided by Bales, we see that she postures in a way that is at least mildly one-down; note, however, that we cannot determine from the description how friendly she is or isn't. Greg (item 2) positions himself one-up; again, we can't tell if he's friendly or unfriendly. Judy (item 3) moves toward, rather than away, from people; we do not know how assertive she is. And Steve (item 4) moves away; we don't know if he puts himself one-up or one-down.

The True Nature of Behavior: Dimensions Versus Categories

Certain human characteristics fall into discrete categories. A woman, for example, is either pregnant or she is not. There is no in-between. In the technical jargon, pregnancy is measured on a "dichotomous" scale, one that has only two values, in this case "pregnant" and "not pregnant." All-or-none characteristics occur much less frequently, however, than those that show up in varying degrees. Such characteristics must be measured on "continuous" scales that, in theory, contain an infinite number of points. Paul and Alex may both be six feet tall. But if we measure more and more precisely, eventually we will discover that one of them is taller than the other. The difference may be trivial, but it is still there.

Notice that the caption for Figure 3.1 contains the word *dimensions* in parentheses. This is to emphasize that interpersonal behavior does not usually fall neatly into categories; it is more a matter of the degree of this or that. There are gradations of moving toward and away, just as there are gradations of moving one-up and one-down. The relational behavior of some people, for example, routinely falls close to the center of the diagram. They move neither up nor down and neither toward nor away. The behavior of others is almost always far from the neutral point on one or both dimensions.

For the sake of speed, it is often helpful, when analyzing interpersonal behavior, to think in terms of categories (dichotomies)—one-up *versus* one-down, toward *versus* away. But it is important to bear in mind that such yes-or-no, on-or-off, this-versus-that thinking is only fiction. Such fiction is useful when interactions are occurring quickly and you have to make sense of them in real time. Still, there is no invisible point at which one-down magically turns into one-up or away suddenly becomes toward. All such interpersonal border crossings are, in the end, arbitrary. People are not friendly *or* unfriendly, for example, as if we could conveniently divide the population of the world into two camps. Toni, Brian, and Kathy may all be friendly, but Toni may, in general, be friendlier than Kathy, who may in turn be friendlier than Brian. This is why we must think and speak in terms of dimensions.

A dimension, for our purposes, is a scale reflecting different amounts of something, such as the number of gallons of fuel remaining in the tank of your car. We "scale" things all the time. If you try to calculate the probability of making it through the next intersection before the light changes or to forecast how much rain will fall in the morning, you are using scales that run, in the first case, from "no chance" to "I've almost cleared the intersection already" and, in the second, from "no rain" to "we're in for a deluge that'll make Noah's seem light."

We turn now to examine the sorts of behaviors represented by each end of our two scales.

How the Two Dimensions Blend Together in Real Life

Moving one-up and one-down cannot be done simultaneously. If you take a one-up stance in relation to Phillip, you cannot in the same instant place yourself one-down to him. The same is true of moving toward and away. If you act coldly toward Brandon, you cannot also act warmly, at least not in the same moment and not genuinely.

Yet as illustrated in Exercise 3.2, moving one-up versus one-down and moving toward versus away have *nothing* in principle to do with each other. Each example in the exercise represented a relatively pure form of one of the four poles (ends) of our dimensions (see Figure 3.1).

Knowing where someone is on one of the two dimensions (axes) gives us absolutely no information about where he or she is on the other. This is partly why the model presented in Figure 3.1 is so powerful. It contains no redundancy.

If someone reports that Thomas, whom we have never met, is assertive, we know that he tends to move to a one-up position. But he could be an aloof and bossy know-it-all or a strong leader who cares deeply about others. If we hear that Rhonda, whom we have not met either, loves people, she could be either a strong charismatic leader or a docile puppy who does whatever anyone else suggests.

In everyday life, a person's behavior typically reflects both dimensions at the same time (some level of assertion and some level of warmth). The two dimensions can be, and usually are, "crossed" so that they reflect themselves in four basic types (quadrants) of action, as depicted in Table 3.1. A person can, for example, move both toward *and* one-down.

○

Exercise 3.3

Classify each of the following statements into one of these four categories: (a) toward and one-up, (b) toward and one-down, (c) away and one-up, or (d) away and one-down. It may help to refer to Table 3.1 as you do this.

1. "OK, you win, just as you always do."
2. "I can do anything better than you can."
3. "I'd be glad to show you how to do that."
4. "I'm willing to do whatever you think best."

○

While it is difficult to know for sure without hearing voice intonations and seeing body language, statement 1 is probably (c), away and one-down; statement 2 is (b), away and one-up; statement 3 is (a), toward and one-up; and statement 4 is (d), toward and one-down.

Situational Differences

To complicate matters further, where the behavior of a specific individual falls on any dimension, such as friendliness, can depend a great deal on circumstance. If we rank-ordered the three people mentioned earlier on a scale from most to least friendly, we would have this: Toni, Kathy, Brian. But such a rank ordering would only be "in general." Depending on the situation (for example, with whom each is interacting), this rank ordering could change dramatically.

Kathy may be friendlier toward telemarketers who call her during dinner than either of the other two would ever be, and Toni may behave with extraordinary intolerance toward them ("I haven't got time for this nonsense— get me off your list and don't ever call again!"). The rank order for warmth in relation to telemarketers becomes this: Kathy, Brian, Toni (who is *unfriendly* toward telemarketers). Yet Brian may be friendlier toward street people (for example, homeless alcoholics) than either Toni or Kathy. Thus in relation to such individuals, the rank order might become this: Brian, Toni, Kathy.

Table 3.1. Behavioral Combinations Implied by Figure 3.1.

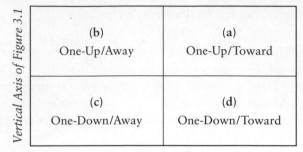

(b) One-Up/Away	**(a)** One-Up/Toward
(c) One-Down/Away	**(d)** One-Down/Toward

Vertical Axis of Figure 3.1

Horizontal Axis of Figure 3.1

While all of us show general interpersonal tendencies (traits)—reflecting how we tend, on average, to act—a good interpersonal analysis *always* takes into account the behavior of the *other* person. It makes little sense, most of the time, to ask about Person A's interpersonal (social) behavior in isolation. We must ask about Person A's behavior in relation to a specific other individual (Person B) or group of individuals (Persons C, D, and E) and perhaps also in a specific situation (for example, maneuvering for the last parking space) and setting (for example, shopping mall versus church parking lot).

Appearances Versus Realities

Most people quickly define themselves on the two dimensions (one-up versus one-down and toward versus away), and therefore, in the majority of cases, we don't need to go sleuthing around for clues. As long as you know what to look for—which is what this book is about—the task is usually easy. People often flood us with so much data that we have trouble keeping up with it all, and we may end up feeling like we're standing in front of the conveyor belt in that well known *I Love Lucy* episode, the one in which Lucille Ball begins to stuff candy into her mouth and under her hat because she can't get it into the wrappers fast enough. Fortunately, it really doesn't matter if we "get it all," because people usually give us a great deal of redundant information.

Nevertheless, it is sometimes necessary to look for the hidden meaning of what others are doing. Although the majority of people provide plenty of valid information about themselves, some offer up almost none. Worse, a certain percentage of individuals are so skilled at deception (dissemblance) that, for a time, you may misread them. They will pretend to be warm but are, in reality, cold and calculating. Some people feign being gracious servant-leaders but, underneath their solicitous behavior, exert a sinister form of Machiavellian control.

In such cases, it is far from easy to make sense of what, on an unseen level, may be going on. "The heart is deceitful above all things, and desperately wicked: who can know it?" (Jeremiah 17:9, NIV). This is yet another reason to make a careful study of interpersonal processes and how the people you encounter position themselves.

More Hands-On Practice

Let's return briefly to Exercise 3.1. For each of the statements uttered by Harriet, try to answer these two questions:

1. Is she moving one-up or one-down?
2. Is she moving toward or away?

In her first statement—"This is how I'd like you to assist me this afternoon"—Harriet is moving to a one-up as opposed to a one-down position. We cannot determine, from the information provided, if Harriet is formally in charge of the decorating or if she's taken it upon herself to be in charge. Regardless, Harriet has moved one-up. She does not, however, appear to be distancing herself or acting in an unfriendly manner. So she is moving toward rather than away.

The second statement—"Would you possibly have time to help me later today?"—also involves moving toward, but it is made from a one-down position. Such a posture may be perfectly appropriate. Harriet is petitioning and, in the process, acknowledging that her friend has the power, and perhaps the right, to say no.

Statement 3, like statement 1, is made from a one-up position but probably not a warm one: "Please make sure you get this done before you leave." While it is difficult to know for sure, her stance seems to be less than friendly. Perhaps the person she's speaking to has previously flaked out on important responsibilities and Harriet is not about to let this happen again.

Harriet's fourth statement—"If you can't help me, just forget it!—I'll do it myself"—appears to convey resentment. Maybe she's asked the person for help many times before and been given one excuse after another.

Harriet is positioning herself one-down; she is also backing away, distancing herself from the other person.

Flexibility and Adaptation

Nothing is inherently wrong with any of these postures because, unless people were willing to move in and out of different roles, social interaction would resemble billiard balls randomly caroming off each other. There would be no predictability to it, and relationships would devolve into chronic confusion. Imagine what it would be like if no one ever deferred to anyone else or, flipping things around, if everyone always deferred. Healthy people are able to assume different postures. They tend to take whatever interpersonal stance best fits the circumstances, unless, of course, there is some higher (for example, moral) reason for doing otherwise.

Psychologically whole people do not, for example, belligerently argue with police officers. Nor do they passively wait for others to take charge ("do something") when they are the only ones around in an emergency. They intuitively sense where to place themselves on the vertical dimension of one-up versus one-down and have no need to remain rigidly fixed at either end of the spectrum. Such people act assertively in one situation and deferentially in another.

They also know instinctively what makes sense on the horizontal dimension. Christians, one would hope, would have a predilection for moving toward rather than away from others. This is because Christianity is inclusive rather than exclusive, affiliative rather than standoffish, warm rather than cold: "I give you a new commandment, that you love one another. Just as I have loved you, you also should love one another" (John 13: 34, NRSV). A warm posture is generally to be preferred.

But as we will see throughout the rest of this book, there are times when moving away from a specific person is necessary and clearly God's will. If we refuse to move away at such times, we are throwing back in God's face the gift of life he has given us as stewards and perhaps also reinforcing bad behavior in others.

Invitations, Requests, Suggestions, or Commands

Just about everything one person does in relation to another contains a bid and an instruction. Person A does something—let's call it "S" for stimulus—that he or she hopes Person B will respond to in a certain way—let's call this "R" for response.

Behavior "S," at the very least, amounts to an invitation. Example: "I'm behaving nicely toward you and invite you to reciprocate."

If A's communication is made with slightly more force, it becomes a request. Example: "I'm being nice to you and ask that you do the same in return."

It is one thing to be invited to a party, with total freedom to accept or decline the invitation. But it is quite another for the host specifically to ask you to attend. The second of the two utterances is therefore the more compelling.

If A communicates—makes a move—from a decidedly one-up position, the invitation or request takes on the character of a recommendation and sometimes a strong one. Example: "I think it would be a good idea—it would be in your interests—to be nice to me."

And if A assumes a pronounced one-up posture, "S" turns into nothing short of an order. No longer an invitation, request, or suggestion, it becomes a directive or an outright command. Example: "Be nice to me—and do it now!"

Establishing and maintaining nourishing relationships depends on the following three abilities:

1. Being able to detect invitations, requests, suggestions, and commands as they come at you in real life.

2. Having the wisdom to discern—in the moment or soon thereafter—whether these invitations, requests, suggestions, or commands are desirable or at least acceptable.

3. Knowing how to decline, ignore, modify, or countermand any of the four when there is merit in doing so.

Learning to detect whether the person with whom you are dealing is moving one-up or one-down and toward or away will give you a good start on ability 1. The rest of this book will help you develop the skills needed for abilities 2 and 3.

Interpersonal Arrangements

It is necessary to introduce one more concept that is fundamental to the study of human interaction and relationships. The behavior of Person A combines with the behavior of Person B to create an *interpersonal arrangement*. As we will explore further in Part Three, such an arrangement reflects an implied contract. The parties to the agreement promise to behave in specific ways and back up their promises with investments of time and energy. Each agrees, usually without conscious awareness, to play a certain role and thus to act according to an implicitly understood script. While both parties intuitively grasp this script, it would be rare indeed for either of them to be able to articulate it with any precision. But living in society for decades, as they have, both individuals more or less instinctively understand what they are to do and also that they cannot deviate too far from the script without consequences. Interpersonal arrangements follow highly predictable patterns that seem, at times, to operate with the force of law.

The following metaphors may give you a preliminary feel for how such arrangements operate, a topic to which we will return again and again:

○ *Table tennis:* Person A's serve determines how Person B returns the ball, which in turn affects how A hits it back, and so on; if the relationship becomes stable, the two players hit it to each other for a long time.

○ *Pendulum:* The pendulum swings in one direction and then in the other, in a series of moves and countermoves. While there are no perpetual-motion machines, some pendulums, once set in motion, carve out the same arc almost endlessly.

○ *Seesaw:* When A goes up, B goes down, and so on.

○ *Dance:* Both partners tacitly agree on who is to lead whom, and the one who is not leading follows.

Interpersonal arrangements resemble all of these things.

Self-Reflection

Before proceeding further, complete this exercise in self-discovery.

_____ ○ _____

Exercise 3.4

Ask yourself the following questions:

1. Do I generally tend to move one-up or one-down in my relationships with others?

2. In relation to whom do I most strongly position myself one-up? How about one-down?

3. Do I tend, in general, to move toward or away from others?

4. In relation to whom do I most enthusiastically move toward?

5. In relation to whom do I most quickly move away?

Then ask two or three people who know you well to answer the same questions about you. How do they see you positioning yourself with others? Try to view yourself through their eyes.

---

o

In the next chapter, we will examine the four basic modes of behavior that emerge directly from Figure 3.1 and the two specific styles associated with each of these modes.

4

MODES AND STYLES
OF ORDINARY INTERACTION

*Live in harmony with one another. . . . Be careful to do what is
right in the eyes of everybody. If it is possible, as far as
it depends on you, live at peace with everyone.*

—Romans 12:16–18 [NIV]

WE EXPLORED, IN CHAPTER THREE, the two fundamental dimensions
(axes) of human interaction: one-up *versus* one-down and toward *versus*
away, as depicted in Figure 3.1. Combining these in various ways, we ar-
rive at four basic modes of interpersonal behavior (such as one-up together with toward). In this chapter, we will examine what these four
modes actually look like in real life. If, for example, a person tends to
move one-up and away, how is he or she likely to act in a group?

Each of these four modes can be expressed in one of two interpersonal
styles, and we will explore these also. Because toxic behavior is often an
exaggerated form of conventional behavior, this will lay the foundation
for our discussion of toxic relationships in Part Three. For our purposes,
we can think of conventional behavior as healthy.

Our focus, in this chapter, remains on what normal people do. I am
using normal in the statistical sense of average. We all have moments of
acting outlandishly and perhaps a few episodes here and there of abject
toxicity, when no sane person would choose to be around us. The only
person ever to have escaped this was Jesus. But for the most part, normal
people act in conventional ways. By this I mean that they do things that
tend to be functional rather than dysfunctional. Although we may not

experience all people who behave in functional ways as nourishing, neither are they especially toxic.

Not everything that normal people do is ideal. Certain behaviors may not fit well at all with what's going on (Stan interrupts a lot at meetings). At times, it may be markedly inappropriate (Betsy routinely pulls out a novel whenever she gets bored with the conversation). But such behavior is not dramatically noxious.

Figure 3.1 presented a skeleton that we must now flesh out. Our immediate task is to supply names—remember Adam's task in Genesis 2—to the four quadrants of conventional behavior summarized in Table 3.1 (for example, "one-up/toward"). Figure 4.1 supplies such names (such as Warm Subordination).

The Nature of an Interpersonal Strategy

In discussing the difference between interpersonal content and process in Chapter Three, we emphasized that, when trying to make sense of what people do to and with each other, it is important to focus on intentions. We also noted that interpersonal intentions are often hidden. Sometimes this is because a person wants to conceal his or her true motives. More often, it is because people—ordinary human beings like you and me—are only dimly aware of what their intentions are. This does not change the fact that we all have them.

When we interact with another person, we are almost always translating into concrete action some kind of strategic purpose. The line between a *strategic purpose,* which is an intention, and a *strategy,* which is an overarching approach, is such a fine one that we will use the terms more or less interchangeably. The important issue is contained in Harry Stack Sullivan's question (noted in Chapter Three): What is this person trying to do with or to me in this situation?

○

Exercise 4.1

What do you suppose is the strategic purpose behind each of the following—what, in each case, is the person trying to do?

1. Warm Assertion

2. Cold Assertion

3. Cold Subordination

4. Warm Subordination

○

Figure 4.1. Four Conventional Modes of Relating to Other People.

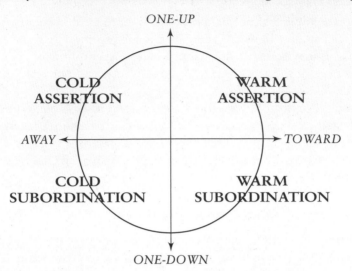

ONE-UP

COLD
ASSERTION

WARM
ASSERTION

AWAY ← → TOWARD

COLD
SUBORDINATION

WARM
SUBORDINATION

ONE-DOWN

Source: © *Relational Dynamics Institute, Inc. Used by permission.*

Figure 4.2 presents one way to think of the four strategies. Each mode of conventional behavior is associated with a characteristic approach to other people. Note that while the four modes of behavior (such as Cold Subordination) are expressed in terms made up of adjectives and nouns, the strategies associated with them are expressed in terms derived from verbs.

Discussion of the Strategies

Caring is the principal strategy of the individual whose behaviors can be classified as Warm Assertion. It is an active strategy in which the person assumes control of the relationship but does so in a benevolent way. Caring is seizing the initiative in a friendly manner and, like the other three strategies, can be expressed through one of two specific styles (to be explained shortly). Caring brings to mind a mother bear looking after her cubs.

Attaching is the strategy most directly associated with Warm Subordination, which combines friendliness with deference. It is more passive than active and hence does not reflect initiative as much as alignment. You might assume, therefore, that the person relying on Warm Subordination has little or no role in shaping the nature of a relationship. To the contrary, the person who relates by Attaching is inviting others to care. Attaching is like the purr of a tabby cat.

Figure 4.2. Interpersonal Strategies Corresponding to the Four Conventional Modes of Relating.

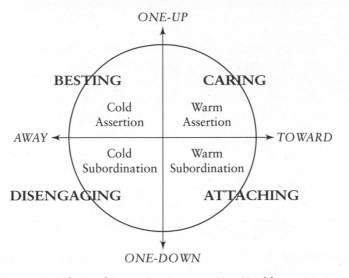

Source: © *Relational Dynamics Institute, Inc. Used by permission.*

Besting others, the strategy associated with Cold Assertion, mixes moving away with moving one-up. Think of it as taking the initiative in an aloof manner. Like the Caring associated with Warm Assertion, Besting is active. It makes things happen by prompting others to react, sometimes sharply. Besting is the striving motif of the racehorse.

Disengaging, like Besting, maintains distance, but it does this in a passive one-down manner. It is the strategy connected with Cold Subordination, a reluctant form of deference. Whereas Attaching involves slow-response feelings (for example, affection), Disengaging often involves fast-response feelings (for example, irritation). As with Attaching, you might initially assume that the person who majors in Disengaging plays little or no part in determining the nature of the relationship. But this is not so. Disengaging can be every bit as much a bid and an instruction (see Chapter Three) as Caring, Attaching, or Besting. Disengaging can resemble the snarl of a mountain lion.

Eight Specific Styles

Each of the four modes of behavior can be expressed through one of two specific styles. The following exercise illustrates why being able to recognize

such styles is important—why it is not enough simply to be able to identify the basic mode of interaction (such as Cold Assertion).

○

Exercise 4.2

Charles is a confident person who takes pride in his ability as a finance
committee chairperson, and he makes no attempt to hide this. From his
behavior, it is clear that he thinks of himself as a more competent financial manager than anyone else on his committee. He does not hesitate
to tell them what he thinks, and they generally regard him as distant.
When he believes strongly in something—whether he's right or wrong—
he will stand firm, and nothing or no one is likely to change his mind.
And he enforces *Robert's Rules of Order* as if they were a religion.
What is his mode of relating to other people (see Figure 4.1), and what
is his principal interpersonal strategy (see Figure 4.2)?

○

His orientation is clearly one of superiority. He shows no reluctance to
assert himself or to use power, and thus he approaches those on his committee from a one-up position. Charles is also aloof, does not seem motivated to make "warm fuzzy" connections, and seems disinclined to
enfranchise others. His mode of relating to others on the committee is
Cold Assertion, and his strategy is Besting.

Based on this information alone, however, we do not know much, if
anything, about the specific way in which Charles strives. Does he focus
more on getting the job done or on making others pay for their mistakes?
Is his emphasis more on driving the agenda of meetings or on making
those who cross him uncomfortable?

Figure 4.3 shows the two specific styles that are associated with each
general mode of relating. You might think of each style as a substrategy.
You can, for example, care for another person by *Leading* or by *Nurturing*. You can attach—warmth plus subordination—either by *Bonding* or
Following. You can strive by *Competing* or *Opposing*. And you can disengage by *Stonewalling* or *Yielding*.

Is Interpersonal Behavior Strategic?

Is everything a person does in relation to another human being purposeful? Does every snippet of interpersonal behavior really embody a strategy? Is it fair, for example, to suggest that those who rely on Besting
others have a different set of motives from those who rely on Attaching
to them? And what about the substrategies? When a person "yields"

Figure 4.3. Eight Conventional Styles of Relating to Other People.

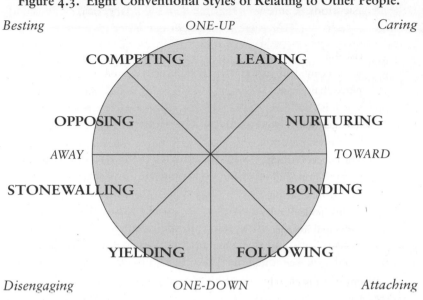

Besting   ONE-UP   *Caring*

COMPETING   LEADING

OPPOSING   NURTURING

AWAY   *TOWARD*

STONEWALLING   BONDING

YIELDING   FOLLOWING

Disengaging   ONE-DOWN   *Attaching*

Source: © *Relational Dynamics Institute, Inc. Used by permission.*

rather than "resists," say, in the wake of an argument, has he or she actually *chosen* one option over the other? Couldn't it simply be a matter of responding automatically—like a reflex?

Interpersonal behavior is indeed reflexive—automatic. Most of what we do in relation to others takes place without conscious planning. We don't think about it; we just do it—which is why it is difficult to change long-term personality patterns. This does not mean that it lacks purpose. One typical purpose is to elicit from others responses with which one is familiar and therefore comfortable. A nasty person who routinely provokes people to distance themselves may become acutely distressed if someone moves closer and acts warmly.

Interpersonal modes and styles operate within a given individual, year after year, because they prove reinforcing. They accomplish something that the person wants—something of which he or she may, however, be largely unaware. A person's behavior in relation to others is intended to do one or more of these three things:

1. Obtain rewards (such as status or security)

2. Avoid punishments (such as criticism or embarrassment)

3. Escape unpleasantness (such as anxiety or uncertainty)

The first is what we usually mean by *positive reinforcement,* and the second and third are forms of *negative reinforcement* (avoidance and escape conditioning, respectively). Note that punishment is *not* negative reinforcement. It is the prevention or cessation of punishment that is reinforcing; all reinforcement, by definition, increases the probability of the behavior that immediately preceded it.

Conscious Versus Unconscious Motivation

But do people *consciously* intend to implement interpersonal strategies and thus to accomplish what they do in relation to others (such as push them away)? How can we know that which, by definition, we do not know? If something is unconscious, we do not know what it is; that's what it means for it to be unconscious in the first place. Do we have two minds, one conscious and the other unconscious, so that much of what we do can be blamed on the latter? "I didn't do it—my unconscious did."

People do *not* have secondary minds inside of them, and there is no concrete barrier between what is conscious and what is unconscious. The boundary between consciousness (awareness) and unconsciousness (unawareness) is fluid and permeable.

Properly used, the term *unconscious* refers to events within us of which we have little or no awareness. It is best to avoid speaking of "the" unconscious, as if we were referring to an entity instead of using a metaphor. Those who refuse to concede this are fooling themselves and sometimes the public also. It is hard for some people to surrender their belief in an elaborate myth, especially when they have devoted years to its study and application. Still, strident insistence on an autonomous unconscious mind is little more than a fanciful journey into the land of psychomythology.

What Determines an Individual's Choice of Style?

Given that each of the four modes of conventional behavior in Figure 4.1 can be expressed in one of two ways, why is it that some people choose one style while others select its alternative? If, for example, someone gravitates toward the strategy of Caring, what determines whether he or she will express this as Leading or as Nurturing? If a person majors in Besting, why would he or she opt for Competing rather than Opposing? If the strategy is Disengaging, why might the style be either Stonewalling or Yielding? And if it is Attaching, why do some people choose Bonding and others Following?

○

Exercise 4.3

Consider the two styles, Leading and Nurturing, that can express the strategy of Caring. Why do you suppose a person would choose one of these styles over the other? It may help to think in terms of an individual's psychological motives (needs) and, referring to Figure 4.1, to play with the words *warm* and *assertion*. Consider them in their usual order, and then turn them around so that *assertion* comes first.

○

A person majoring in Warm Assertion can emphasize *either* moving one-up or moving toward but not both at the same time. This is one of the features of a circular model. Suppose, in Figure 4.1, that you were at the edge of the circle right in the middle of the upper right quadrant, Warm Assertion, and therefore equidistant from both one-up and toward. If you begin to move north, in the direction of one-up, you must simultaneously move west. On the other hand, if you move east, in the direction of toward, you must also move a bit south.

A person who relies on the strategy of Caring will express it through Leading if, and only if, being one-up is *more* important to him or her than relating closely. If, by contrast, emotional closeness is more important than superiority, the style selected is likely to be Nurturing.

○

Exercise 4.4

For each of the other three modes—Besting, Disengaging, and Attaching—which specific style will be chosen if assertion versus subordination is more important to the individual, and which will be chosen if emotional climate (warm versus cold) is more important?

○

If superiority is more important to someone with a Besting strategy, Competing will be the style of choice, whereas if emotional distance is more important, it will be Opposing. If subordinating is more important than emotional distance to someone who relies on Disengaging, his or her style is likely to be Yielding; if, on the contrary, emotional distance predominates, the chosen style will be Stonewalling. Finally, for someone who relies on the strategy of Attaching, Bonding will be the choice if emotional closeness is paramount, but it will be Following if subordination is primary.

Returning to Exercise 4.2, if Charles is mostly interested in achieving and excelling, his style will be Competing. If, however, he is more motivated to challenge others and do battle with anything or anyone he considers to be wrong, his style will be Opposing. The emphasis in Competing is on winning, on becoming and remaining one-up, and if this requires keeping one's distance from others, so be it. Sacrificing interpersonal warmth is merely a necessary evil, not the driving motive. The emphasis in Opposing, by contrast, is on combating anything or anybody that needs correcting and thus on moving away or against. Interpersonal distance is more important than achieving and excelling.

Tactics Associated with the Eight Styles

Figure 4.4 displays the tactics most closely associated with each of the eight styles. The difference between a strategy and a tactic is somewhat arbitrary, but it helps to think of a *strategy* as a general approach that reflects an overarching purpose and of a *tactic* as one among many activities that support that approach. The following exercise may help fix the distinction in your mind.

○

Exercise 4.5
Sandra is a sixteen-year-old high school student who decides she wants to graduate from a top-notch college. Getting into at least one such college becomes her goal. She decides to submit applications of such high quality that few, if any, of her chosen colleges will reject her. She further decides to write superlative essays, maintain an A average, and participate in well-chosen extracurricular activities. Identify her strategy and tactics.

○

Sandra's strategy, designed to support her goal of getting into at least one top-notch college, is to submit stellar applications. Her tactics are to write great essays, keep up an A average, and participate in extracurricular activities.

I will not elaborate further on the tactics associated with each style because they are more or less self-evident, and we have other matters to which we must now turn our attention.

Social Value of the Eight Styles

Conventional behavior—the kind ordinary people demonstrate every day—does not, as I have suggested, always conform to the ideal. At the

Figure 4.4. Tactics Associated with Each of the Eight Conventional Styles of Relating to Others.

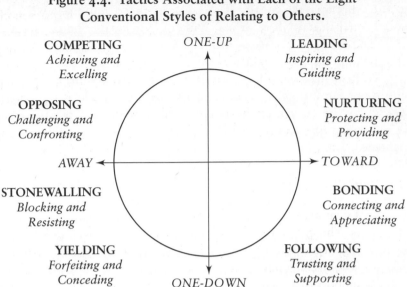

Source: © *Relational Dynamics Institute, Inc. Used by permission.*

same time, I doubt very much if God wants us to be clones of each other, walking around like visitors from another planet in an episode of *The Twilight Zone,* with wooden smiles on our faces, feeling only a zombielike sense of contentment.

Some of the differences between us are undesirable. Certain people love violence, and certain others care only about themselves. Yet many more of our differences are what, I suspect, the Creator of the Cosmos especially values and enjoys about us. I can see God smiling, as it were, over the difficulty some of us have with directions or the trouble others have in trying to carry a simple tune. Just as earthly parents enjoy differences among their children, God may relish such differences—and idiosyncrasies.

Society could hardly function without what sociologists call a division of labor—people doing different jobs. Think of what would happen if we all had to grow our own food, build our own houses, or assemble our own automobiles. Just as we need people who do different jobs, we also need people to play different interpersonal roles—for example, those who will keep us on track when there is something worthwhile to accomplish and those who will keep us feeling good while we accomplish it.

Here are some of the benefits associated with each of the eight styles represented in Figure 4.3:

○ *Leading:* We *need* those who can sense where the rest of us should go and who have the confidence to take us there, especially when we would prefer to stay where we are. Without individuals who can act with vision and have the courage of their convictions, governments would falter, corporations would stagnate, and churches would wither and die.

○ *Nurturing:* People who can nurture us are also important, not just within our families but also in the organizations to which we belong. Mentors, coaches, and sponsors are all nurturers. They feed us when we're hungry, lift us up when we're down, and comfort us when we're frightened. These are the people who, when called on, will give everything they have.

○ *Competing:* Without those who enjoy competing and do not shrink from contests, civilization would advance at a glacial pace. Those who achieve and excel move us forward because it is on their shoulders that we all, as part of society, ride. Such individuals inspire us when we see them perform in the Olympics. They are also the backbone of our economic system and, en route to winning Nobel Prizes and Pulitzers, come up with vaccines against diseases such as polio or perhaps write great literature.

○ *Opposing:* Where would we be without those who will stand up, persons who are willing to put themselves on the line for us? Our national security and the safety of our streets depend on people who are willing to place themselves at risk. They have the fortitude to thwart those who prey on the weak. These are the valiant champions of right.

○ *Stonewalling:* When something is going wrong, there have to be people around who are willing to dig in their heels and counter it—when, for example, someone with sinister motives attempts to impose his or her will on the rest of us. These are the individuals who refuse to go along with the program simply because doing so would be easier. They block and resist harmful trends and movements, even if it makes them unpopular.

○ *Yielding:* To everything there is a season (Ecclesiastes 3:1). There are times when all of us have to concede. We've argued our case, we've made our best points, and still the group wants to go another way. People who cannot forfeit and capitulate, when it is proper to do so, become obstacles. No one can win all the time.

○ *Bonding:* We all need those who are comfortable receiving and appreciating what we have to offer and, in the process, who connect strongly with us. Regardless of how they interact with other people, we need the people in our families to bond with us. Bonding is, of course, the core of romantic relationships as well as friendships.

○ *Following:* When we lead, as we all must sometimes do, we need people who, instead of competing with or opposing us, will follow. Without followers, there can be no leaders, and if there were no leaders, society would quickly stall. Without people who adopt the Following style, we'd never be able to agree on what to eat for dinner, which film to see, or where to spend the weekend. We need people in our lives who trust and support us.

All eight of these styles have value. In their more rigid and extreme forms, however, they become toxic, as we will see in Chapters Six through Fourteen.

Interpersonal Flexibility

Although it may seem as if we could associate one, and only one, style with every normal (nontoxic) person we know, the reality is more complicated. We typically move through the styles, adopting this one for a while today and that one for a while tomorrow—changing styles to fit the occasion. And that is how it should be. Although all people gravitate toward certain styles rather than others, we cannot classify people rigidly into types. A fully functioning person will be able to move into and out of all eight styles.

As we will see in detail when we get to Part Three, problems arise when people are unable, for whatever reason, to adapt to circumstance, when they get stuck in a preferred mode or style.

Summary

To give you an opportunity to consolidate your learning of the material in Chapters Three and Four, I want to summarize the major concepts we have discussed.

o There are two primary axes (dimensions) of interpersonal behavior: one-up *versus* one-down and toward *versus* away. Moving one-up is to assert one's power and superiority, while moving one-down is to acknowledge the other person's power and superiority. Moving toward is to act in a warm and friendly manner, while moving away is to act in a cool and less friendly one.

o Because these two axes are independent of one another, it is appropriate to draw them at right angles, which produces four quadrants, each one reflecting a *mode* of interaction:

1. Warm Assertion
2. Cold Assertion

3. Cold Subordination

4. Warm Subordination

○ Each of these modes is associated with a *strategy* of relating to other people:

1. Caring (Warm Assertion)

2. Besting (Cold Assertion)

3. Disengaging (Cold Subordination)

4. Attaching (Warm Subordination)

○ These four strategies can each express themselves through one of two *styles:*

1. Leading or Nurturing (Caring)

2. Competing or Opposing (Besting)

3. Stonewalling or Yielding (Disengaging)

4. Bonding or Following (Attaching)

○ Finally, each style typically involves the use of specific *tactics:*

1. Inspiring and Guiding (Leading)

2. Protecting and Providing (Nurturing)

3. Achieving and Excelling (Competing)

4. Challenging and Confronting (Opposing)

5. Blocking and Resisting (Stonewalling)

6. Forfeiting and Conceding (Yielding)

7. Connecting and Appreciating (Bonding)

8. Trusting and Supporting (Following)

Figure 4.5 presents much of the same information in the form of an easy-to-read chart.

The Christian's Stance Toward God

Before closing this chapter, I want to take up the question of how a Christian ought to relate to God. What posture are we to assume? A cold stance is inherently defiant, so we can eliminate the left side of Figure 4.1. But what about the upper right quadrant? Are there times when a Christian ought rightfully to act assertively in relation to the Creator-Provider-Sustainer?

Figure 4.5. Conventional Modes, Strategies, Styles, and Tactics.

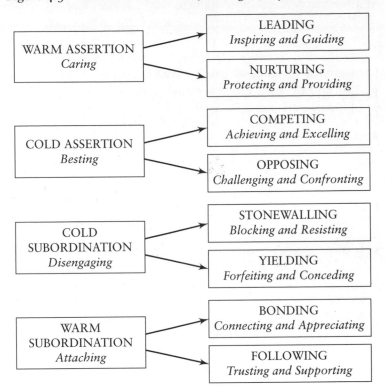

Source: © *Relational Dynamics Institute, Inc. Used by permission.*

The answer depends on how we define acting assertively. If we mean taking charge, assuming control, claiming superiority, giving orders, or grabbing power, assertion has no place in the spiritual life of the Christian. If, however, we mean feeling comfortable enough with God to address Him as our loving Father, imploring Him for noble purposes, assertion may actually reflect a holier posture than one that is formal (see Luke 11:5–13). There is, after all, a certain coolness to formality, and coolness in God's sight may not be a very good thing (see Revelation 3:15–16).

The Christian's stance toward the Lord of the Universe ought ordinarily to be Warm Subordination. Our job is to get in step with God, not to pull away or to try to tell Him how to run the world. And yet there may be times when we should, in the most reverential sense, passionately express our desires to Him.

In relation to other people, there are circumstances, as we shall see, when it is necessary and appropriate to use behaviors from all regions of Figure 4.1. This is, again, largely because we are all fallen creatures in a fallen world.

In the next chapter, we will discuss how certain interpersonal maneuvers prompt and reinforce specific kinds of responses. The discoveries on which this knowledge is based are among the most important to have emerged from behavioral science.

5

THE HIDDEN RULES
OF HUMAN RELATIONSHIPS

*Knowing their thoughts, Jesus said, "Why do you entertain
evil . . . in your hearts?" Jesus knew what they were thinking and
asked, "Why are you thinking these things in your hearts?" But
Jesus would not entrust himself to them, for he knew all men.*

—Matthew 9:4; Luke 5:22; John 2:24 [NIV]

UNLIKE JESUS, WE CANNOT read minds and hearts, which is one reason
why we are told not to judge (Matthew 7:1). But there are two principal
meanings of the word *judge,* and it is important to distinguish between
them. We are commanded to give others the benefit of the doubt and not
to judge them in the sense of *condemning.* That is the first meaning of the
term. The other is to discern or draw the right conclusion, which is what
Paul means in 1 Corinthians 10:15 when he writes, "I speak to sensible
people; judge for yourselves what I say" (NIV).

Although we, as mortals, can never reach a final conclusion about
another person's heart—that's God's job—we can and should become
skilled at *discerning* the nature of specific interpersonal motivations and
maneuvers. People—all people—are spiritual beings and, as such, are capable of far more good and evil than we typically recognize. Let me emphasize, as we begin this chapter, that it is important to reflect on our own
behavior, not just on other people's.

Insights from Relational Psychology

Only a small number of discoveries in any science ever radically alter it. These discoveries are those rare and fundamental advances that change how people working in a particular scientific discipline think. Such advances make it impossible for scientists ever to return to their old paradigms. What I am going to share with you in this chapter is of that magnitude. As the eminent psychologist and psychotherapist Hans H. Strupp noted years ago, "We stand on the threshold of a revolution." This revolution has to do with psychology's movement away from the study of the individual, more or less in isolation, to the study of the person interacting dynamically, and in real time, with other persons. Person A does X, Person B does Y, A then does X_1, B responds with Y_1, A does X_2, and so on.

This foundational shift has been facilitated and accelerated by the following pivotal insights, which lie at the core of everything we are discussing:

1. We continually *train* others and they, in turn, train us.
2. Interpersonal behavior occurs *instantaneously* and without much conscious control.
3. People make social *overtures* to others in the hope that these will be accepted.
4. Specific interpersonal acts prompt *predictable* responses from others.
5. Relationships must involve interpersonal *compatibility* to become stable.

We will explore each of these ideas in detail.

But there is another insight that you will not find in textbooks of psychology; for it, you will have to turn to scripture. Unless a Christian is going to engage in the folly of trying to erect a wall between the spiritual and the secular—church on Sunday and work on Monday—this insight will have to be reckoned with. It must be taken seriously and never trivialized, and it is this: although interpersonal styles are usually difficult to alter, people who experience a life-changing encounter with the resurrected Christ sometimes show dramatic and enduring changes in their behavior toward others. "With God all things are possible" (Matthew 19:26, KJV).

I mention this to discourage, once again, any tendency you may detect in yourself to embrace psychology as if it were a new and better religion, which it is not. Psychology is not some new mystical discipline that has magical powers to transform human personality in a way that God, without its assistance, cannot. Properly undertaken as a science, kept in its proper place, and correctly applied as an art, psychology is a wonderful boon to the Church. Misguidedly pursued, inappropriately embraced, and wantonly misapplied, psychology becomes a disappointing illusion and, in the end, a form of idolatry.

How People Train Each Other

We continually teach other people how to respond to us. Such teaching goes on so automatically, however, that it is probably better to use the word for this that most interpersonal experts do: training. *Teaching* brings to mind conscious awareness of what is going on—deliberate intention. *Training,* by contrast, suggests a process of which we may be completely unaware.

Whenever we spend time with another human being, we begin to suggest how he or she might best act in relation to us. We communicate, through what we say and do, that the other person is superior or inferior in some sense, and to what extent we want the relationship to be friendly. The other person does the same thing in return as we attempt to work out a way of interacting that will allow both of us to feel comfortable.

○

Exercise 5.1

You can make great strides forward in life by figuring out how you train others to act toward you. Are you teaching them to respect or disparage you? To treat you with tenderness or brutality? To criticize or support you? Of one thing you can be certain: you *are* training them and, to some extent, allowing them to train you. The important question is how.

○

It has been said that all relationships involve a power struggle. Most probably do. But not all. Truly excellent relationships involve no fixed sense of who's one-up and who's one-down, who enjoys the most power and who the least, and so forth. The vertical (one-up versus one-down) dimension of relating in Figure 3.1 becomes highly fluid, with the participants taking turns, as it were, at assuming the one-up position. If Person A is more competent to call the shots for a particular activity (for example, following directions), then A will be more assertive during that activity. If Person B is more competent in another area (for example, locating entertainment), this will be established as one of his or her domains of superiority. It usually takes a long time for a relationship to reflect this level of interpersonal achievement, and before it does, A and B have to work out the steps to the dance.

Far from occurring haphazardly, the mutual training that enables them to do this is systematic, purposeful, and driven by strong inner needs. Yet as noted, it rarely goes on with anything close to full awareness. People who feel most comfortable taking care of others automatically train those around them to respond with attachment and affection. Those who want to control others train them to go along with their programs. And those who feel most at ease when they are insulated from emotional closeness, perhaps by setting themselves against other people, train them to argue or in some other way distance themselves. Those who feel most at ease when they are defending themselves—and there are many people like this— actively invite others to attack them. Again, all of this happens without anyone thinking much about it or realizing that it's happening.

The following exercise will give you a sense of how subtly interpersonal training can, and often does, occur—and how rich in material a simple social encounter can be.

○

Exercise 5.2

Wilson arrives at a party where people, in groups of two or three, are chatting up a storm. He isn't in the room long when he and another man, Johnson, strike up a conversation. When they first begin to talk, Johnson nods his head in agreement whenever Wilson voices an opinion about anything, such as a recent film. Wilson responds with more eye contact and by leaning forward. Then Johnson disagrees with Wilson on some minor point about the film's script. Wilson turns away slightly and suddenly seems disinterested. Johnson, noticing this, suggests that Wilson was probably right and that he, Johnson, may not have listened carefully enough to the actors' lines, adding that he appreciates the fact that Wilson has taken the time to point out the fine merits of the screenplay. Wilson again shows interest, but a minute or two later he emits a barely audible sigh as if he were beginning to feel bored. Johnson quickly remarks on how knowledgeable Wilson is about films, and Wilson responds with more eye contact. Johnson then scrambles off to fetch him a beverage.

Analyze the foregoing vignette. What exactly has happened? How have Wilson and Johnson trained each other?

○

Wilson is a skilled player (trainer) who seems routinely to maneuver himself into the one-up position. He does not climb onto a chair and proclaim that he expects others, such as Johnson, to defer to him. Political dictators may do things like that, but in ordinary life that is not how social exchanges work. Interpersonal training takes place more covertly.

It is almost certainly the case that Wilson gradually conditions others to do what he wants without even realizing it. He does this by slowly and artfully shaping their conduct. Wilson makes it harder and harder for them to get his attention and approval. And so they must act ever more deferentially and, by implication, agree with his opinions and comply with his wishes. Note how, when Johnson "nods his head in agreement," Wilson immediately reinforces him with "more eye contact and by leaning forward." But eventually, Wilson makes it more difficult for Johnson to get attention. He "emits a barely audible sigh."

Johnson, sensing that he is losing his audience, "quickly remarks on how knowledgeable Wilson is." For this, he is favored with renewed "eye contact." When Johnson "scrambles off to fetch him a beverage," there is no longer any question about the nature of their relationship. Wilson is the one-up teacher and Johnson the one-down student.

This entire sequence, of Wilson making it increasingly difficult for Johnson to obtain favorable attention and to feel good about himself, has taken only a few minutes. But it establishes their pattern of interaction so powerfully that it would be hard, if not impossible, for Johnson to change it. Note in passing that if Wilson is rigidly dominant, Johnson could not have changed it anyway. Unless he proved willing to play the subordinate role, one of them would probably have terminated the interaction.

Something else, far more subtle, has also happened. Johnson has trained Wilson. It may seem otherwise because Wilson is the more active party, but even this is part of how, together, they are defining and structuring the relationship. The person assuming the one-up position typically takes the initiative. As soon as Wilson begins to express opinions, "Johnson nods his head in agreement," which reinforces Wilson and encourages him to move even further up.

Perhaps deciding, on some level, that *he* wants to make a run at assuming the superior position, Johnson "disagrees with Wilson on some minor point." Exactly what he disagrees about is trivial; it is what we referred to in Chapter Three as content. Anything will do. It is Johnson's attempt at repositioning himself that matters here; the choice of subject is irrelevant.

When this attempt proves unsuccessful—Wilson "turns away slightly and suddenly seems disinterested"—Johnson resumes his prior mode of training with a vengeance, by emphasizing that Wilson was "probably right," that he, Johnson, "may not have listened carefully," and that he appreciates how "Wilson has taken the time to point out the fine merits of the screenplay." And when Wilson sighs with boredom, Johnson redoubles his training efforts by remarking on "how knowledgeable Wilson is" and then by scrambling off "to fetch him a beverage."

It takes two to play the game, and for it to work optimally, neither person can refer explicitly to what's going on. What's happening between them must be kept implicit. If, for example, Wilson had insisted flat-out that Johnson defer to him, they might have ended up in an overt struggle, if for no other reason than that Johnson's pride would have prevented him from admitting to himself or Wilson that he was deferring. Thus one of them, probably Johnson, would have ended the conversation and, with it, the relationship. Johnson, in leaving, would have moved into the mode of Disengaging (see Figure 4.2) and probably would have perceived Wilson as unduly Besting him. And Johnson would have been right, because whenever dominance struggles occur, the more assertive of the two people typically moves to the left (away) side of the diagram.

The Nanosecond Nature of Human Interaction

As mentioned in Chapter Four, interpersonal behavior is reflexive, a point that warrants additional emphasis. How we respond to what other people do happens so quickly that we rarely have time to think about it, much less plan it out. As we develop and mature, we all make choices, and these choices play a major part in molding us into the persons we become. Yet once interpersonal reflexes have been trained into us by others (for example, parents, siblings, and friends) or we stamp them into ourselves, they operate with the speed of a firecracker and, sometimes, the force of a bulldozer. Here are some examples of relational reflexes:

- ○ Doreen smiles—we react by smiling or by scowling.
- ○ Kathy hugs us—we hug back or stiffen up.
- ○ Glenn cuts ahead of us in line—we object or seethe in silence.
- ○ Sarah tells us what to do—we comply or refuse to be bossed around.
- ○ Maggie treats us irritably—we overlook it or start a fight.
- ○ Michael acts overbearingly—we go along or put a stop to it fast.

And of course, in each instance there are many more options than the two I have cited. Such interpersonal reflexes are largely the stuff of which a happy or unhappy life is made.

○

Exercise 5.3

Answer these questions in terms of yourself and at least one other person with whom you are close. What is your instantaneous response when another person (a) cuts you off in traffic, (b) asks if you need help, (c) treats you impersonally, and (d) smiles at you in an elevator?

○

Interpersonal Overtures

We discussed, at the end of Chapter Four, how just about anything one person does in relation to another contains a bid and an instruction. On a scale ranging from low to high insistence, it is an invitation, request, suggestion, or command. It is, in the most general sense, an *overture,* for which the *American Heritage College Dictionary* provides this definition: "An act, an offer, or a proposal indicating readiness for a course of action or a relationship." For the overture to be successful, the other person must accept it.

Our interest in this chapter is to illuminate exactly how overtures work. As we will see, each type of overture proposes the establishment of a specific kind of relational arrangement. Once you understand the significance of a given interpersonal act, you will no longer be confused about the meaning of what someone else is doing with or to you. You will know. Keep in mind, however, that we are all fallible and, as indicated at the beginning of the chapter, none of us can read minds—it is inevitable that you will make mistakes. We all do.

We turn now to the unwritten rules of social behavior. These are the hidden rules or principles according to which overtures function. But first, I want to mention a few more characteristics of our model of behavior.

The Circular Model of Interpersonal Behavior

Our two-dimensional model is in reality a "circumplex." Do not let this term daunt you because it is easy to understand and quite useful. A circumplex is an arrangement of behaviors in which the ones closest together (on a circle) are most similar and the ones farthest away from each other are least similar.

Cold Subordination, for example, is more closely related to both Warm Subordination and Cold Assertion than to Warm Assertion: Cold Subordination shares one property with Warm Subordination (Subordination) and one with Cold Assertion (Coldness) but no property with Warm Assertion.

Similarities and Differences

Birds of a feather flock together, we are told, but also that opposites attract. Which is it? Let's begin with this exercise, designed to give you practice in detecting interpersonal similarities and differences.

○

Exercise 5.4

Imagine four men—Nick, Ben, Larry, and Phillip. Nick is compassionate, extraverted, and the first to put together a new effort to help those in need. Ben is career-oriented and ambitious and likes to win, but he does not care all that much about what others think of him. Larry is reserved, prefers to keep to himself, and sullenly resists whenever someone else presses him to do something. Phillip has lots of friends, gets along well with everyone, and is known as a good team player. Which of the four are the least similar? The best way to approach this exercise is to decide, for each one, whether he tends to posture himself more one-up or one-down and whether he tends to move toward or away from others. Referring to Figure 4.1 as you do this may help.

○

If you look back at that figure, you will see that Nick and Ben tend to act assertively while Larry and Phillip are more inclined to behave subordinately. You will also see that Nick and Phillip move toward people while Ben and Larry are more inclined to move away from them. From this, you can see that, when it comes to interpersonal behavior, Nick and Larry have little or nothing in common. The same is true of Ben and Phillip. Now try this exercise:

○

Exercise 5.5

Imagine that the four men in Exercise 5.4 are going to be marooned on two deserted islands—Lucha and Pelea. Two of the men will go to each island, but since the islands are roughly equivalent, it doesn't matter which island any one of the four is marooned on. But making it off either island is not going to be easy, and the two men will have to get along well for this to happen. Into what pairs should the men be sorted?

○

The answer to this exercise will give you a great deal of useful insight into how similarities and differences operate in relationships.

Assigning Nick and Ben to the same island could lead to trouble, because they might be inclined to engage in contests of will. Both of them generally want to take charge. Putting Nick and Larry on the same island could also create problems, since Nick is friendly and, by comparison, Larry is not. Assigning Ben to the same island as Phillip is unlikely to work out well because Phillip is friendlier than Ben, which could leave Phillip depressed and unmotivated, especially since Ben is more dominant. And if you left Larry and Phillip together, there could be a crisis of leadership, with each waiting for the other to organize their efforts and make something happen. This leaves us with the following best matches: Nick and Phillip for, say, Lucha, and Ben and Larry for Pelea.

The important point to note is that, for all four men, they are with neither the person they are least like nor the one they most resemble. Neither birds of a feather nor the attraction of opposites has given us the right answer. As we have noted, for example, Nick is least like Larry but is just as similar to Ben as he is to Phillip. So then, why pair him with Phillip? This brings us to the heart of the chapter and, indeed, of this entire book.

What Warmth and Assertiveness Prompt

The following exercise will get us started down the path of discovering the simple but powerful rules of what behaviors prompt what responses—of how interpersonal overtures work in real life.

---
o

Exercise 5.6

Relying only on your personal experience, answer these questions:

1. If someone is warm to you, are you more inclined to respond warmly (move toward) or coldly (move away)?

2. If someone is cold to you, how are you likely to respond?

3. If someone assumes a subordinate position, would you tend to assert or subordinate yourself?

4. If someone acts assertively, would you be more or less likely to behave in a subordinate manner?

---
o

Taking each of the four in order, most people respond to warmth with warmth (item 1) and to coldness with coldness (item 2). But in response to subordinate behavior, they tend to respond with assertion (item 3), and in response to assertion, with subordination (item 4).

There are exceptions. Some people are so rigidly assertive that they can subordinate themselves to no one, while others almost never assert themselves. Some are routinely warm and others routinely cold. But what I have described is the way relationships usually work. In a nutshell, here are the four basic principles of what psychologists call *interpersonal complementarity* but what, for ease of communication, we shall simply call *compatibility.* This word has taken on some undesirable overtones because of its frequent use in divorce proceedings. Still, it is a perfectly good word and the one that I think works best. The four principles can be summed up succinctly as follows:

- Warmth begets Warmth.
- Coldness begets Coldness.
- Assertion begets Subordination.
- Subordination begets Assertion.

Psychologists who study interpersonal processes speak of *correspondence* (similar response) on the dimension of Warmth and of *reciprocity* (opposite response) on the dimension of Assertion. Warmth or Coldness prompts the other person to mirror it—to behave in the same way—while both Assertion and Subordination tend to induce their opposites. There is no need for you to remember the technical terms for this, but it is crucial to understand and remember the underlying principles. It may help to glance at Figure 5.1 and spend a minute or two thinking through the four "rules" I have just stated. Together, these rules capture the essence of interpersonal *compatibility,* by which I mean that they define how certain types of behavior fit best with certain other types.

These findings lead to some surprising conclusions, one of which is that interpersonal compatibility, as we saw in Exercise 5.5, is *not* based on across-the-board similarity *or* dissimilarity. Whether similarity or dissimilarity prompts two people to get on well together depends on which axis (one-up versus one-down or toward versus away) we're talking about. As noted early in this chapter, although interpersonal behavior will never be entirely predictable, it is far more predictable than most people think.

○

Exercise 5.7
Using the conclusions we came to for Exercises 5.5 and 5.6, which pair of interpersonal combinations works best together from the following

choices (see Table 3.1): (a) One-Up/Toward, (b) One-Up/Away, (c) One-Down/Away, or (d) One-Down/Toward? How, in other words, should the strategies of Caring, Besting, Disengaging, and Attaching be *paired* to maximize compatibility?

○

The answers can be seen in Figure 5.1. Remember that each strategy *invites* and *reinforces* compatible behavior. Besting and Disengaging invite and reinforce each other, and so do Caring and Attaching.

Figure 5.2 shows how the styles associated with the four basic modes invite and reinforce each other. The eight styles are arranged in matching pairs. Leading induces and reinforces Following, and vice versa, and the same symbiotic relationship exists for the other three pairs: Nurturing and Bonding; Competing and Yielding; and, Opposing and Stonewalling. *Symbiosis* means "mutual dependence." Both members of the pair need, and provide for, the other. Figure 5.3 zooms in to illustrate how this works for tactics.

Leaders induce others to follow them by inspiring and guiding, and followers trust and support their leaders, thus encouraging them to continue to lead. People who provide nurturance through protecting and providing induce others to bond with them via connecting and appreciating—which

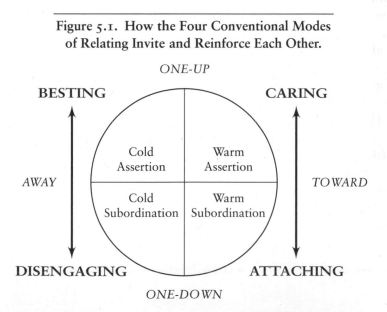

Figure 5.1. How the Four Conventional Modes of Relating Invite and Reinforce Each Other.

Source: © *Relational Dynamics Institute, Inc. Used by permission.*

Figure 5.2. How the Eight Conventional Styles Invite and Reinforce Each Other.

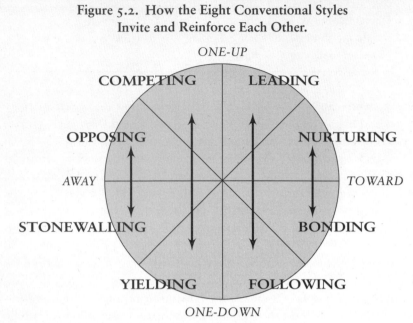

Source: © *Relational Dynamics Institute, Inc. Used by permission.*

leads to more nurturance. Individuals who compete with others by achieving and excelling induce them to yield by forfeiting and conceding, while those who yield encourage and promote further competing. Finally, those who oppose by challenging and confronting prompt others to stonewall them by blocking and resisting their efforts (forms of disengagement), which in turn provokes continued opposition.

To solidify your mastery of how such interpersonal transactions work in real life, try the following challenging exercise. You will have to use some imagination for this one, since it takes us well beyond what we have discussed in this chapter or the last two—it is a preview of what's to come in Part Three.

○

Exercise 5.8
For each of the following behaviors demonstrated by Ted, select the most probable response by Joni. *Ted's behaviors:* (1) Presses Joni to show more initiative and have more backbone. (2) Blames Joni for showing up late. (3) Scurries to do what Joni wants. (4) Draws back from Joni, who is abusive. *Joni's responses:* (Q) Becomes even bossier.

(R) Becomes even more passive. (S) Increases her level of aggression. (T) Puts herself down and makes excuses.

o

Note that while we are looking for the "most probable" response from Joni, this does not necessarily mean the response that all people would give. In response to behavior 1 on Ted's part, for example, Joni might react with even more aggression than Ted demonstrates by "railing." Still, here are the best answers—best being defined by what is most likely to happen: 1-R; 2-T; 3-Q; 4-S.

Exhorting someone to show more initiative and develop a spine (behavior 1) is very assertive (one-up) behavior, and such behavior tends unintentionally to induce further subordination—exactly the opposite of what Ted intends. Blaming another person (behavior 2) is assertive (one-up) and overtly aggressive (away) and so is likely to induce one-down reactions. Rushing in to do what another person wants (behavior 3) reflects a strong one-down stance that is also defensive, which tends to encourage even more bossiness. And retreating from someone who is abusive (behavior 4) tends, often, only to increase the level of aggression.

Figure 5.3. How the Tactics of Conventional Styles Invite and Reinforce Each Other.

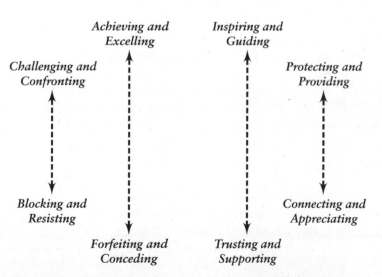

Source: © *Relational Dynamics Institute, Inc. Used by permission.*

This exercise was not easy. If you had difficulty with it, don't worry. We will discuss these sorts of toxic transactions thoroughly in Part Three.

A Quick Review

It may be easier to remember the principles of interpersonal compatibility if you put them in spatial terms:

North and South

Remember that Assertion is at the top of Figure 5.1, whereas Subordination is at the bottom. Assertive people do best with those who do not struggle with them over who is to be more one-up. Who wants to engage in an endless power struggle? Assertive behavior is an invitation for the other person to go along with the program. Subordination, by contrast, is an invitation for the other person to take charge and lay out the program—whatever it may be.

East with East and West with West

Recall also that friendliness is on the right side of Figure 5.1, while distance and coldness are on the left. Friendly people are most comfortable with other friendly people. Warm behavior is an invitation for the other person to be warm in return. Emotional distance, similarly, calls forth the same kinds of behavior in others.

Compatibility *always* operates north-south (up and down) in the figures, never east-west (across) or diagonally. Note, however, that a diagonal match (for example, Besting and Attaching) is more compatible than one that runs east and west (for example, Besting and Caring). This is because, with diagonal pairings, there is at least compatibility on the Assertion-Subordination dimension. With an east-west pairing, however, there is no compatibility on either axis.

The Quest for Compatibility

In Exercise 5.2, Wilson and Johnson found each other. Wilson was unconsciously looking for someone who would go along with him and, having located one, quickly began the process of "shaping." They might as well have been playing a duet on the piano. Johnson, whether he realized it or not, was looking for someone to tell him what to think and do—as much as, in moments, he might have resented this.

People seek out others who behave in ways that fit their emotional needs and hence people who exhibit compatible social patterns. It is as if we were continually sending out high-frequency signals that advertise who we are and what we're looking for or as if we were posting a personal ad in the newspaper or on the Internet.

We unconsciously but actively search for, and usually find, people with compatible styles. These are the ones whose interpersonal purposes and strategies match and reinforce ours. Because not all such matches are beneficial, it is important to understand how they develop.

Much has been written about "codependence" but little about what drives it, which is interpersonal compatibility. As I've suggested, each of the four pairs of styles represents a potential symbiotic relationship, indicated by vertical dotted lines in Figure 5.3.

Note that both selection and training are going on here. We find people who seem open to our overtures to behave in a particular way—they also find us—and then we help them perfect their game.

In Chapter Six, we will do what a popular television chef is fond of saying: kick it up a notch. We will preview the eight toxic interpersonal styles and examine how interpersonal complementarity operates within toxic relationships.

6

OVERVIEW OF INTERPERSONAL TOXICITY

Do not fear those who kill the body but cannot kill the soul;
rather fear him who can destroy both soul and body in hell.

—Matthew 10:28 [NRSV]

Behold, I send you forth as sheep in the midst of wolves:
be ye therefore wise as serpents, and harmless as doves.

—Matthew 10:16 [KJV]

THE TENTH CHAPTER of the Gospel of Matthew is filled with no-nonsense warnings about the implications of interpersonal behavior, especially in relation to Christ and other Christians. It makes clear, for example, that we are not to shrink back from acknowledging—owning up to—our faith in God because of what others may threaten to do to us. In a world populated by "sophisticated" people who regard genuine religion as a taboo topic and who view sincere piety as indicative of backwoods ignorance, shoddy education, or significant psychopathology, owning up is not always easy. Whereas in most of the Western Hemisphere, you may be ridiculed for your beliefs, in other regions of the globe, you could be put to death. Nonetheless, Jesus insists, it is not physical but spiritual injury that we should fear.

As we spend our days on earth, as quasi-aliens in a world that has largely turned its back on its Creator, we are to refrain from hurting others, which occasionally demands restraint. When someone insults or abuses us, it is not always easy to inhibit the impulse to return the favor. The rich young ruler (Luke 18:18–23) had trouble surrendering his wealth. We, more typically, have trouble surrendering our pride—not defending what we take to be our honor.

Living graciously, however, does not mean being naïve or stupid. Nor does it mean inviting others to do harm. This is why we are also told to be wise. When Jesus advises his disciples to be "wise as serpents and harmless as doves," he is not suggesting that we refuse to notice the evil around us or to allow others arbitrarily to inflict it on us. Because human beings are spiritual creatures, psychological injuries affect their spirits, for better or worse. Recall that the Greek term *psyche,* from which the word *psychology* derives, means "soul."

Only God fully comprehends the intricate connections between interpersonal and spiritual toxicity. At what point, for example, does the emotional injury sustained in a toxic relationship bleed over into spiritual damage? Is it possible to kill another person's spirit and, in the process, turn him or her away from God? Am I, in fact, my brother's and sister's keeper (Genesis 4:9)? Is soul murder just a metaphor? "Occasions for stumbling are bound to come," warns Jesus, "but woe to anyone by whom they come! It would be better for you if a millstone were hung around your neck and you were thrown into the sea than for you to cause one of these little ones to stumble" (Luke 17:1–2, NRSV). Sobering words.

Some experts believe that Jesus is focusing on those who put temptation in the way of Christians, but I think his words have wider implications. Precisely because we are spiritual beings, *everything* we do in relation to another person influences that person's spiritual well-being. Although no mortal can completely grasp the complex interpenetrations between the spiritual and the interpersonal, you can be sure that they exist (see Part One). What we do to other people is not trivial. Nor is what they do to us. Both matter far more than we typically realize.

We will preview, in this chapter, eight toxic relational styles. Nearly everything in the chapter builds directly on the information presented in Chapters Three, Four, and Five. Those chapters had to do with conventional behavior, whereas this one begins to home in on toxic behavior, our central concern. As you read this chapter and the ones in Part Three, look inside as well as outside, at yourself as well as others, for this is what the Lord expects of us and what, as Christians, we ought to expect of ourselves.

The Nature of Interpersonal Toxicity

Despite the valuable discoveries made over the past half-century by psychologists who study person-to-person interaction, most of them—myself included—made a fundamental mistake. We assumed that, in the realm of interpersonal conduct, abnormal (toxic) behavior was in every instance only an exaggerated or rigid form of normal (conventional) behavior. The pioneers of interpersonal research promoted this hypothesis, and we accepted it on faith, partly because it seemed so credible.

A good deal of toxic behavior does, in fact, look like an exaggerated or inflexible form of conventional behavior. A person who smothers you to the point of intruding mercilessly into your life (see Chapter Nine), for example, might actually be someone who moves further "toward" and further "one-up." The traditional argument runs that if this person were less warm and assertive, he or she would be a conventional "Nurturer" (see Figure 5.2). But with such unbounded affection, the person's behavior has turned toxic. This line of reasoning, as I will demonstrate, does not hold up to close scrutiny.

One of the ways in which the horizontal (toward *versus* away) axis of our model has sometimes been labeled, and therefore construed, is as the dimension of love. The more a person moves toward someone else, it has been assumed, the more he or she loves that person. Such an analysis reflects, at best, only a superficial understanding of love and, at worst, a fundamental misunderstanding of its nature. We need not address the different varieties of love (for example, eros, agape)—for this, see *The Four Loves* by C. S. Lewis. All we have to do here is note that there is an egocentricity to smothering that is not found in healthy nurturance. It is *not* that the person who smothers "loves more" and that the person who nurtures loves less. Rather, it is that the two people love differently, if we may even call what an intrusive smotherer does "love." There is a *qualitative* difference between healthy and toxic behavior in this instance. In other instances, the difference between healthy and toxic behavior is only a matter of degree.

We cannot explore this subject in any more detail here, and, frankly, I'm not sure that I or anyone else could do it justice at this point in the history of psychological thought. The issue is certainly one that I continue to think about. For our immediate purposes, it is enough to remember that, at times, the *nature* of the boundaries between conventional and toxic conduct are sometimes permeable and sometimes not. In many instances, toxic behavior *is* just an exaggerated or rigid form of normal behavior, while in others it shows an entirely different character.

Four Toxic Modes of Relating

Figure 6.1 is a modification of Figure 4.1. Note that the horizontal axis no longer begins with *away* at the left but instead begins with *against*. There is a close relationship between the two. Moving emotionally or physically away from another person can be a potent form of moving against that person, especially in an intimate relationship where the person depends on you for human contact. It has been pointed out, for example, that the most powerful form of control over another person is, in the end, contact control ("She's too busy to see you today . . . and, no, she doesn't have time to return your call").

The names of the four quadrants have also been revamped. *Warm Assertion* (upper right) is now *Affiliative Dominance*. This reflects two noteworthy changes that we must make in our thinking as we move from our discussion of conventional to toxic behavior.

First, we have substituted the idea of affiliation for warmth. It is possible to become strongly connected to (affiliated with) another person without the existence of much, if any, genuine affection—a reality that is obscured by psychologists who use the terms *affection* and *affiliation* interchangeably. In certain toxic relationships, there is the *appearance* of love while, in truth, there is only a syrupy symbiosis.

Second, instead of the word *assertion,* we are now using the word *dominance.* There comes a point at which moving one-up—assuming a superior position—goes beyond simple assertion and qualifies as dominance. Being dominant is not necessarily the same as being dominating or domineering, both of which are aggressive forms of dominance (upper left quadrant). In behaving assertively, a person is focusing primarily on himself or herself moving one-up, while in behaving dominantly, the individual is more intent on ensuring that the other person is one-down. This is the subtle difference that psychologists refer to as "focus on self" versus "focus on other."

Cold Assertion (upper left quadrant) in Figure 4.1 is called *Aggressive Dominance* in Figure 6.1, and *Cold Subordination* (lower left quadrant) has been relabeled as *Hostile Submission*. These changes, too, are important.

Both aggression and hostility are forms of moving against others. Although the terms are often used to mean the same thing, there is a distinction. Aggression is active and applies when a person takes the initiative to threaten or injure someone else. Hostility, by contrast, is passive and applies when there is only a readiness to respond to aggressive behavior. Aggression is more of an action and hostility a reaction. Hence the use of the two different terms in the upper left and lower left quadrants of Figure 6.1.

Figure 6.1. Four Toxic Modes of Relating to Other People.

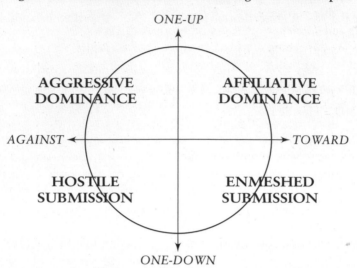

Source: © *Relational Dynamics Institute, Inc. Used by permission.*

As with the transition from assertion to dominance, there is a point at which subordination—deference—becomes outright submission. This is reflected in the use of the latter term in the lower quadrants.

Finally, the lower right quadrant has been changed from *Warm Subordination* to *Enmeshed Submission*. Although we could apply the concept of enmeshment broadly, to mean any enduring toxic relationship, we are reserving it to mean an arrangement in which one person is behaving in a way that encourages another person to become inappropriately and excessively involved in the details of his or her life. Enmeshment is what happens when two people are so emotionally intertwined that it is harmful to both of them.

A Useful Simplification

More than three decades ago, Robert C. Carson of Duke University wrote a fine book titled *Interaction Concepts of Personality*. In it, he proposed using the following four names for the quadrants that appear in Figures 4.1 and 6.1: Friendly Dominant (upper right), Hostile Dominant (upper left), Hostile Submissive (lower left), and Friendly Submissive (lower right).

Although Carson's model does not pick up some of the nuances we have considered, such as the difference between aggression and hostility, it is elegantly simple and, for that reason, practical. For one thing, it requires that you keep only two pairs of words in mind—*friendly* versus *hostile* and *dominant* versus *submissive*—which is a great advantage when things are happening quickly. It is relatively easy to decode behaviors into these four shorthand abbreviations:

FD = Friendly Dominance

HD = Hostile Dominance

HS = Hostile Submission

FS = Friendly Submission

Try this exercise.

○

Exercise 6.1

Using Carson's shorthand—FD, HD, HS, FS—decode each of the following statements:

1. "Please stop picking on me—it bothers me a lot."

2. "I'm going to take you to dinner on Friday."

3. "You did it wrong again—can't you do anything right?"

4. "I'll be ready on Friday—what should I wear?"

○

Statement 1 is HS (Hostile Submissive), statement 2 is FD (Friendly Dominant), statement 3 is HD (Hostile Dominant), and statement 4 is FS (Friendly Submissive). With a little practice, you will learn to do this sort of decoding quickly and easily. Now, try the next exercise, which will give you a preview of where we're going in Part Three.

○

Exercise 6.2

Which interaction modes are the most compatible if paired up? This does not mean that they are desirable or healthy—just that they are likely to invite and reinforce each other. It may help to look back at Figure 5.1.

○

Even without referring to the diagram in Chapter Five, it is more or less obvious, I think, that the Friendly Dominant and Friendly Submissive styles are compatible. Look back at Exercise 6.1. In sentence 2, the FD person is telling the other that they will be having dinner together on Friday, and in sentence 4, the FS person is cooperating nicely. Thus FD and FS are optimally compatible. Note that these are the upper and lower right quadrants, what we described in Chapter Five as north and south. It may be less intuitively obvious that the Hostile Dominant and Hostile Submissive styles are also fully compatible. In Exercise 6.1, the HD person in sentence 1 is criticizing and the HS person in sentence 3 is more or less pleading for the behavior to stop. This is also a north-south combination.

Toxic Strategies

Figure 6.2 makes the same sorts of modifications to Figure 4.2; Figure 6.2 depicts the strategies that correspond to the four toxic modes of interacting. What used to be Caring (upper right quadrant) is now *Engulfing*. Besting, by taking on a more aggressive character, is now *Attacking*. Disengaging has turned into all-out *Retreating*. And Attaching has taken on the enmeshed form of *Submerging*.

Eight Toxic Styles

Figure 6.3 summarizes in graphic form the eight toxic relational styles. In Part Three, we devote an entire chapter to each of these. For now, it is enough simply to know that they exist and to familiarize yourself with their names. Note that Nurturing in Figure 4.3 is now *Intruding,* Opposing is now *Victimizing,* Following is now *Drifting,* and so on.

Toxic Tactics

The tactics associated with each of the eight toxic styles are depicted in Figure 6.4. Note that while Achieving and Excelling are the tactics associated with the conventional (normal) style called Competing, the tactics associated with the corresponding toxic style of Humiliating are *Demeaning* and *Belittling*. Quite a change! The same sort of intensification can be seen as we turn from the tactics for Following (*Trusting* and *Supporting*) to those for Drifting (*Obeying* and *Conforming*). And so on for the other six.

Parallel to what we did in Figure 4.5 for conventional behavior, Figure 6.5 summarizes in one diagram the modes, strategies, styles, and tactics of toxicity.

Figure 6.2. Interpersonal Strategies Corresponding to the Four Toxic Modes of Relating.

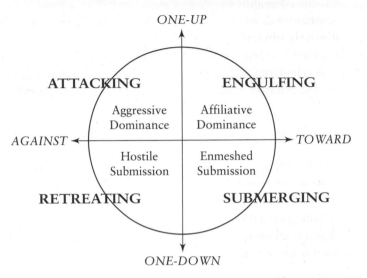

Source: © *Relational Dynamics Institute, Inc. Used by permission.*

Figure 6.3. Eight Toxic Styles of Relating to Other People.

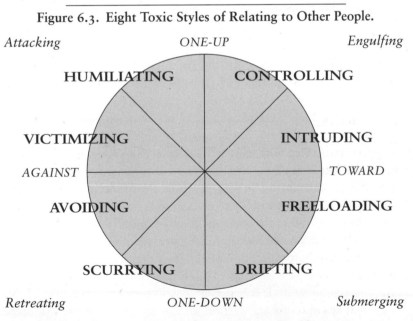

Source: © *Relational Dynamics Institute, Inc. Used by permission.*

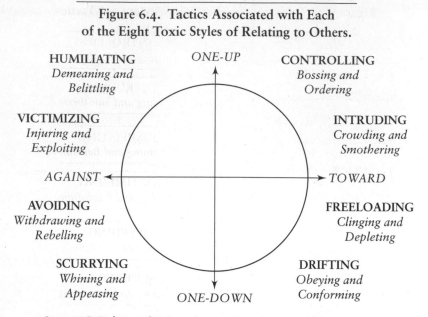

Figure 6.4. Tactics Associated with Each
of the Eight Toxic Styles of Relating to Others.

Source: © *Relational Dynamics Institute, Inc. Used by permission.*

How Toxic Modes and Styles Perpetuate Each Other

We saw in Chapter Five how the four conventional *modes* and *strategies* of behavior invite and reinforce each other (see Figure 5.1). Figure 6.6 demonstrates how this works for the four toxic modes. Engulfing and Submerging are compatible pairs, and so are Attacking and Retreating.

Many people, in response to toxic behavior, will *not* respond in a compatible fashion. If someone tries to meddle excessively in our affairs, for example, we may quickly counter this by putting an end to it fast and perhaps backing away.

That many people are unable to engage in such relationship modification is central to Part Three—stopping and exiting fail to occur in toxic relationships. Both people merely perpetuate the toxicity.

In Chapter Five, we also examined how conventional *styles* invite and reinforce each other (see Figure 5.2). Figure 6.7 illustrates how this works for the corresponding toxic styles. People who major in *Intruding* into the lives of others have an uncanny genius for linking up with those who spend their lives *Freeloading*—and vice versa. As with Wilson and Johnson in Exercise 5.2, they would somehow manage to find each other in a room

Figure 6.5. Toxic Modes, Strategies, Styles, and Tactics.

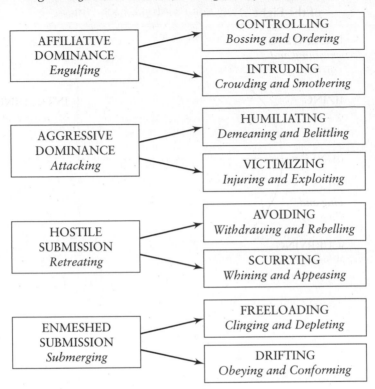

Source: © *Relational Dynamics Institute, Inc. Used by permission.*

of hundreds. Those who relish *Humiliating* and *Scurrying* do the same, as do those with styles of *Victimizing* and *Avoiding* and those with styles of *Controlling* and *Drifting*. We will explore all of this in detail later.

How the Tactics of Toxicity Invite and Reinforce Each Other

Finally, we reach the issue of how the *tactics* associated with the eight toxic styles invite and reinforce each other. This is summarized in Figure 6.8.

Note, for example, that the best way to get someone to demean and belittle you is to whine and appease—to try to buy the person off (see Chapter Twelve). The best way to induce another person to boss you around is to give in to everything the person wants (see Chapter Eight). And so on.

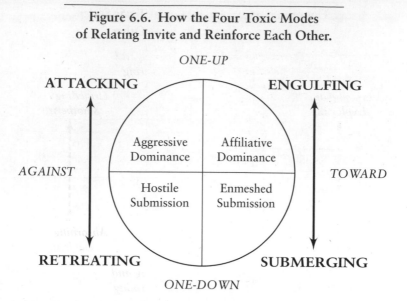

Figure 6.6. How the Four Toxic Modes
of Relating Invite and Reinforce Each Other.

Source: © Relational Dynamics Institute, Inc. Used by permission.

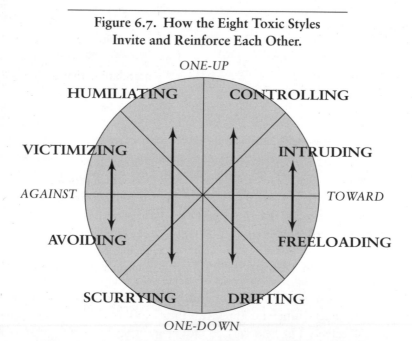

Figure 6.7. How the Eight Toxic Styles
Invite and Reinforce Each Other.

Source: © Relational Dynamics Institute, Inc. Used by permission.

Figure 6.8. How the Tactics of Toxic Styles Invite and Reinforce Each Other.

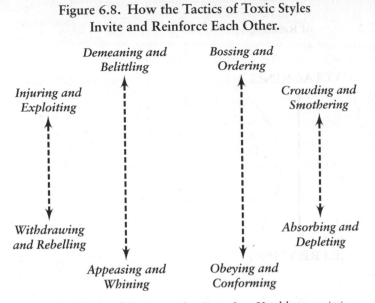

Source: © *Relational Dynamics Institute, Inc. Used by permission.*

A Realistic Example

You will probably find the following exercise difficult. But it is useful to work through because it represents a type of interchange that goes on in thousands of households every day.

○

Exercise 6.3

Analyze the following conversation between a mother and her seventeen-year-old daughter. In which of the four toxic modes is each person operating (Figure 6.2)? Throughout the conversation, the mother remains in the same toxic quadrant (mode). And except for one minor exception near the end of the dialogue, so does the daughter. After you determine their respective *modes* of toxicity, try to determine the specific *style* reflected in each statement (Figure 6.3). I have numbered each statement for convenience.

1. MOTHER: You did it again, didn't you? Left school early and spent the afternoon with that Thorndike boy.

2. DAUGHTER: Why are you always criticizing me?

3. MOTHER: If you did what you were supposed to, I wouldn't have to criticize you. You're a big disappointment, that's all I can say.

4. DAUGHTER: [*Looks away and says nothing.*]

5. MOTHER: [*Frustrated by her daughter's silence.*] Say something!

6. DAUGHTER: I have nothing to say.

7. MOTHER: I'll bet you don't.

8. DAUGHTER: [*Holds up her left hand and inspects her fingernails.*]

9. MOTHER: What's wrong with you? Is that all you care about, whether your nails are chipped? Why don't you talk to me? Why do you have to associate with losers all the time?

10. DAUGHTER: Maybe because I'm a loser. That's what you tell me, isn't it?

11. MOTHER: Go to your room! I can't stand the sight of you.

○

Without worrying about who started it, or who's at fault, let's analyze what's going on between them. Reduced to essentials, the mother is Attacking and the daughter is Retreating. The more the mother attacks, the more the daughter retreats; the more the daughter retreats, the more the mother attacks. This is what we would expect based on our model. What, however, are the styles that go along with each of the statements?

Statement 1, by the mother, is Humiliating: "You did it again, didn't you?" She's using the tactics of belittling and blaming.

The daughter responds (sentence 2) by whining, which is one of the tactics associated with Scurrying: "Why are you always criticizing me?"

To this, the mother responds with an utterance that seems designed to injure (sentence 3), and so she has now moved to Victimizing: "You're a big disappointment."

As Figures 6.7 and 6.8 would lead you to predict, the daughter withdraws and detaches (statement 4), tactics for Avoiding. She looks away and says nothing.

Statement 5 by the mother ("Say something!") is ambiguous, but it seems more like Humiliating than outright Victimizing, so we can assume that she's become slightly less aggressive.

To this, the daughter again responds with walling off (sentence 6), but this time she actually says something, which is more giving (affiliative) than silence: "I have nothing to say." She seems to be on the border between Avoiding and Scurrying.

The mother resorts to sarcastic attack (sentence 7): "I'll bet you don't." It seems as if she has moved back toward the style of Victimizing.

Now the daughter reacts with even more passive defiance (statement 8)—inspecting her fingernails, as if the mother weren't even in the room. Recall how moving away can be a potent form of moving against. The daughter is again withdrawing and rebelling—in other words, Avoiding. And once again, there is no speech. Note the defiant nature of the daughter's detachment.

This maneuver has succeeded in further frustrating the mother, who tries to reengage the daughter by once again attacking (sentence 9): "What's wrong with you? . . . Why do you have to associate with losers?"

It's difficult to know for sure whether the mother is Humiliating or Victimizing at this juncture. Such ambiguity is true to life. Just as physical bodies do not always conform to anatomy textbooks—organs and blood vessels are not always where they're suppose to be—interpersonal behavior does not always match the interpersonal model. But it is rarely far off and, in this instance, may not be off at all. The mother seems to have become a bit less hostile in sentence 9. Perhaps sensing that she is losing all touch with her daughter, she moves ever so slightly away from Victimizing and back toward Humiliating.

Predictably, the daughter (in sentence 10) engages in self-deprecation, which is correlated with Scurrying: "Maybe because I'm a loser." Then, for good measure, she adds, "That's what you tell me, isn't it?" The daughter is now doing a little Victimizing of her own.

The mother then responds (sentence 11) with the trump card of ending the conversation. She does this, in part, by stopping the daughter's aggression: "I can't stand the sight of you."

Comparing Conventional and Toxic Styles

By way of review, it may be helpful to place the eight conventional and the eight toxic styles on the same circle. Figure 6.9 shows how all sixteen styles—functional (conventional) and dysfunctional (toxic)—relate to each other and also to the two primary dimensions of interpersonal behavior.

Default Modes and Styles

We noted earlier that people tend to move in and out of different styles and that interpersonal flexibility is a sign of psychological wholeness. Even so, all of us gravitate toward some modes and styles more than others. These are what I think of as Default Modes and Default Styles, and we

Figure 6.9. Conventional (Inner) and Toxic (Outer) Styles of Relating to Other People.

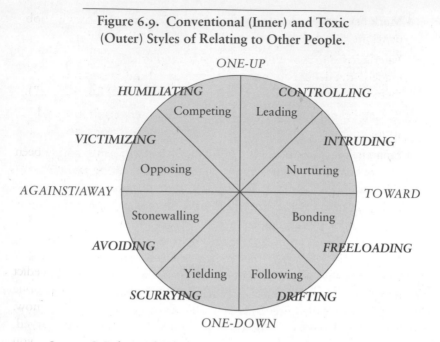

Source: © *Relational Dynamics Institute, Inc. Used by permission.*

all have them. People who spend their lives in toxic relationships sometimes cling rigidly to only one or, at the most, two styles.

A Default Style is one to which an individual naturally reverts, especially under stress. It is that person's characteristic way of relating to others. Default Styles that are intense or inflexible are not easily changed and are therefore a kind of interpersonal fingerprint. Note that for each Default Style (for example, Scurrying), there is always a corresponding, underlying, and more general Default Mode (for example, Hostile Submission, with its accompanying strategy of Retreating). Here are some examples of Default Styles as they might be expressed in everyday behavior:

- Sheldon insists on making all the decisions in his family, including what the family members watch on television and what they eat for dinner (see Chapter Seven, "Controlling").

- Rachel usually wants to be told what to do and asks one person after another for advice on the same issue (see Chapter Eight, "Drifting").

- Amanda invites herself to meetings that she has no reason to attend and constantly offers unwanted advice to her friends (see Chapter Nine, "Intruding").

○ Mark asks his mother for more money every time he loses his job or wants to buy a new car (see Chapter Ten, "Freeloading").

○ Valerie loves to make the other women in her tennis club feel inadequate, delights in flaunting her money, and makes fun of them when they miss a shot (see Chapter Eleven, "Humiliating").

○ Patrick cannot stand up for himself when others insult him and seems to invite their abuse (see Chapter Twelve, "Scurrying").

○ Ethan is hot-tempered, gets into fights with coworkers, and has been arrested twice for assault (see Chapter Thirteen, "Victimizing").

○ Bernice avoids people, rarely goes out of the house, and does not want to get to know her neighbors (see Chapter Fourteen, "Avoiding").

If you pay attention to what goes on around you, you will come to recognize such Default Styles quickly. This, in turn, will enable you to predict how people are likely to act in the future: not perfectly, of course—no one can do that—but with a lot more accuracy than you probably enjoy now. Will Gary, for example, be dictatorial or compliant, intrusive or reserved, demanding or withdrawn? When you meet someone for the first time, you will usually be able to map his or her Default Style or Styles and therefore know what to do and, what is sometimes more important, what not to do ("She's an Avoider—I won't crowd her"; "Feels like a Humiliator—I'd better not whine or placate").

You will also understand the kinds of reactions that each Default Style "draws" or "pulls" from others. And perhaps most important of all, you will better understand your own interpersonal patterns.

Try to answer the questions in the following one-minute exercise.

○

Exercise 6.5
Without looking at any of the figures, what is likely to happen if you do each of the following?

1. Automatically go along with everything someone else says or wants.

2. Grovel, bargain, and try to appease an individual who relentlessly needles you.

3. Resentfully back away from a person who repeatedly and deliberately hurts you.

○

The answer to item 1 is that the other person is likely to attempt to control you even more—the demands will escalate. In item 2, the other person may be inclined to pick on you with renewed enthusiasm. And in item 3, the person will probably keep hurting and bullying you. Dealing with abusive people is no trivial matter and requires skill. This is a topic to which we will return in later chapters.

Once you know which behaviors invite and reinforce which other behaviors—the focus of this chapter and the previous one—you are in a position to *change* behaviors that don't work, in yourself and sometimes in others. The implications of all this, as we will see, can be staggering. When you find yourself in a relationship that isn't working, you may quickly sense why: "He wants me to defer to him and accept his opinions as law—he may even try to punish me if I do not go along with him." And when others cause you grief, you may be able to figure out how to stop them: "I'm not going to slink off in an angry fashion, or he'll become even nastier—I'd better stand up for myself."

From this point on, we will refer to people who employ the various styles using a sort of shorthand: people who rely on the style of Controlling will be called Controllers, people who rely on Avoiding are Avoiders, and so on through the list. Keep in mind, however, that applying these names is simply a matter of convenience. You will encounter very few people who demonstrate one, and only one, toxic style. Figure 6.10 presents the personality types that go along with the eight toxic Default Styles.

Where We've Been and Where We're Going

We began Part Two with a simple model of interpersonal behavior (see Figures 3.1 and 3.2), built around two axes: toward *versus* away and one-up *versus* one-down. In Chapter Four, we moved on to discuss the four modes of everyday behavior (Figure 4.1), the major strategy flowing from each one (Figure 4.2), the eight related styles (Figure 4.3), and the tactics most closely associated with each style (Figure 4.4). Then, in Chapter Five, we explored the rules of compatibility—how certain interpersonal maneuvers invite and reinforce specific responses. We noted how the rules of compatibility operate for the four modes of conventional behavior (Figure 5.1), the eight related styles (Figure 5.2), and their associated tactics (Figure 5.3). Finally, in this chapter, as an introduction to our detailed exploration of toxic relationships in Part Three, we performed the same sorts of analyses on toxic behavior.

Each of the chapters in Part Three concerns one of the eight toxic styles. We will discuss the following for all eight:

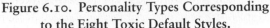

Figure 6.10. Personality Types Corresponding to the Eight Toxic Default Styles.

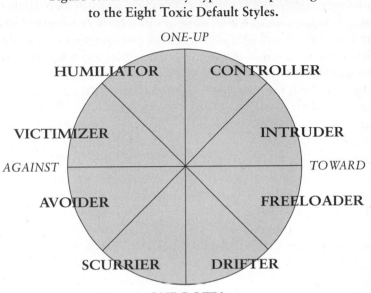

Source: © *Relational Dynamics Institute, Inc. Used by permission.*

- The life script that the person tends to live by
- Benefits of the style in its milder forms
- How it tends to be justified by the person using it
- Psychology of the individual who adopts the style
- Payoffs associated with implementing it
- What the person who favors that style typically avoids
- Exactly what he or she attempts to train you to do in response
- What happens when the relationship (contract) breaks down
- The person's probable life history
- What happens when you try to establish a close relationship with the person

How we behave, of course, has a powerful influence on how others behave toward us. So in exploring the eight toxic Default Styles, we will have a dual purpose: to look at the interpersonal styles of others but also to examine how our relational behaviors affect the way others treat us.

In Parts Three and Four, we will tackle the thorny problem of how to counter the troublesome behavior that is associated with each toxic style. We will turn the searchlight on ourselves as well as on others. If there is anything a Christian should not be, it is interpersonally toxic, and so we will devote considerable attention to the challenge of ensuring that we prove nourishing to people. We will also discuss when it is realistic to try to change another human being's interpersonal style—and when it's not.

PART THREE

EIGHT WAYS OF DISAPPOINTING THE FATHER

THE EIGHT CHAPTERS in Part Three may spark the keenest interest among readers of this book. This is because these chapters examine toxic styles and relationships in considerable detail. We saw in Chapter Six ("Overview of Interpersonal Toxicity") how the rules governing toxic interactions are similar to those governing conventional ones.

Chapter Six did in relation to toxic behavior what Chapters Three through Five did in relation to normal or conventional behavior. It explained the nature of interpersonal toxicity and, parallel to the four basic modes of ordinary interaction, outlined the four modes of toxic relating (for example, Aggressive Dominance). As with the four normal modes, each toxic one reflects a strategic purpose (for example, Attacking). And again parallel to the eight ordinary styles, in that chapter we introduced eight styles of toxicity (for example, Humiliating) and the tactics associated with them (in this example, Demeaning and Belittling). Chapter Six also highlighted which modes, strategies, styles, and tactics invite and reinforce each other.

The eight chapters in Part Three—each illustrated with examples from the Bible—explore in detail the range of toxic relationships, from those based on aggression and hostility to those based on a kind of warped connectedness masquerading as affection. We will explore the inner psychological workings and outer toxic maneuvers of people with the following styles:

- Controlling
- Drifting
- Intruding
- Freeloading
- Humiliating
- Scurrying
- Victimizing
- Avoiding

There is a natural pairing embedded within these styles. As we saw in Part Two, people with compatible styles—which does not necessarily mean desirable ones—show great skill at finding and linking up with each other: Controllers and Drifters, Intruders and Freeloaders, Humiliators and Scurriers, and Victimizers and Avoiders. It is a good idea, therefore, to read the chapters in pairs, which is how I have arranged them in the book. As you read, remember to look into your own heart and at your own conduct, as well as at the behavior of others.

7

CONTROLLING

BOSSING AND ORDERING

Jesus said to them, "Be on your guard against the yeast of the Pharisees and Sadducees." [The disciples] discussed this among themselves and said, "It is because we didn't bring any bread." . . . Jesus asked, "Why are you talking among yourselves about having no bread?" . . . Then they understood that he was not telling them to guard against the yeast used in bread, but against the teaching of the Pharisees and Sadducees.

—Matthew 16:5–12 [NIV]

CONTROLLERS ARE RIGIDLY DOMINANT and uncomfortable in situations they cannot orchestrate. They expect others to respond to them with respect and obedience, to be impressed by their abilities, and above all to allow them to take charge—even if what they're taking charge of is someone else's life. The Controller's version of the Golden Rule is, "Do as I say, not as I do." Exhibit 7.1 summarizes the Controller's main characteristics.

The Controller is goal-directed, committed to establishing and maintaining superiority, and likely to present himself or herself as a hero or savior. Such a person insists on being recognized as possessing definitive knowledge, infallible judgment, and correct opinions. Since he or she majors in "telling," the Controller prescribes what should be done and demands that others do it without question. If many people are like sheep, uncertain of where to go next, Controllers are like shepherds who are

Exhibit 7.1. Profile of the Controller.

Theme	"I'll tell you what to do and how to think."
Self-Presentation	Confident, strong, focused, and self-sufficient; authoritative and competent; states or implies that he or she has the answer and, sometimes, is the answer.
Additional Characteristics	Commanding and autocratic; intolerant of challenge, disagreement, or opposition; inclined to lecture and instruct; quick to give orders and directions; often ambitious and frequently stubborn; intense and insistent; opinionated; energetic and forceful; methodical and organized; willing to use power to ensure compliance; believes he or she exists to lead and direct; expects others to agree and go along.
Responses Induced in Others	Compliance and conformity; if not too overbearing, may induce respect, admiration, loyalty, comfort, and a sense of security; if dictatorial, and others are willing to play compatible roles, obedience and a willingness to surrender their independence of thought and action; if this style intensifies, those once willing to submit may revolt.
Healthier (Milder) Version	Leading through inspiration and providing helpful and confident guidance; acting with vision and courage; moving society forward by taking the initiative and boldly going where others have not yet ventured; providing necessary structure to and for organizations.

more than eager to direct them. Because they are usually confident, they especially appeal to those who are unsure of their own opinions and are not well grounded. This is precisely why Controllers can be troublesome, whether in society at large or within a spiritual community.

Your initial reaction to a Controller may be to go along with what he or she wants. Many Controllers take charge smoothly, if not hypnotically, which may leave you thinking, here's someone, finally, who knows how to make things turn out right. This style of relating to others is managerial and, when not too dictatorial, can be valuable (see Chapter Four and

Exhibit 7.1). Taken to extremes, however, the Controlling style is oppressive and tyrannical. Few people want to be treated like robots.

Controllers who "don't know when to stop" can become objects of resentment, especially if they move over to the left side of Figure 6.3, toward Humiliating (see Chapter Eleven) or, worse, Victimizing (Chapter Thirteen).

The Controller's Script

While most of us play several different roles in life (for example, friend, spouse, employee, parent, child), each of us develops a core script that embodies our principal Default Style and therefore guides what we say and do. Scripts operate largely outside of awareness. We may sense, on some level, that we have a script but usually remain oblivious to what it actually is.

Some people, for example, play the victim. They will do almost anything to remain in a one-down position that perpetuates their pain and seem to feel secure only when they are suffering. Scurriers (see Chapter Twelve) frequently exemplify this script. Others arrange their entire lives so that they can play the martyr. They insist on sacrificing themselves and appear, at first glance, to be embodiments of love and caring. On closer inspection, however, they often turn out to be smothering if not overwhelming, stifling those whom they are ostensibly trying to help. Intruders (see Chapter Nine) act out this script.

The Controller's life script is to set agendas, not just for himself or herself but for everyone else as well. And he or she will do whatever it takes to guarantee that these agendas are followed. The Controller's motif is that of a benevolent dictator. In the film *Meet the Parents*, Jack Burns is this kind of person. He hands out printed schedules for his daughter's wedding rehearsal and is given to saying such paradoxical things as "We have plenty of time—thirteen minutes and forty-four seconds." Consider this realistic example:

○

Case 7.1

George drives his wife, Tabitha, crazy with his endless tasks and assignments. When he gets home each evening, he grills her about whether she's done what he asked. His requests routinely sound like commands.

"Did you call the insurance company?"

"Yes, this morning."

"What did they tell you about the deductible?"

"We'll have to pay it."

"Were you able to get through to the pastor?"

"He's out of town until tomorrow."

"What about the vet? Can we take the dog in on Saturday?"

"They're booked."

"Did you ask them if there's a waiting list?"

"No."

"Did you make the dinner reservation?"

"Yes."

"Did you get the name of the person you talked to?"

"Sorry, I forgot."

"You should always get a name."

This sort of thing goes on every night, usually before he's taken off his coat. Before he leaves each morning, and often while she still has a toothbrush in her mouth, George gives Tabitha an oral to-do list and frequently calls her from his car to add to it. Ironically, Tabitha is extraordinarily competent, handles many things better than he does, and was for years chief administrative officer for a medium-sized company.

○

Despite the fact that Tabitha is competent, George is relentless in trying to dominate and control her, which illustrates the compulsive nature of his style.

Benefits of the Behavior

In its milder forms, the Controlling style is not without substantial benefits to society. Civilization is moved forward mostly by those who know how to take charge. Someone has to understand what to do and where to go so that the rest of us don't bump our heads while stumbling through the dimly lit corridors of ignorance and chaos. Every building or highway had to be designed and built by people who were assertive enough to "make it happen." Every invention and discovery, from antibiotics to electricity, had to be imagined and gone after. Controllers are the czars of progress, whether in politics, commerce, philosophy, or science.

While it may not be obvious, teaching is by nature a Controlling activity, even when conducted by the most introverted professor. The student is, by definition, one-down and the professor one-up. Deeply embedded within all pedagogy is the message, "I know more than you do," which is why teachers are often willing to work for modest wages. Their real compensation comes in the form of power, status, and impact. Recall the controlling style of the Pharisees who asked Jesus, "Why are your disciples picking grain on the Sabbath? They are not supposed to do that!" (Mark 2:24, CEV).

Justifications for the Style

The Controller may use any number of justifications to ensure superiority. Rank or office—what is usually called the authority of position or position power—can serve this purpose nicely. A military officer, for example, needs no other rationale for the right to command than epaulet bars or other insignia. But there are subtler platforms on which the Controlling style can be based, and if you challenge the preeminence of a Controller, he or she will usually fall back on one of these justifications for imposing his or her will on you.

Authority of competence. A Controller may know more than others about a given subject (for example, accounting or history) or be more capable in some other way (for example, organizing or planning).

Natural persuasiveness. The Controller may have the looks and bearing of a born leader. It is well known that, all else being equal, the taller man is likely to win the election. And often, so is the most attractive woman, or the person who speaks most eloquently.

Abundance of financial resources. Money talks, goes an old saying, and what it says is captured in the wry version of the Golden Rule, "He who has the gold makes the rules." Few behaviors establish one's claim to dominance more conclusively in our society than wealth. I am not saying that this should be so, only that it often is.

Moral authority. This hinges on others' believing that the Controller has special access to its source, which may in some instances be taken to be God. Some of the most controlling people in congregations are those who insist that they are more spiritual than others.

Physical strength. At least among males, this can establish, and back up, one's right to command, from the football field to the construction yard.

Academic achievement. Intellectuals are more control-oriented than you might think. In the name of scholarship, art, or science, they can demonstrate a lust for power that would have prompted the admiration of a pharaoh. Having attended a good college also helps establish this basis of superiority.

These—singly or even several at once—are the excuses that the Controller will offer.

Psychology of the Controller

Controllers rely on power to manage their anxiety. They are driven to dominate others because they feel most secure when they're in command. Their aim is to win approval by playing a role that society idealizes— authoritative leader—and their need to play this role underlies their ambition, whether it's artistic, scientific, social, financial, organizational, or even spiritual.

Those who constantly need to demonstrate their competence and effectiveness are worried that they may be incompetent or ineffective, although the odds of their ever admitting this, even to themselves, are small. Perfectionists, for example, are afraid to make a mistake and go through life dreading that others will criticize them. They can be among the world's most accomplished Controllers.

Such people make a religion of duty. They internalize and come to cherish what they have been forced to say or do by their parents or other early role models. In the words of the psychoanalyst, they "identify with the aggressor." Because of this, Controllers feel most comfortable when they imitate the behavior of the powerful. Unfortunately, the immense self-satisfaction they derive from doing this makes them quick to defend their opinions and wishes. Few people are as pleased with themselves as the self-righteous Controller, whose proclaimed righteousness is far more the product of man-made rules than of a living relationship with God.

It should come as no surprise that many Controllers have strong unconscious needs to rebel against order and regimentation. Their scrupulous adherence to precision and convention is a form of reaction formation: substituting in consciousness the opposite of what one really thinks, feels, wants, or believes. Many Controllers admire their parents, whom they see as capable and independent, and openly support their parents' values. Unconsciously, however, they may despise and resent them.

Controllers tend to perceive weakness in others where it doesn't exist, which makes them all the more likely to take over. Such imperialism trains others to think of themselves as ineffective and incapable, which can eventually result in their becoming genuinely weak and incompetent. Children of demanding high achievers sometimes emulate them but may also turn into pathetically incompetent adults. A nasty self-fulfilling prophecy is potentially at work in any relationship with a Controller. Through the Controller's arrogance and determination, the other person becomes less confident and capable each day. What this does to self-esteem is not pretty.

In addition to using the defense mechanism of reaction formation, Controllers rely on displacement: expressing their frustrations toward people who had nothing to do with creating them. The textbook example of displacement is kicking your dog when you're mad at your boss, spouse, or friend. Controllers take out on others what, on a deeper level, they would like to take out on their parents or themselves. Not only do they displace their feelings, but they also rationalize such displacement with moralistic speeches about how their actions are not just reasonable but desirable. Such actions, they insist, are for everyone else's good.

Among the most chilling depictions of what it is like to be in the clutches of a strong Controller is the film *The Passion of Ayn Rand*. You may recall that Rand was the author of such best-selling novels as *The Fountainhead* and *Atlas Shrugged*. From the 1940s until her death in 1982, she was a celebrated intellectual whose secular philosophy of "heroic self-interest" was anything but Christian. It embodied the antithesis of the Christian ideal of making the welfare of others as important as our own. She insisted on the virtues of uncompromising individualism—every person for himself or herself—and glorified those who defied convention to pursue their ambitions. Rand justified selfishness by insisting that it was somehow founded on logic, and she excused her own selfish actions accordingly. Like most Controllers, she did not fare well when her philosophy was turned back on her, and this is brought out poignantly in the film.

Controllers in the Bible

First-century Pharisees provide many examples of the Controlling style. "The Pharisees and teachers asked Jesus, 'Why don't your disciples obey what our ancestors taught us to do? Why do they eat without washing their hands?'" (Mark 7:5, CEV). And "That night Matthew invited Jesus and his disciples to be his dinner guests, along with his fellow tax collectors and many other notorious sinners. The Pharisees were indignant. 'Why does your teacher eat with such scum?' they asked his disciples" (Matthew 9:10–11, NLT). Theological experts of the day even took issue with his eating habits: "The religious leaders complained that Jesus' disciples were feasting instead of fasting. 'John the Baptist's disciples always fast and pray,' they declared, 'and so do the disciples of the Pharisees. Why are yours always feasting?'" (Luke 5:33, NLT).

The early church was challenged by many episodes of excessive control. In one instance, the problem was with Pharisees who had become Christians. As you can see from Paul's responses in the following passage, even by coming to faith in God through Christ it was difficult for them to modify their Controlling style: "But some believers who belonged to the sect of the Pharisees stood up and said, 'It is necessary for [Gentile

Christians] to be circumcised and ordered to keep the law of Moses.' . . . [Paul said] in the early days God made a choice . . . that I should be the one through whom the Gentiles would hear the message of the good news and become believers. And God, who knows the human heart, testified to them by giving them the Holy Spirit, just as he did to us; and in cleansing their hearts by faith he has made no distinction between them and us. Now therefore why are you putting God to the test? . . . We will be saved through the grace of the Lord Jesus, just as they will" (Acts 15:5–10, NRSV).

The Arrangement Sought

The Controller invites people to follow without question, and as long as this happens everything works fine. Over time, however, many Controllers tend to become dictatorial and increasingly to dominate and command others. They want disciples who automatically carry forth their messages and missions, work to achieve their goals and objectives, never challenge their proclamations or assertions, and remain loyal and steadfast even if those who want to control them no longer prove worthy of such dedication.

From Figures 6.7 and 6.8, you can see that the Controller wants to link up with people who have no mind of their own and who will submit and conform without questioning. The most compatible Default Style, therefore, is Drifting (see Chapter Eight). The Drifter has no firm sense of self, doesn't quite know what to think or feel, and is forever searching for someone to furnish an identity for him or her—a self—and to provide a set of prepackaged attitudes, beliefs, and opinions.

Controlling is flanked on the circle (see Figure 6.7) by Humiliating and Intruding, which means that the Controller will also attract a certain number of Freeloaders (see Chapter Ten) and Scurriers (see Chapter Twelve). The former tend to become sycophants, servile flatterers who endlessly reassure the Controller of how wonderful he or she is, while the latter tend to play the role of devoted follower but, in reality, are resentful malcontents without the backbone to assert themselves—lest the Controller become angry.

Payoffs for the Controller

It is gratifying to be admired and respected. Who among us is not secretly drawn to status and power? It is marvelous to have others obey and look to us for guidance.

By imposing their wills on other people, Controllers reassure themselves that they are competent and, secondarily, loved. Such reassurance is bolstered by the fact that others defer to them. Such respect and compliance provide Controllers with evidence of their consummate value and thus protect them from the anxiety that comes from being one-down or feeling undervalued. Napoleon once quipped that kings wore fine clothes to remind themselves of their importance. Controllers induce the admiration of others partly to persuade themselves of how capable and appreciated they are.

People with the most status in any society enjoy the most rewards. Rulers, for example, are routinely better off than their subjects. It is the Controllers in any society who are most likely to become rulers of the land and, along the way, to benefit from whatever riches are to be found there. Assertiveness, when it is affiliative and not so oppressive that it alienates others, is a substantial aid to earthly success.

What the Controller Avoids

The Controller refuses to think that he or she is *not* in control—a terrifying notion! Thus the realization that others are dissenting, even possibly revolting, has the potential to plunge the Controller into despair. Persons who rigidly define themselves as in command and in the know block out of their awareness even the possibility that things might be otherwise. The Controller tries never to feel needy, even when such feelings would be appropriate. Such a person lives as if he or she had memorized those military leadership manuals advising that the leader is "never uncertain, never afraid, never hungry, and never tired." Vacillation and self-doubt create anxiety for the Controller, who avoids all feelings of subordination.

Controllers are largely unable to communicate deference and will do so only if it becomes clear that subordination is necessary. Such rigidity fuels no end of conflict at the top of organizations. Controllers are also reluctant to relax and let their hair down. They may be skilled at working a room but approach everything with an earnestness that prompts others to suggest that they lighten up. And they convey intolerance for ineptitude, negligence, or laziness. Since emotional openness might cause them to convey uncertainly, Controllers are reluctant to self-disclose, a characteristic that can prove frustrating to people who attempt to get close to them.

The Controller runs from any behavior implying or suggesting passivity or dependence. He or she refuses to accept assistance, unless directing others to provide it, and tries not to demonstrate such behavior as Drifting (see Chapter Eight) or Freeloading (see Chapter Ten). Nor is he or she likely to act with an Avoiding style (see Chapter Fourteen)—for example, by disengaging, which can make it hard for the Controller to withdraw from a losing battle. The Controller is even less inclined toward self-abasing Scurrying (see Chapter Twelve) and so will rarely admit to being wrong.

What the Controller Trains You to Feel and Do

Controllers try to get you to respond with friendly compliance. They are mostly in the business of recruiting and training Drifters. Their mission is to induce you to respect and admire them, to surrender any right you may have to raise objections, and periodically to serve up morsels of admiration. Your failure to produce such fawning obedience will result in a decrease in your social standing and, sometimes, in excommunication. Of the eight Default Styles, it is the Controller who, in training others, most relies on the giving and taking away of status.

Most Controllers also use contact control to ensure compliance. To have access to the Controller, especially if he or she is in demand, you must deliver what the Controller wants, which can mean indulging a lot of arbitrary wishes and whims. The more dominant the Controller, the less patience he or she will show with anyone who fails to get in step. Possessing a strong opinion on everything and everyone, Controllers will rarely allow others to do to them what they rarely if ever do to themselves, which is to question the soundness of their own judgments. The Controller expects others to provide unquestioned acceptance, and those who do not provide it suffer. "Because I said so" is taken to be a sufficient rationale for just about anything.

The Controller wants and expects automatic agreement. Your acquiescence and allegiance is to be noncontingent (not dependent on what the Controller says or does), since the Controller's words and actions are, by definition, right and proper. The Controller's approval, by contrast, is never unconditional, and he or she grants it only to those who pay proper homage. You will be favored to the extent that the Controller deems you enlightened and deferent. There can be no criticism, and if you offer any you will find yourself placed immediately on probation. In more extreme instances, success may require the complete merging of your identity into that of the Controller, which is what often happens in cults.

When the Arrangement Breaks Down

If a Controller becomes too heavy-handed or punishing, the other person may resent it and, when conditions permit, revolt. Rebellion is unlikely to occur, of course, if the Controller enjoys consequence control, which is power over other people's outcomes, such as whether they keep their jobs or remain on prestigious committees. When such control exists, resentment will quietly fester until a suitable opportunity arises for its expression. Like Mack at the bottom of the stack in the Dr. Seuss story *Yertle the Turtle*, those who have gone along with the program may simply reach a point where they have had enough—and hiccup.

Recall that Controlling is flanked, in Figure 6.7, by Intruding and Humiliating. When others begin to question what the Controller wants, he or she may quickly move either toward crowding and smothering, the tactics of the Intruder, or demeaning and belittling, the tactics of the Humiliator. These are, in a sense, opposite maneuvers.

Moving in the latter direction, toward Humiliating, is for the Controller to become less affiliative and more aggressive. This is the strategy of trying to whip errant disciples into shape, lest they decide that they can think for themselves. Moving in the former direction, toward Intruding, is for the Controller to become more affiliative and less aggressive. This is the strategy of attempting to reenfranchise those who have strayed, by indulging and micromanaging them, lest they forget the goodies that the Controller has the power to bestow on them.

Revolt is made more likely when the Controller moves to the aggressive side of the circle (see Figures 6.6 and 6.7), that is, if he or she begins to humiliate or victimize those who have previously given their unflagging allegiance. Such persons did not sign on to Scurry, for example, and may refuse to do so. By changing into a Humiliator (see Chapter Eleven), the Controller violates the arrangement and, with it, the implied agreement with those who prove unwilling to appease, whine, and placate, that is, to behave in a Scurrying manner (see Chapter Twelve).

The Controller who gives his wife whatever she wants, for example, but who increasingly tries to restrict her freedom may get away with it for a while. She may rationalize going along with his micromeddling by telling herself that he's only doing it because he loves her. If, however, he begins to attack her as a person, demeaning and humiliating her, the relationship will show the strain. She may get back at him in any of a thousand ways, from refusing to do the dishes, if that has been her responsibility, to running up the balances on their charge cards. And if things get really bad, he may come home some evening just in time to watch the moving van pull away. The only thing left in the house may be a note informing him that she's drained their bank accounts.

Life History

Many Controllers were raised by parents who stressed proper and responsible conduct. As we shall see again and again, people do unto others what they do to themselves. And they do to themselves what others have done to them.

The Controller was expected to perform and, often, to be the perfect child—responsible and conscientious. He or she later takes on the role of the limit-setting parent and expects others to support this. Many Controllers were expected to achieve. They were urged to follow the rules but also to be assertive, to put themselves out in front, as objects of admiration and envy.

Oldest children tend often to become Controllers because they were saddled with excessive responsibility at an early age. Such children served as their parents' lieutenants and assistants and were frequently charged with caring for siblings. This, naturally, turned them into Controllers early on.

A role reversal sometimes occurs between parent and child. This can happen when one or both parents are medically or psychologically impaired. The child of an alcoholic may become the most responsible person in the home, which is why it has been quipped that the first child in an alcoholic family *is* the parent. Such a child is, in this way, induced to engage in Controlling behaviors and, unwittingly, to adopt Controlling as his or her lifelong Default Style. The same pattern is also prevalent in the history of those who develop an Intrusive style (see Chapter Nine). It commonly shows up, therefore, in the life histories of persons who relate to others through Engulfing (see Figure 6.6). In such cases, it is not so much that the child identifies with the parents and internalizes their values but that the Controlling style arises as the natural match to parental dependence and incompetence—to their psychological Drifting. In response to parental weakness and inadequacy, the child learns to be exceedingly strong, excessively directive, and unusually self-sufficient. Such parents are unable to give much emotionally, and so the child comes to feel that there is no one there. He or she grows up too early and concludes that it is one's destiny in life to take charge.

Intimacy and the Controller

Default Styles, when they are exaggerated, prevent people from obtaining what we all need—intimacy. These styles protect them from anxiety and real or imagined hurts, at the cost of depriving them of emotional satisfaction. As soon as they begin to get close to another human being, to share feelings on an adult-to-adult level, the toxic Default Styles kick in and bring all this to a halt.

The Controller is driven to tell others what to do, how to think, and how to feel. This makes it difficult for Controllers to express what is going on inside. Without the freedom to do this, no real closeness can develop and, even if it does, it will not last. Intimacy requires mutuality, as we touched on in Chapter Two, and it is difficult to experience true give-and-take with someone who is trying to choreograph each and every step of your life.

What makes things worse is that, as soon as you tell a Controller that you are troubled about something, he or she will immediately set about solving the problem. Instead of listening, which is often what you most need, the Controller will attempt to fix whatever caused your discomfort, and you will end up feeling more alone than if you'd never said anything about your uneasiness in the first place.

The Controller's strong task orientation crowds out the free exchange of feelings and thus the deepening of the relationship. As soon as you start to watch the sunset with a Controller, he or she will begin to look for a place from which to get a better view. The mood will be lost and, with it, the moment, which may not come again. Intimacy thrives on spontaneity, and this is not something the Controller either facilitates or tolerates well. He or she may occasionally act spontaneously but is unlikely to be at ease when others do the same.

Spiritual and Moral Choices

As with any other Default Style that is inflexible or extreme, it is not easy for Controllers to change their ways. One reason is that such people are great to have around when there is a crisis, and so others keep reinforcing them for exaggerated dominance. They take charge, and because they are often competent they will see you through to safety. The problem is that it is difficult for them to *stop* directing and commanding others when the crisis is over. Their mentality is that if they don't take charge of everything, from when to take the trash out to how to boil an egg, the world will fall apart. Thus they reflexively intervene, manage, and arrange anything they can.

Christians have a duty to guard against tendencies to dominate others. We should be even more on guard against any inclination we have to rationalize such domination. If you were not competent, you probably wouldn't be reading this book, and so you may have a tendency to operate with a Controlling style. If so, keep in mind these words of Jesus: "You know that in this world kings are tyrants, and officials lord it over the people beneath them. But among you it should be quite different" (Matthew 20:25–26, NLT).

There ought to be a relaxed softness to how we relate to others. Is this difficult to achieve for a person who automatically moves toward people in a dominant way and truly cares about how well things turn out—someone who is willing to put his or her shoulder to the wheel?

You bet it is!

SELF-ASSESSMENT

To get a quick sense of how much you may rely on this Default Style, ask yourself the following questions. Although these questions do not constitute a test, they may give you a rough idea of where you stand. Please consult www.relationaldynamics.com for information about more sophisticated methods of assessment.

1. Do you routinely tell others what to do and insist on teaching and instructing them?

2. Are you quick to assert the correctness of your views, with little tolerance for opposition?

3. Do you tend to take over in meetings and convey to other people that you're in charge?

ANTIDOTES TO TOXICITY

I am now going to provide you with two sets of suggestions. The first may help you reduce any tendency you find in yourself to operate in the Default Style we have discussed in this chapter. Before trying out any of these suggestions, it would be wise to read Part Four of this book, particularly Chapter Fifteen, on myths about behavior change. The second set of suggestions may help you respond more effectively to others who relate to you through this Default Style. These suggestions are of necessity general and therefore may not work with a specific individual. So use them wisely and judiciously, and above all do not apply them mechanically or put yourself in danger. Although people with certain interpersonal styles tend to be more troublesome and combative than those who rely on other styles, it is best to err on the side of caution. When in doubt, consult those with publicly sanctioned expertise in personality disorders, such as mental health professionals.

If You Tend Toward Controlling . . .

Here are some suggestions that may help you reduce this tendency:

○ Try not to do everyone else's work for them. Controlling sometimes reflects taking on too much responsibility, which trains others to take on too little. Empower people instead of treating them like children.

- Expect those around you to be competent. People tend to perform at the level of others' expectations. If you communicate that you think they will be conscientious, they are more likely to be exactly that. Of course, there are no guarantees.

- Work to understand that your standards of performance may be unrealistically high. While you may demand perfection from yourself, and may even achieve it sometimes, you will get perfection from only a small number of others.

- God places a high value on human freedom (see Chapter One). Acknowledge that it is wrong of you to value it any less. Do not restrict other people's freedom of choice unless absolutely necessary, and admit that what you think is "necessary" often may not be.

- As hard as it may be, let others make their own mistakes. If you continually try to protect them, they will never learn to deal with life's harsher realities.

- Value relationships more and tasks less. Controllers are often strongly committed to getting things done and relatively unconcerned with how others feel along the way. Remember Martha and Mary (Luke 10:40–42), and do not rationalize your way out of what this incident communicates about how Jesus viewed tasks and relationships.

- Recruit Anchors to help you (see Chapter Sixteen).

How to Respond to Controlling

If someone else is relating to you through Controlling, here are some potential countermeasures:

- Do not reward others for controlling you by complimenting them when they begin to take over—which is what you may feel inclined to do.

- Express your own opinions even if it means that the Controller will disapprove.

○ Refrain from asking for advice and guidance, since this only increases the tendency in the other person to dominate and direct.

○ Stick to your position if and when the Controller attempts to chide or punish you for this; remember that Controllers, when they sense that they are losing their viselike grip on others, will often move to the left side of our interpersonal model (see Figures 3.2 and 4.2).

○ Above all, resist any tendency in yourself automatically to obey the Controller.

○ Tell the Controller that you feel controlled—and expect that, when you do, it is unlikely that the Controller is either going to understand what you are saying or own up to what is going on. Nevertheless, labeling the Controlling behavior for what it is may decrease it.

8

DRIFTING

OBEYING AND CONFORMING

_____

*King Solomon loved many foreign [pagan] women along
with the daughter of Pharaoh . . . from the nations concerning
which the Lord had said, "You shall not enter into marriage with
them . . . for they will surely incline your heart to follow their
gods" . . . [but] when Solomon was old, his wives turned him
after other gods; and his heart was not true to the Lord his God.
. . . Solomon did what was evil.*

1 Kings 11:1–6 [NRSV]

LIKE SOLOMON WHEN HE WANDERED away from God, Drifters spend
their lives "going along" with the people around them and, as a result,
lack clear identities. They are human mirrors who mostly reflect the views
and opinions of others and, even when pressed, hardly know who or what
they are. While they may have likes and dislikes, they are so focused on
what other people want that even as adults they have few distinct preferences and lack anything resembling a strong sense of themselves and who
they are. They are unassertive and largely without passion, and they
impress others as interpersonally weak, emotionally flat, and sometimes
incompetent. The Drifter's version of the Golden Rule is "Say unto me
and I will do." Exhibit 8.1 outlines the key attributes of the Drifter.

You will automatically feel powerful in the presence of a Drifter and
therefore inclined to provide him or her with the benefit of your views

---

Exhibit 8.1. Profile of the Drifter.

Theme	"You're right—I'll think and do whatever you say."
Self-Presentation	Uncertain, tentative, and insecure; lacking in confidence; willing, perhaps eager, to be instructed and enlightened; more respectful of others than self; disinclined to express personal views and opinions; grants more status and power to others than to self.
Additional Characteristics	Passive and compliant; timid and quick to concede or compromise; uninspiring and shallow; often incapable of making decisions and only marginally adequate; reactive rather than proactive; dismissive of own worth or importance; underdeveloped self-concept and blurred or confused identify; few strong opinions or passions; little or no originality of thought; inclined to "shop" many people to obtain counsel and to agree with each along the way.
Responses Induced in Others	Guiding, advising, and directing; may elicit dominating behavior even from those not typically forceful; if excessively bland or vacillating, others may "give up" out of boredom or exasperation.
Healthier (Milder) Version	Following others when appropriate to create healthy compliance and alignment; refusing to compete when doing so would be counterproductive; honoring and supporting organizational and social structures; behaving in a manner that others can count on, that puts others at ease, and that others find helpful.

---

and opinions. It will be clear that the Drifter expects you to assume control, and even if you are not dominant by nature you will probably do so. When it dawns on you that the Drifter's readiness to agree has more to do with a need to please and defer than with the substance of your arguments, you may feel deflated. And when you finally realize that the Drifter is without much of a self—is almost a hollow person—you may back away from the relationship. It is difficult, if not impossible, to establish genuine closeness with someone who lacks a mind or will of his or her own.

The Drifter's Script

The script of the Drifter is to submit and, in this way, establish a place in the world, a niche, where he or she can feel accepted. Because many people in society are looking for someone else to dominate, or at least feel superior to, the Drifter can easily purchase acceptance by granting such persons control. Under such an arrangement, he or she can usually count on benevolent oppression from the other person, who will typically operate with a Controlling Default Style. The Drifter's strategy is to fit in by fading into the woodwork and, if conditions are right, by playing the part of the devoted fan or follower.

○

Case 8.1

Randy has survived for decades in his company, primarily by doing whatever his boss wants. Although he is what most people would describe as a good citizen, he has quietly done some unsavory things over the years—from falsifying corporate documents to "losing" information. In each instance, he did what was asked of him. His coworkers have little respect for Randy because, to them, he has no spine. He will align himself with whoever is in power and nod his head even when he knows that their ideas are ridiculous. What Randy doesn't yet understand is that he will never be promoted much beyond where he is in the company because of his Drifting style, which reflects a lack of leadership.

○

This example illustrates an important characteristic of the Drifter, one that can actually result in an otherwise timid and reserved person's becoming menacing and, on rare occasion, dangerous. The desire to be accepted can lead the Drifter to commit acts that a person with a more crystallized sense of self or character would never do. Under certain conditions, the Drifter can transform—"morph"—into an automaton who carries out the instructions of malevolent masters. Because the Drifter's allegiance can generalize to a social or political group, he or she will sometimes mutate from a harmless lapdog into a savage beast, capable of whatever atrocity is prescribed by those in power. It is a great paradox that the soul who is, by nature, the most compliant occasionally becomes, in the end, the most ferocious. The insecurity that impels the Drifter to seek approval can also turn him or her into a hatchet person. This, however, is unusual. Under ordinary circumstances, the Drifter simply goes along with the program and attempts to win acceptance by pleasing those who insist on taking command.

○

Case 8.2

Linda, mother of four and a graduate of a top university, is a joiner. She is involved in two church groups and works hard for both. Most of her friends take her for granted. They give her the most menial jobs when they plan an event—from stuffing envelopes to fetching coffee. Sometimes, after a morning meeting, several of the women will go to lunch and, occasionally, invite her along. Linda rarely knows what she wants to eat, typically asks the waiter for advice on what to order, and afterward says only that her lunch was "good" or "nice." Whenever the women consider a controversial topic or proposal, Linda says that she's fine with it or declines to express an opinion. She offers few suggestions and says nothing that could prompt anyone's disapproval.

○

Benefits of the Behavior

Drifters, like Freeloaders (see Chapter Ten), get along reasonably well in society and its various organizations. They are respectful, unlikely to cause trouble, and willing to contribute. What they contribute, however, can be ordinary, uncreative, and run-of-the-mill because they are not disposed to take risks, and innovation usually involves risk taking. Still, society functions best when conflict is kept within manageable limits, and Drifters assist enormously with this. They help keep organizations running smoothly and can be a refreshing contrast to individuals who are confrontational, argumentative, or contentious. Others are likely to describe persons who relate with a Drifting style as nice people who can be trusted. Drifters are quick to get out of the way.

Justifications for the Style

The Drifter, if questioned about this deferential or lackluster behavior, will respond in a way that reaffirms his or her unworthiness, be at a loss for words, begin to mist up in response to feeling criticized, or start to express resentment, thus moving to the left side of Figure 6.7 by adopting the Scurrier style (see Chapter Twelve). Here are some of the specific ways in which Drifters justify their submissive approach to others:

Absence of any right to assert. The Drifter will tell you that it would be wrong to act more assertively. He or she may be quick to point out that others are more entitled to be respected, listened to, and obeyed. If indeed, for all of us, a central issue in life is how much to take care of ourselves versus how much to take care of other people, the Drifter has resolved this dilemma largely in favor of others.

Absence of competence. He or she will express doubts about his or her abilities or capacities. If only he or she were more intelligent, educated, cultured, well financed, experienced—whatever—the Drifter would be more definite in voicing opinions and making demands. As things stand, however, the Drifter has no basis for doing anything of the sort.

Awkward silence. Some Drifters are so unassertive that, when challenged, they do not even respond. While a more assertive person might say anything from "I'm doing what I want to do" to "Mind your own business," the person with an extreme and rigid Drifting style may clam up. He or she will, of course, be frustrated in the process, because you are doing the one thing the Drifter dreads, making him or her the center of attention and, on top of that, expressing disapproval.

Displays of injury. The Drifter may be cut to the quick by your challenge and become misty-eyed. By words or actions, the Drifter is "doing the best I can" and is silently asking you to affirm this.

Whining and appeasing. A Drifter may complain that you are hurting him or her and ask, even beg, you to stop. Such pleading is more characteristic of the Scurrier (see Chapter Twelve), but under pressure the Drifter may engage in it.

All these maneuvers by the Drifter are prompted by others' expressions of disenchantment, frustration, or exasperation and are therefore reactive. They reflect the very characteristic for which the Drifter is being criticized, that is, refusing to assume responsibility for his or her own existence.

Psychology of the Drifter

The Drifter attempts to get on in life by giving other people status and power at his or her own expense. Unlike the Freeloader (see Chapter Ten), who goes along with others only as long as this gets something he or she wants, the Drifter goes along even when this doesn't happen. He or she hopes that by surrendering the right to express preferences and make choices, others will accept him or her. The Drifter thus trades self-respect and personal autonomy for inclusion and affirmation. Great anxiety is aroused when the Drifter does anything that makes him or her stand out, and so the Drifter's principal strategy is to blend in. He or she communicates, in a thousand ways, a sometimes desperate need for others to provide guidance and direction, a willingness to comply with whatever they say, and a pronounced inability to make independent decisions.

Drifters structure their interpersonal worlds so that others outrank them and are therefore superior. Such structuring is the one area in which Drifters are assertive. Paradoxically, they strongly but covertly assert their intention to remain unassertive. Drifters make compliance into an art form. They keep their anxiety in check by observing whatever boundaries others establish for them, and they feel most secure when others supply them with clear boundaries. And Drifters do mentally what they do behaviorally, which is to stay within prescribed lines. They simply do not allow themselves to think or acknowledge certain things.

There is a difference between repression and denial that is worth noting. Repression is blocking out of awareness things that are inside of you. Denial, by contrast, is refusing to acknowledge things that are outside of you. Drifters are no strangers to repression, and it is common, therefore, to find them confused about their feelings, unable to acknowledge anger in themselves, even when others can see it plainly in their faces, and unsophisticated about their inner workings. Yet they are even more prone to engage in denial, especially when it comes to misconduct by those to whom they have connected themselves. They are especially oblivious to hostility in others and gladly absorb it without seeming to notice that it's there. If someone with an exaggerated Drifting style asked you for guidance about which sport to take up and you said "javelin receiver," such a person might thank you for your constructive advice. Drifters may come across as too stupid to be insulted, but in most instances this is not the case. Rather, they merely refuse to notice what's in front of their noses.

Drifters are born disciples but not necessarily disciples of the one true God. They are inclined to comply with the wishes of any strong authority figure. They not only deceive themselves about how much they tend to defer but, more important, the extent to which they are empty persons.

○

Case 8.3

Toni has been dating Andrew for seven months and, although she was initially impressed by his good looks and manners, she is having second thoughts. Although Andrew often asks what she would like to do for the evening, he has no suggestions of his own. When they go to dinner, it is Toni who chooses the restaurant, and before they order Andrew asks what she is going to have and then orders the same thing. When they go to the theater, Toni selects the show, and if, after seeing it, she asks Andrew for his critique he says it was "fine" and immediately wants to know what she thinks. Whatever she says—that it was the best or worst show ever—Andrew agrees. And if they have an argument, he is quick to admit that it was his fault, as if he wants to sweep the issue under the rug as soon as possible. When Toni recently asked him if he'd ever thought about their getting married, Andrew said that he hadn't but that it seemed like an "OK" idea. He gave her the same go-along-with-the-program answer when she asked about children—he'd be glad to do whatever she wanted, either have them, adopt, or grow old together alone. While Andrew is academically bright and has a good job, Toni has begun to wonder if he has a mind of his own. She also wonders if he has ever had a personal encounter with God or if he is merely parroting others in their Bible study group.

○

Andrew is relying on the Drifting style, and Toni, who is anything but a Drifter, may be subtly encouraging this style by taking charge. Drifters are most at ease when they have someone to look up to and admire, someone to tell them what to think and feel, a sort of psychological commandant. They are therefore inclined to identify with the aggressor, a phenomenon that sometimes occurs between Controllers and their parents (see Chapter Seven). Yet while Controllers adopt the styles of those who dominate them because they want to become like them, Drifters identify in a more selective way. They take on the values, opinions, and attitudes of those to whom they defer. But they will not act assertively unless instructed to do so, in which case they may become tyrants. Drifters do whatever they have to do in order to enjoy the comfort of having someone else manage their lives, including behaving like a Caspar Milquetoast.

Most Drifters have positive feelings about their relatives and, if they are married, about their spouses. This, after all, is what's expected of them. As noted, they tend to excuse bad behavior in others, rather than to reckon with it for what it is (for example, nasty), and this promotes a certain superficial peace within the family.

Like most people with a toxic Default Style, the Drifter is not inclined to engage in much self-exploration. If the Drifter did such introspection, he or she might have to own up to the fact that his or her entire life is based on paying ransom. Drifters bribe potential dominators to accept them by paying tribute, that is, by promising and delivering obedience and conformity. Although Drifters may seek help in the form of advice and guidance, they do not always want to follow the guidance that they are given, particularly if it involves acting freely and independently. They are wooden, like Pinocchio, only unlike that fictional character they prefer to remain so, since becoming a real person would involve unbearable risk. Others, after all, might get angry with them for daring to have opinions of their own. Becoming a genuine person, with nonconforming thoughts and passionate feelings, would require that they step out in front, where they could be criticized and rejected—a horrible thought.

Drifters in the Bible

Scripture is filled with people who drifted at a key moment in their lives because they were not sufficiently anchored (Lot and Aaron are good examples). Jesus gave the disciples this sobering parable about drifting:

> A farmer went out to sow. . . . This is the meaning of the parable: The seed is the word of God. Those along the path are the ones who hear, and then the devil comes and takes away the word from their hearts, so that they may not believe and be saved. Those on the rock are the ones who receive the word with joy when they hear it, but they have no root. They believe for a while, but in the time of testing they fall away. The seed that fell among thorns stands for those who hear, but as they go on their way they are choked by life's worries, riches and pleasures, and they do not mature [Luke 8:5, 11–14, NIV].

Rehoboam provides an example from the Old Testament of someone without a clear sense of self and what this led to. "So King Rehoboam established himself in Jerusalem and reigned. . . . He did evil, for he did not set his heart to seek the Lord" (2 Chronicles 12:13–14, NRSV). There was nothing inside of Rehoboam to serve as a compass to keep him from veering off course or from what, in today's language, would be called strategic drift.

The Arrangement Sought

People who need to feel weak characteristically pair up with those who are strong. Stronger people benefit from the contrast they can draw between themselves and their weaker associates and also from having others around who will do whatever they're told. Such obedience comforts those who are strong and validates their right to command. This is what we saw in Chapter Seven, when we examined the psychology of the Controller.

Weaker people, for their part, benefit from associating with those who accept them and provide guidance. The arrangement sought, from the point of view of the Drifter, goes something like this: "You lead and I'll follow; you command and I'll obey; you dictate and I'll conform; you demand and I'll comply. And by the way, who *am* I anyway, apart from you telling me? I'm but a shell of a human being, afraid to take the risk of developing my own ideas, attitudes, or opinions."

Payoffs for the Drifter

The principal emotional reward that comes from adopting the Drifting style is that it brings with it peace and certainty. Drifters know whose opinions count—those in power—and enjoy the security of knowing exactly whom to obey. Their manner of existence provides them with relief from the anguish that comes from not being able to answer the most basic questions in life, such as who and what they are. The Drifting style also fends off the anxiety that comes with opposing those in power, since powerful people can punish you for opposition. Drifters therefore declare such opposition unthinkable and, by implication, out of bounds.

A Drifting style brings with it two related social benefits. One is that Drifters are usually well liked. While those who have to endure the boredom that sometimes comes from living with them may be less charitable, most of their acquaintances find them pleasant. They do not realize that the Drifter has little in the way of an inner life. And unless they come to despise the Drifter for groveling (for example, before his or her boss), they will automatically accept him or her. The other social benefit of the Drifting style is that Drifters, owing to their eagerness to cave in during conflict, rarely cause others to become angry. At most, other people are likely to feel only mild irritation at the Drifter's lack of initiative—for example, if he or she is put on a committee and fails to produce results.

What the Drifter Avoids

Drifters fretfully avoid thinking of themselves as better than others. Sentiments of superiority run counter to their whole approach to life. They will rarely, if ever, define themselves as experts, leaders, bosses, or even caregivers except in the most general sense. And of course, they are even more unlikely to think of themselves as aggressors. While on the surface this may look like Christian humility, it is not.

Their feelings tend to follow their thoughts. Drifters do not sense themselves to be one-up and therefore rarely have the feelings that go with this—feelings, for example, of strength and effectiveness. If they allowed themselves to feel strong or effective, they might provoke humiliation at the hands of others, and so they stick to the business of *acting* humbly. They keep their emotional heads bowed and paste fake smiles on their faces. As noted, however, what looks like humility is not always motivated by love of God and fellow humans. It sometimes comes from fear and insecurity.

The Drifter does not usually think out loud, at least not candidly. Most people will tell you what they feel if you ask them. Not so the Drifter, who will tell you what he or she calculates you want to hear. It is not that the Drifter is a manipulative schemer who is trying to work you for selfish ends. That's what Victimizers do. It is rather that the Drifter desperately wants your liking and approval. As a result, the Drifter is not forthright and may at times come across as evasive and duplicitous. Yet it is not that the Drifter intends to deceive, only that he or she is inclined to agree with you, or anyone else he or she is with. On those rare occasions when you can get the Drifter to offer a genuine opinion, it will not be anything close to "This is what I think and why."

It is unlikely that you will find the Drifter debating or arguing. Such a person backs away from competitive contests and power struggles, preferring simply to forfeit or yield in a quiet manner. An expert in compliance, the Drifter will rarely display anger, much less become involved in rebellious activities of any kind, unless of course this is what a Controller wants. The Drifter will neither challenge authority nor stand up for himself or herself, unless the circumstances are extreme and he or she absolutely has to.

What the Drifter Trains You to Feel and Do

Drifters induce in others, at first, a sense of strength and adequacy. Those interacting with Drifters naturally feel competent, empowered, and, by virtue of the uncertainty shown by Drifters, more self-assured than they otherwise would. Such others tend to feel increasingly confident of their opinions and to take on the mantle of capable leaders. So far, so good. There's nothing wrong, and perhaps plenty right, with working out a relationship in which one person leads and the other follows. That, however, is not quite what's going on.

Those interacting with Drifters are inclined, over time, to become ever more dominant. Even relatively unassertive people who generally steer clear of a Controlling style may begin to provide firm direction, and eventually they may even take on the hostile edge of the Humiliator (see Chapter Eleven). Without realizing it, they will firmly and sometimes insistently prescribe tastes (for example, food or clothing), attitudes (for example, religious or political), and opinions (for example, doctrinal or liturgical). Such dominance may escalate until they take Drifters completely for granted. Others may lose all respect for Drifters and trivialize whatever they say. They may even proclaim the Drifter an insufferable bore—with good reason. And if others carry around a lot of resentment, they may begin to take this resentment out on the Drifter simply because he or she is there and will put up with this.

It is not as if others learn to dehumanize Drifters without their participation. Ironically, Drifters *actively* teach others to dismiss them through practiced *passivity.* Not only are Drifters willing to bear such unpleasantness, but unconsciously they welcome it. The question, of course, is why.

Drifters, like most of us, are least anxious when they play roles with which they are familiar. But Drifters have learned only one role, and it is this inflexibility that causes problems. By communicating to others that they have no right to be respected as *persons,* they attempt to ensure that others will not abandon them and, further, that they will not have to take on the weighty responsibility that comes with freedom of choice. Since Drifters have no significant freedom of choice, having long ago surrendered it, all they have to do is what they're told.

Authoritarian societies are not made up only of Controllers (see Chapter Seven), Humiliators (see Chapter Eleven), and Victimizers (see Chapter Thirteen), all of whom are dominant in style. Such societies would collapse without Drifters to sustain them. Drifters look for and attract those who are forceful, assertive, and capable. The Drifter is, at root, an obedient follower who is forever looking for an authoritative, if not authoritarian, leader who will accept responsibilities that the Drifter shirks.

When the Arrangement Breaks Down

The stronger person, as we have seen, may become bored with the weaker person—in this case, the Drifter—precisely because the latter has no clear identity or direction. Such boredom, since it proves frustrating, may turn into anger and, eventually, rage. At this point, the Controlling style transforms itself into a Humiliating or even a Victimizing one. If and when it does, the relationship may dissolve.

Marriage therapists are fond of saying that, for couples, whatever brought them together is often the very thing that is driving them apart. Frank marries Kathryn because she's vivacious and laughs a lot, and Kathryn marries Frank because he's serious and responsible. Ten years later, Frank may be frustrated because Kathryn "can't be serious," and Kathryn may be frustrated because Frank "can't relax and have fun."

You can sometimes see how such attractions turn to frustrations in couplings of people with Controlling and Drifting styles. The Controller, above all, wants someone who will go along with the program without challenge. Who on earth could be better at *not* challenging than the Drifter? The Drifter, for his or her part, wants someone to provide such a program and does not want to be left without direction. Who is better at providing direction than the Controller?

But there can be trouble in paradise. An old comedy skit goes like this: Wanting to improve the quality of their marriage, the wife persuades her argumentative husband to listen each morning to a radio program about relationships. The husband, knowing that his marriage is in trouble and wanting to please, begins to agree with everything she says. This goes on for days. As he continues to agree, she smiles ever more radiantly. They are enjoying a happy arrangement, one founded on the match between someone with a Controlling style (wife) and someone with a Drifting style (husband). Then one morning she realizes that her husband has been insincerely going along with her, whereupon they have a ferocious argument during which she accuses him of having "no mind of his own" and he, in turn, tells her what he "really" thinks.

Although, initially, the Controller may be happy to have someone who will conform and comply, he or she may later realize that such conformity and compliance have no substance and are not based on the Drifter's appreciation for what the Controller says but rather on the need for acceptance and approval. At this point, the Drifter may become an object of persecution. This may not become overt, however, if the Drifter remains useful as a supporter or constituent.

The arrangement may also break down if the Drifter begins to develop a sense of self—an independent identity. Most of us know formerly docile people who, in their thirties or forties, returned to school or work and soon began to act differently. Fed up with living vicariously through others and saying yes to everything, they reinvented themselves and redrafted the "rules of engagement" operating in their closest relationships. Most of us have also known people who in midlife, claiming to have found their true selves, started to assert and redefine themselves bizarrely, with disastrous consequences. Although such radical personality change is unusual, it does occur, and when it does, relationships change, for better or for worse.

Finally, the contract can break down because the person in the dominant position either becomes more vindictive than the Drifter expected or turns out to have been so all along. When Drifters enter into romantic relationships, they tend to choose partners whom they perceive to have Controlling styles, people who will help manage their lives. They do not, however, do well with partners who are or become *aggressively* dominant (Humiliators or Victimizers). Drifters prefer affiliation to antagonism. They are on the right side of our model depicted in Figure 6.1. Drifters want to be with *benign* dictators.

Because of their passivity, however, Drifters sometimes have a hard time breaking out of relationships with Humiliators or Victimizers. Such people are dominant and inclined, therefore, to continue to tell the Drifter what to do—for example, to remain in the relationship. Note that, as we discussed in Chapter Six, there is a certain amount of compatibility between the Drifting style, on the one hand, and both the Humiliating and Victimizing styles on the other. Although they are not compatible on the affiliative (horizontal) axis, they *are* compatible on the dominance-submission (vertical) one. Even when the arrangement breaks down and turns seriously destructive, the Drifter may remain in it. This, of course, is often what happens in physically abusive marriages.

Life History

Most Drifters were raised in conventional homes by dominating parents. As a child, the Drifter was taught to be seen and not heard and to win approval by staying out of the way and causing no trouble. Self-expression was not encouraged; conformity was.

It is not unusual to discover that a Drifter was reared in a family that was generally benevolent but, at the same time, authoritarian. A premium was placed on obedience, and affection was expressed indirectly (for example, through gift giving) rather than directly (for example, via hugging). Conspicuously missing was any encouragement for the child to excel, stand out, or become a leader. Emotional warmth and personal encouragement were in short supply. The message "I believe in you" was rarely communicated.

Some Drifters were raised by militaristic parents who, from the day they were born, barked orders at them. Such parents, while intending to teach self-discipline, succeeded only in breaking, or at least dampening, the child's spirit.

Intimacy and the Drifter

The Drifter may, at first glance, seem like the ideal person with whom to enjoy an intimate relationship. He or she is motivated to please and accommodate, disinclined to argue or fight, and capable of saying exactly what you want to hear. Then, one day, you realize that everything the Drifter says has been scripted. It strikes a false note, as if it had been rehearsed and designed to curry favor or to mollify. You get the vague impression that you are talking to an android, programmed for your enjoyment and gratification, and you may eventually conclude that the individual with whom you are trying to establish intimacy is hardly a *person* at all. A relationship with a Drifter can therefore prove to be a lonely experience. You end up feeling as if you're talking to yourself, and whatever mutuality you seem to develop evaporates quickly; it turns out to have been largely an illusion.

Spiritual and Moral Choices

Even for the most devout Christian, there are times when life is frightening, and there is nothing like fear to set one adrift. You get a phone call informing you that something terrible has happened. Your doctor tells you that you have a serious medical problem that needs immediate attention. The church splits in two because of a troubling doctrinal debate or because someone on the staff has done something controversial or unconscionable. These are the times that try one's faith. They are also the times that require courage. If you study scripture carefully, you will see that courage is not optional for a Christian and that the courage demanded of us is often moral. It has to do with making difficult *decisions* and firm *commitments*. Such courage is precisely what the Drifter lacks and needs to cultivate.

We have a responsibility to develop a solid and unshakable identity as a child of God. This, in part, is what it means to be a Christian. We are told, for example, not to buy in to the values of secular society, a message that is brought home powerfully by substituting the expression "world system" for "world" in the following passage: "Do not love the world or the things in the world. The love of the Father is not in those who love the world; for all that is in the world—the desire of the flesh, the desire of the eyes, the pride in riches—comes not from the Father but from the world. And the world and its desire are passing away, but those who do the will of God live forever (1 John 2:15–17, NRSV).

One problem with Drifting is that it leaves a person vulnerable to forming unholy alliances. It is not always easy to hold firm to the faith that has been delivered to us. But this, above all, is what we must do: "I know your deeds, your hard work and perseverance. . . . I know that you have . . . endured hardships for my name, and have not grown weary. Yet I hold this against you: You have forsaken your first love" (Revelation 2:2–4, NIV). God wants people who are grounded in Him and know who they are.

SELF-ASSESSMENT

To get a quick sense of how much you may rely on this Default Style, ask yourself the following questions. Although these questions do not constitute a test, they may give you a rough idea of where you stand. Please consult www.relationaldynamics.com for information about more sophisticated methods of assessment.

1. Do you find yourself agreeing with the last person to express an opinion?

2. Are you quick to go along with whatever other people want?

3. Do you often find yourself puzzled or unsure about what you think, feel, or believe?

ANTIDOTES TO TOXICITY

I am now going to provide you with two sets of suggestions. The first may help you reduce any tendency you find in yourself to operate in the Default Style we have discussed in this chapter. Before trying out any of these suggestions, it would be wise to read Part Four of this book, particularly Chapter Fifteen, on myths about behavior change. The second set of suggestions may help you respond more effectively to others who relate to you through this Default Style. These suggestions are of necessity general and therefore may not work with a specific individual. So use them wisely and judiciously, and above all do not apply them mechanically or put yourself in danger. Although people with certain interpersonal styles tend to be more troublesome and combative than those who rely on other styles, it is best to err on the side of caution. When in doubt, consult those with publicly sanctioned expertise in personality disorders, such as mental health professionals.

If You Tend Toward Drifting . . .

Here are some suggestions that may help you reduce this tendency:

○ Spend plenty of time writing down your thoughts, feelings, attitudes, and opinions. Make journaling a regular part of your life. Keep this famous line from E. M. Forster

(1879–1970) in mind: "How do I know what I mean until I see what I say?" Writing will help you clarify your thinking and thus your identity as a human being.

○ Be wary of those who offer to guide and advise you, especially if you are tempted to curl up in their psychological laps and have them take care of you. Such counsel may help you in the moment but stunt your long-term growth.

○ Do not reinforce controlling behavior in others by automatically going along with what they want or by routinely adopting their positions on issues. God should be your Controller, not the man or woman next door or at the office.

○ Take the risk of asserting yourself, which means that those whom you've already trained to take you for granted may become irritated by what they may see as presumptuousness. You have a right to a voice just as much as they do.

○ Refrain from opinion shopping, the tendency to move from person to person in the hope that someone, finally, will tell you the right thing to do. Many times, such shopping is merely an avoidance of deciding for yourself. It can also be a nonmedical form of doctor shopping—going from physician to physician until you get the diagnosis you want.

○ Recruit Anchors to help you (see Chapter Sixteen).

How to Respond to Drifting

If someone else is relating to you through Drifting, here are some potential countermeasures:

○ Resist the temptation to take over, make the Drifter's decisions, or fix the problem—whatever it may be. Such Controlling behavior entrenches Drifting even more deeply. Whatever assistance you provide may, in the long run, simply foster further dependence. Understand how seductive but counterproductive it can be to ride in on a stallion and come to the rescue. Avoid falling into the trap of Controlling.

○ Be patient. It can take a long time for another person to firm up an identity. Many people drift along for years, not knowing what they think or feel, but eventually become full persons. Default Styles often take a long time to change.

○ Employ lots of active listening. This means saying back to the person what he or she says to you. Rather than asking and answering questions, try to function like a human mirror. By reflecting the emotional meaning of what the Drifter says, you may help solidify his or her human core. Any good therapist or counselor should be able to teach you the basics of such reflection. Strive for nondirective empathy as opposed to authoritarian problem solving.

○ Try to provide the Drifter with warmth that is sincere but, at the same time, not controlling. Be accepting without being directing or dominating.

○ Be weak in order to make the Drifter strong. The more you need the Drifter's help, the more able and self-directed he or she is likely to become.

9

INTRUDING

CROWDING AND SMOTHERING

The Lord said to Eliphaz . . . , "My wrath is kindled against you
and against your two friends; for you have not spoken of me
what is right. . . . Go to my servant Job [who] shall pray for you,
for I will accept his prayer not to deal with you according to
your folly. . . . And the Lord restored the fortunes of Job.

—Job 42:7–10 [NRSV]

LIKE JOB'S THREE MISGUIDED FRIENDS, Intruders rush in to help even when their help is neither needed nor desired. They insist that their motives are selfless and demand that others agree. While they use the words of a consultant ("This is what you could do"), they convey the urgency of a grade school teacher ("This is what you must do"). The Intruder's version of the Golden Rule is "I will do unto you—and you will be thankful."

Such a person is imposing, defensive, prideful, and without self-insight. Convinced of his or her virtue, the Intruder is willing to use personal resources to buy the right to meddle. He or she is inclined, therefore, to offer financial and other kinds of support, such as time, energy, and expertise. The price for this assistance is that others do what they are supposed to, which is adapt their wills to the Intruder's. Exhibit 9.1 summarizes the Intruder's principal characteristics.

Your initial reaction to an Intruder is likely to be positive. Most of us are happy to run into someone who shows an interest, gives thoughtful ad-

Exhibit 9.1. Profile of the Intruder.

Theme	"Always remember that I know best."
Self-Presentation	Competent, mature, and knowledgeable; conventional, dependable, predictable; states or implies that your best strategy will be to allow him or her to take care of you and that you will not fare well without help.
Additional Characteristics	Pressuring, doting, and overwhelming; strong, caring, and protective; generous and giving; understanding, sympathetic, reasonable, and fair; long-suffering; quick to proclaim noble motives and deny self-interest; obliquely but nonetheless clearly makes known how much he or she has endured and sacrificed; defensive, brittle, and sensitive to criticism and confrontation; willing to use guilt to ensure bonding; believes he or she exists to nurture and provide; expects others to remain grateful.
Responses Induced in Others	Attaching and merging; if not too overpowering, will induce acquiescence, dependence, gratitude, and self-indulgence; if excessively stifling, will be resented and ultimately rejected; invites and rewards exploitation.
Healthier (Milder) Version	Nurturing; provides protection and caring, not just in families but in organizations as well; mentoring, coaching, and sponsoring; ready to provide for others, to feed the hungry, lift up the downtrodden, and comfort the frightened; tends to give everything possible when called on to do so.

vice, and genuinely cares. But unless you are a Drifter (see Chapter Eight) or a Freeloader (see Chapter Ten), you will soon feel trapped, as if the walls of your life were closing in around you, and when this happens you may experience an urgent need to escape. An individual who relates through the Intruding style is difficult to oppose, however, because the Intruder justifies his or her behavior with statements like "I'm only doing it for you, dear." Who among us can criticize a saint?

Intruders are reluctant to admit anything about themselves that does not enhance their altruistic image. If, on the one hand, you go along with what they advise, you will probably end up doing something you never wanted to do and, in the process, reinforcing their intrusiveness. If, on the other hand, you refuse to go along, you may end up feeling guilty. And you may be punished: "If that's the way you feel, maybe you should find someone else to watch your kids."

Both Controllers and Intruders are determined to manage others, and both therefore prompt and reinforce compliance. While the Controlling style emphasizes deference, however, the Intruding style stresses affiliation. An Intruder cares mostly about attachment, while a Controller cares primarily about submission. You could say, therefore, that the Controlling style trains others in affiliative submission and the Intruding style trains them in submissive affiliation.

The Intruder's Script

The Intruder's script is to dominate others through giving, coupled, when necessary, with the induction of guilt. He or she acts out, on the private level, what the domineering philanthropist does on the public level. While such a philanthropist attempts unduly to influence nonprofit organizations to which he or she contributes, the Intruder attempts unduly to influence individual lives to which he or she contributes.

○

Case 9.1

Dolores, now in her sixties, is the mother of four sons and three daughters. When her first husband died sixteen years ago, she married a successful surgeon and is consequently rarely short of funds. Yet instead of taking expensive vacations or buying designer dresses, she spends most of her money on two of her children, Natalie and Larry. Natalie, who is forty years old, has never quite found herself, has been on welfare most of her adult life, and cannot seem to hold a job. Why should she? By supplementing what Natalie gets from the state, Dolores ensures that her daughter's material needs are met. There is, of course, a blemish on the landscape of Natalie's paradise, which is that she can do almost nothing without Dolores, who tells her what to eat, how to style her hair, and even where to buy groceries. Larry is a thirty-eight-year-old ex-plumber who four years ago announced that he wanted to go to college. He has never taken more than one course a semester, rarely opens a book, and has less interest in learning than a tired frog. Dolores pays his tuition and keeps him supplied with cash. Not a bad life, you might conclude, until you notice that Larry is at his mother's beck and call. He cannot even date without her approval. She picks out his clothes, shows up unannounced at his apartment, and insists that he take her out to dinner at least once a week. The surgeon doesn't mind because she's as intrusive with him as she is with her children. On those rare occasions when Natalie or Larry tries to go it alone, to think or act independently, Dolores reminds them of how much she's sacrificed. And if that doesn't work, she breaks into sobs, talks about how no one cares whether she lives or dies ("Maybe it'll be better for everyone if I'm gone"), and locks herself in the bathroom. Because she once swallowed a bottle of pills, this makes short work of any attempt on their parts to separate from her.

○

While Dolores may mean well, she is not necessarily doing her children a favor. And for their own growth and development, they should find ways to make it in life on their own. An individual with an Intruding style typically clings to the one-up position and to getting others to validate his or her goodness, generosity, and worthiness. The Intruder's intention, conscious or not, is to place others in his or her debt, thus making it difficult for them to criticize the intrusion. It is also to persuade them that they need the Intruder, who hints at the catastrophes that await those who refuse assistance. This tactic works especially well on the insecure, who are susceptible to warnings like these:

"Without my guidance, you'll fail."

"Without my help, you're doomed."

"Without my support, you'll starve."

"Without *me* . . . there's no hope for you!"

These are highly toxic statements.

Benefits of the Behavior

People with mild Intruding tendencies are the caregivers of the world. They will bind up your wounds and be there for you when you need them. Since their basic inclination is to give, they are routinely available for advice, support, and comfort. If you need help cleaning your kitchen or fixing your roof, they are usually willing to provide it without complaint.

If those with a Controlling style lead society, those with an Intruding style sometimes keep it glued together. Unlike many in our fast-paced world, Intruders are the Good Samaritans, the ones who, when they find you downtrodden, will pick you up, dust you off, and set you on your way again. Those who relate to the world with a mildly Intruding style are therefore its Florence Nightingales and Albert Schweitzers.

Justifications for the Style

Intruders are sometimes called on to justify their invasion of others' privacy and tendency to stick their noses where they don't belong. Their response to such challenge characteristically takes one of the following forms:

Altruistic motives. The Intruder cares about the welfare of others. Surely, in light of his or her noble intentions, the tendency to come on too strong, now and then, can be overlooked and forgiven.

Willingness to risk. While others remain safely on the sidewalk, the Intruder will go into the street to stop crime. The Intruder puts himself or herself on the line and will do whatever it takes to rescue those in peril. This, the Intruder asserts, earns the right to be included and to offer constructive advice.

Readiness to share. Others may hoard their resources, but not the Intruder, who offers whatever he or she has to those in need. People should therefore be more than happy to welcome the Intruder into their midst and accept his or her wise counsel.

Social or spiritual obligation. Because the Intruder has special gifts of wisdom and discernment, the Intruder is obligated, indeed burdened, to share what he or she knows. This, in fact, is the Intruder's calling, and those whom the Intruder attempts to help are correspondingly obligated to defer to him or her and perhaps even pay homage.

Prior investments. All along, the Intruder has given generously, and it is his or her right, therefore, to expect a certain measure of honor in return. The Intruder points out that he or she does not seek medals or flashy awards but simply wants to be invited to participate and to be consulted. Consider the following case.

○

Case 9.2

Ever since Jeff's mother ran off when he was nine years old, his father, Dan, has given everything he could to his son. When Jeff was thirteen, he decided that he wanted to take up horseback riding; Dan not only paid for costly lessons but also bought him his own horse. Then Jeff decided that he wanted to attend the most expensive college on the East Coast, and again Dan was there to provide. He took out a second mortgage on his house, cosigned for loans, and ran up his credit cards. Jeff is now at work on a master's degree. If you talk with him, he will tell you how much he loves Dan, who has been the most wonderful father imaginable. When you get to know them a little better, however, you get the distinct impression that there is something peculiar going on. As soon as Jeff started graduate school, for example, Dan sold his home in Connecticut and moved a block away from Jeff and his wife, Tonya. Dan goes to their home almost every evening for dinner and stays until midnight. Although they would prefer to be alone once in a while, Jeff and Tonya feel obligated to invite him, especially when he says things like "It's awful to be alone, staring at the walls of that apartment, with no one to talk to." The same thing happens when they try to get away for a weekend. Dan tags along, and they reassure him, half sincerely, that he is welcome. Dan's intrusive presence is beginning to get to Tonya, who increasingly believes that Jeff puts his father ahead of her. "He'll be sleeping with us soon," she quips. Dan's intrusiveness is also getting to Jeff, but he doesn't know how to stop it, particularly when Dan says, "Everything I do is for you, son—I have never thought about myself."

○

Both Jeff and Tonya are clearly being intruded on. And Dan has fallen into a pattern of insensitive Intruding.

Psychology of the Intruder

Intruders decrease their insecurity by ensuring that they are loved and, above all, needed. They strive to position themselves as benefactors, and when they cannot achieve this they become uncomfortable. A person with a strong Intruding style comes across as caring, involved, responsible, gregarious, capable, and superior. He or she artfully coordinates the need to control others with *their* need to be cared for and, in doing so, can be as suffocating as a boa constrictor.

Actively embracing the ideal of service, Intruders are partly motivated by a genuine desire to help. Caring for others is what they consciously want to do. Unconsciously, they want others to take care of *them*. But Intruders can neither express nor admit this, because if they did they would have to own up to their own neediness and perhaps to the emptiness of their lives as well. The best defense against having to reckon with one's own needs is constantly to be focused on meeting the needs of others.

Although Intruders induce those around them to employ the defense mechanism of denial—"The Intruder is not dominating me"—their own preferred defenses are repression and reaction formation. They diligently re-press all awareness of their drive to dominate others. Then, through reaction formation—turning unconscious ideas into their conscious opposites—they convince themselves that their deepest wish is to enable others to become self-sufficient. But somehow the Intruder is never convinced that they are quite ready. Always, there is just one more thing that must be done for them, whether it's to prepare lunch or fix the faucet. Sheer benevolence keeps the Intruder at the center of their lives and justifies the constant interference.

○

Case 9.3

When Charlie's wife died, he telephoned his thirty-five-year-old son, Jack, in Tucson. "Guess it's time for me to move closer so that I can help out a bit." Prior to his retirement two years ago, Charlie sold insurance for a large firm. A year before retiring, he was promoted to sales manager, but this didn't work out, so he was demoted to his prior position. Jack, not wanting to offend his father, said, "Sure, Dad," but knew that he'd made a mistake. Charlie, then sixty-one, promptly sold his home in Florida and relocated to Arizona. He was eager to "assist the boy," Charlie told his friends, and "give him a few pointers on the business." Jack, who owned a thriving insurance agency, was shocked when, without warning, Charlie showed up one morning at the office wearing a suit and tie. "Where would you like me to start?" he asked. Caught off guard, Jack replied, "In accounts receivable." A week later, one of Jack's best employees quit; on the way out, he said, "I told you the day after your father arrived that he interferes constantly and doesn't know what he's talking about." It wasn't long before Charlie started on Jack. "Don't you think your employees take too much time for lunch? You need to get tough with those guys—who's running this place, anyway, you or them?" Having been trained to heed his father's advice, Jack began to make the changes Charlie recommended and within three months had nearly dismantled a business that had taken him fifteen years to build.

○

This case shows how hard it is sometimes to stop an accomplished Intruder. But as you can see, if you don't, the consequences can be disastrous.

The Intruder's tendency toward engagement, rather than disengagement, often results in overcommitment. He or she promises more than can be delivered and offers what he or she cannot supply. Such overtures of caregiving can prove irresistible to people desperately in search of nurturance. They can feel sorely disappointed, however, when they recognize the gap between what the Intruder pledges and what he or she actually provides. It is not as if the overreaching Intruder occasionally fails to come through but that his or her entire life is geared toward doing whatever it takes to be *viewed* as the provider. And sometimes this means placing himself or herself in hock. The Intruder is the sort of person who, after losing his or her job in the morning, buys an expensive suit for someone else in the afternoon.

As you might expect from someone who gives but cannot receive, the Intruder is angry at how one-sided life is and at how it is "always" he or she who does the giving. This, of course, is exactly the reality that the Intruder strategically creates. Oblivious to this, however, the Intruder is inclined to induce guilt in others when he or she feels slighted. The Intruder tells them how unappreciative they are and indicts them for their selfishness.

If Intruders become frustrated enough, they are capable of attacking others in order to bring them back in line. Such individuals may shock you with their occasional nastiness. But such nastiness is aimed at enforcing compliance. Because the Intruder is not by nature sadistic, hurting other people is rarely engaged in for its own sake. This potential for Intruders to become aggressive illustrates how even people with intensely affiliative Default Styles can move to the left side of Figure 6.1 when it suits their purposes. Moreover, the rigidity of their life scripts prevents Intruders from getting their emotional needs met and, so, leaves many of them mightily frustrated with existence. Quite aside from strategies and tactics, such frustration brings with it the potential for angry discharge.

Violent crimes are generally committed by three kinds of people. The first is the psychopathic deviant with a defective conscience who maims or kills while committing another crime (for example, robbery) or in an angry and demented quest for thrills. The second is the paranoid person who is afraid of harm. The third, however, is the pleasant person next door, the one who wears nice clothes to work and always smiles. One day, the person snaps, and no one understands why. Most of the time, it is because he or she can no longer contain the immense resentment felt over others' having disappointed him or her. This person, as we have seen, has always been the giver.

Intruders in the Bible

We began this chapter with what God said to Job's misguided advisers. Next we'll see what they had told Job. Note that on the surface, nothing in what they said seems bizarre. Yet they did not know what they were talking about, which made their intrusive behavior all the more troublesome.

> [Eliphaz the Temanite said,] "The wicked writhe in pain . . . because they stretched out their hands against God. . . . Agree with God, and be at peace; in this way good will come to you." [Bildad the Shuhite said,] "How long will you say these things? . . . Does God pervert justice? . . . If you will seek God and make supplication to the Almighty . . . surely then he will rouse himself for you and restore to you your rightful place." [Zophar the Naamathite said,] "If iniquity is in your hand, put it far away. . . . Surely then you will lift up your face without blemish; you will be secure, and will not fear" [Job 15:20, 25; 22:21; 8:2–6; 11:14–15, NRSV].

The disciples were not above intruding either. Once, his listeners became so captivated by what Jesus said that they started to bring their children to him, hoping that he would touch these little ones. When the disciples saw what was going on, they rushed in to protect Jesus. But in doing so, they were interfering far more than the parents were. "Jesus called the children to him and said, 'Let the little children come unto me, and do not hinder them, for the kingdom of God belongs to such as these. I tell you the truth, anyone who will not receive the kingdom of God like a little child will never enter it'" (Luke 18:16–17, NIV).

Another time, when Jesus took Peter, James, and John up the mountain to pray, his face changed, his clothes became dazzlingly white, and two men—Moses and Elijah—appeared and began conversing with Jesus. "Just as [the two men] were leaving him, Peter said to Jesus, 'Master, it is good for us to be here; let us make three dwellings, one for you, one for Moses, and one for Elijah'—not knowing what he said" (Luke 9:33, NRSV). There seemed, sometimes, to be no end to Peter's impetuosity and resulting tendency to intrude, which in this case caused him no small amount of emotional pain:

> He then began to teach them that the Son of Man must suffer many things and be rejected by the elders, chief priests and teachers of the law, and that he must be killed and after three days rise again. He spoke plainly about this, and Peter took him aside and began to rebuke him. But when Jesus turned around and looked at his disciples, he rebuked Peter. "Get behind me, Satan!" he said. "You do not have in mind the things of God, but the things of men" [Mark 8:31–33, NIV].

The Arrangement Sought

Whereas the Controller manages others through power, the Intruder manages them by creating emotional connections. These connections can emerge in a number of ways. The Intruder can establish them by providing for others materially. Or he or she can indoctrinate others with the idea that it is wrong to resist the Intruder's wishes; even parents of adults in middle age can get away with this. Or more perniciously, the Intruder can persuade them that without his or her involvement, terrible things will ensue. Some Intruders use all these methods at once. Regardless of how the bond is formed, it is rooted in obligation, and this, above all, is the arrangement that the Intruder creates.

The perfect match for an Intruder is someone who is affectionate, wants to be taken care of, and is willing to surrender a great deal of personal freedom. Such a person must be able to maintain a deferential frame of mind. He or she must be someone who demonstrates, or can be trained to demonstrate, submission and affiliation at the same time.

Sometimes a sociopath will attempt to prey on an Intruder by *pretending* to conform. But a sociopath can feign subordination for only so long. Angry impulses eventually surface and become overwhelming, and when they do the arrangement is threatened. A successful relationship with an Intruder requires that the other person maintain a posture of gratefulness, and a sociopath can rarely do this.

Both Victimizers and Freeloaders exploit people. Whereas the Victimizer ordinarily does this with one-shot predatory spectaculars (for example, fraudulent business schemes), the Freeloader does it through the slow, more or less affectionate, long-term depletion of the Intruder's resources.

Payoffs for the Intruder

Several psychological payoffs come with the Intruding style. One is that it enables a person to feel strong. That the Intruder is the giver, and others receivers, allows the Intruder to convince himself or herself that there is nothing to fear. Because the Intruder is forever taking care of and protecting others, he or she *must* be powerful and therefore secure, and the more the Intruder clings to this role, the safer he or she feels. Another payoff is that the Intruding style insulates the person from feeling helpless, alone, or angry. Because the Intruder's stance toward the world is active rather than reactive, the Intruder is not inclined to feel like a victim. He or she takes action and does something about whatever obstacles arise. The Intruding style also prevents the person from feeling lonely for long because whenever he or she begins to feel that way, the Intruder can invade someone else's life-space. Finally, for Intruders who cannot allow themselves ever to feel angry, the ones who smile plastically and chronically, assisting others is a wonderful defense. How can the Intruder be angry with someone he or she is trying to help?

The social benefits of the Intruding style are, first, that it fosters a sense of power. If you place another individual in your debt, you increase your hold over that person. While the Intruder is primarily motivated toward affection, he or she is also drawn toward acquiring power. The Intruder can exercise considerable influence without ever having to admit it.

Second, there is the public acclaim that comes along with a reputation for altruism and generosity. It is validating to be known in one's community as a person of great virtue. This "community" can be the family, local congregation, professional association, labor union, charitable organization, ethnic subgroup, or political constituency—in short, almost any collection of individuals. Because others would feel ungrateful if they thought ill of such a giving person, members of such groups are often beclouded about the price that the Intruder exacts for benevolence, which has more strings attached to it than a stadium full of people with balloons.

What the Intruder Tries to Avoid

For the Intruder's manipulations to work, he or she has to be on good terms with others. The Intruder therefore shows a decided preference for positive over negative attitudes and tends to be an optimist, accentuating other people's virtues and downplaying their faults—provided, of course, that they do what he or she advises. Were the Intruder to think negatively about others, it would be more difficult to move toward them. The Intruder also refuses to view himself or herself in an unfavorable light.

The Intruder's need to see the world through rose-colored glasses yields a restricted, if not impoverished, emotional life. The refusal to acknowledge anything but the good, the true, and the beautiful, especially within, limits the Intruder's range of awareness and thus his or her personal reality. Human beings experience ecstasy only to the extent that they can experience agony. Joy is possible only if misery is also possible. By walling themselves off from all but the most superficial emotions, Intruders can turn into one-dimensional people who merely go through the motions of living. Refusing to feel the unpleasant, they become incapable of feeling deeply about almost anything.

Clinging to an optimistic, if not Pollyanna, view of life, the Intruder is not easily daunted and does not, therefore, communicate pessimism. Among the last things an Intruder is going to say is that he or she is out of ideas for solving a problem, is devoid of resources with which to assist, or is personally demoralized. Where there's a will, there's a way, asserts the Intruder, and he or she just about always has the will.

The Intruder is more or less conventional. He or she has been well socialized, accepts the rules, manners, and customs of society, and counts on others to do the same. Although covert power struggles are his or her métier, the Intruder attempts to avoid overt conflict. Since the Intruding strategy depends on fostering the illusion of closeness and an imitation intimacy, the Intruder will try hard to avoid anything that might threaten this. The Intruder also avoids openly competing, especially with those he or she wants to place in debt, because of its potential to kindle anger and trigger estrangement. There *can* be competition, but it must remain implicit. The Intruder will run the other way if his or her competitive strivings threaten to become visible. And that is the great art form of the Intruder—dominating others while conspiring with them to deny that this is happening.

What the Intruder Trains You to Feel and Do

The Intruder invites you to respond with friendly compliance. Intruders are in the business of recruiting and training others to depend on and defer to them. If you refuse to do this, the Intruder will decrease whatever resources he or she is providing and eventually withdraw affection as well. Of the eight Default Styles, it is the Intruder who most uses the giving or withholding of *love* as a method of training; recall that the Controller most relies on the granting and withdrawing of *status*.

Intruders, like Controllers, teach others to agree with them and to carry out their wishes. Unlike Controllers, however, Intruders try to get others to feel beholden as they comply. It is not enough for the Intruder to train others to go along with the program. He or she must train them also to feel grateful, indebted, and, as the occasion requires, unworthy. To feel grateful is to feel indebted, and to refuse to pay one's debts is to feel unworthy.

All of this breeds resentment, which is why those who attach themselves to Intruders often turn on them. Even the most docile person involved with an Intruder may show occasional and seemingly inexplicable outbursts of fury, followed by strong feelings of guilt. These feelings only breed more resentment: no one likes to be turned into one's own persecutor. This guilt is further encouraged by others' failing to acknowledge how stifling the

Intruder is. They wrongly conclude that, as the Intruder suggests, it is *they* who have been arbitrary, unfair, and unreasonable. Such others do not understand that the Intruder's allegations of disrespect and ingratitude are part of an overall strategy to keep them in line. What has led up to such allegations is usually that, while others consciously accepted the Intruder's definition of reality, they unconsciously knew better and rebelled.

Still another source of guilt is the stance of martyrdom assumed by Intruders. Skilled at communicating how they have been misunderstood, Intruders make it clear that they have been wounded, thus turning the spotlight away from their intrusive dominance. All along, proclaim Intruders with sadness, they have "only" wanted what's good for others, and now, it seems, they stand accused of interfering.

If you dare to suggest to an Intruder that he or she is dominating, you may be set straight with a ferocity that would rattle a general. Paradoxically, the Intruder will forcefully deny that he or she is forceful. The Intruder's intense reaction occurs because you have threatened to expose the game, to make explicit what he or she strives hard to keep implicit: overbearing instincts and tyrannical methods. For intrusive social maneuvers to work, the Intruder has to persuade others *not* to recognize them.

The Intruder not only refuses to acknowledge that his or her style is dominating but teaches others to do the same. Such double-edged denial by others has two important results. First, it allows them to preserve their dignity. By emphasizing the Intruder's benevolence while deemphasizing his or her domination, they avoid admitting to themselves, or anyone else, that they have been bought. Second, it ensures the growth of their repressed anger. Instead of openly opposing the Intruder's control, they try to weather it and so continue to poison their own hearts with unexpressed resentment.

There is one thing that Intruders diligently train others *not* to do, and that is to take care of them, because, except in small doses, this would disrupt their entire game plan. If you try to give to Intruders, which is exactly what they need and have needed all their lives, they will either refuse your gift (for example, deny the need for it), break off the relationship (for example, refuse to respond to your messages), or, in the extreme, embarrass you (for example, suggest in public that you cannot afford whatever it is that you're attempting to give).

When the Arrangement Breaks Down

If an Intruder becomes overly domineering, those close to him or her may revolt. Knowing just how far one can push is therefore a necessary skill for perfecting the Intruding style. When an Intruder misjudges and goes over the line, smoldering animosities within others tend to flare up. The loss of personal freedom they experience is no longer worth the tending they receive from the Intruder.

Desperation may set in if the other person sees no way out—for example, if he or she is financially reliant on the Intruder and thus caught between anger and need. Such desperation often leads to despair, which can in turn lead to hopelessness. It is worth noting that often it is not so much depression that prompts people to commit suicide as lack of hope. And so Intruders may hold in their hands the very lives of those they have induced to depend on them. As Saint-Exupéry wrote in *The Little Prince,* we become responsible for what we love. Nowhere in life does this notion seem more apt.

The arrangement may also break down if the Intruder can no longer provide. A break is unlikely if the emotional connection to the Intruder has been created by brainwashing (for example, "You cannot make it without me"). But it does occur when the bond has been established on the basis of tangible resources (for example, food and lodging). Once the Intruder is without resources to buy the right to intrude, the party may abruptly come to an end.

Life History

Many Intruders, like a fair number of Controllers, have spent their childhoods putting an intoxicated father to bed or caring for a troubled mother. Sometimes one of the parents repeatedly threatened suicide. Such threats are terrifying to a child and, like little else in life, can foster a profound sense of responsibility for others. The role reversal—parent becoming child and child becoming parent—that typically accompanies living with a suicidal parent is perhaps the ultimate form of intrusion training.

Another path to the Intruding style is growing up with a sibling who is gravely ill or in some other way requires special care. Such a child gets the lion's share of parental attention. The budding Intruder, whose emotional needs are neglected, gives up all hope of ever being nurtured and turns the whole thing around. The Intruder first represses his or her emotional needs and then inverts them. Instead of wanting to be cared for *by* others, the Intruder cares *for* others. As long as the Intruder focuses on other people, the Intruder cannot focus inwardly, on his or her own unmet needs and the pain associated with them.

Finally, some parents endlessly communicate to a child how wonderful it is that he or she is so mature and self-sufficient. While in some families this instills confidence, in others it teaches the child that it is not OK to have emotional needs. Which of these messages the child hears depends largely on what the parents intend. If they are sincere in their affirmations, the child may thrive. If, however, they send the child the subtle message (metamessage) that expressing affectional needs will burden them, the child may develop into someone who tries to meet his or her own needs vicariously by tending to others. The child learns that *his or her* needs will routinely go unmet and that there is therefore no point to admitting that these needs even exist.

Intimacy and the Intruder

The Intruder's need to move in on others, coupled with the demand that others respond with warmth and appreciation, makes intimacy difficulty. For intimacy to exist, it must be rooted in affection. And for genuine affection to develop, it has to be spontaneous. Insisting that others behave affectionately makes it impossible for them to do so. This is because such insistence creates a situation reminiscent of the spontaneity paradox: If I say to you, "Be spontaneous at two o'clock," you will be unable to comply. Certain things in life simply cannot be commanded because, by nature, they have to be voluntary.

Intruders may say things that sound highly affectionate, and they sometimes overflow with doting adoration, but much of what they express stems from a sense of duty. It comes more from the head than the heart. Such duty-based love just about guarantees that whatever affection others express to Intruders will, in return, amount to little more than duty.

Because Intruders so compulsively force themselves on others, they unwittingly build into their relationships strong pursuer-avoider paradigms. The more Person A moves closer, the more Person B backs away, which prompts A to move closer still, and so on. Anthropologists, watching conversations between people from different parts of the world, were the first to notice this pattern. A person from one area of the globe, for example, who is used to short physical distances during a conversation, keeps moving forward, while the conversation partner, from another part of the world, who is used to more personal space, continues to back up. It is not unusual for the two to begin in the middle of the room and, a few minutes later, be standing near a wall.

Intruders become emotional stalkers who relentlessly close in. Whatever their conscious intentions, they just cannot bring themselves to allow others the freedom necessary for true intimacy to emerge. Instead of feeling warmth, the other person gets claustrophobic. As discussed in Chapter Two, intimacy requires mutuality, a kind of free and easy meeting of the minds. It is hard to be free and easy when someone is trying to suffocate you. What you mostly experience is panic.

The tragedy in all this is that the Intruder sincerely wants to be close. Although most Intruders are not creatures of great self-insight, they are eminently clear about the fact that intimacy is important. This very clarity may torture them, because no matter how hard they try, true intimacy continues to elude them. They try so hard to become close that they drive others away.

Spiritual and Moral Choices

The line between loving and hovering is sometimes thin. When you genuinely care about someone and strongly believe that you know what's good for that person, it can be difficult *not* to apply pressure. The more you care, the harder it is to refrain from crowding and micromanaging. If, for example, a family member is behaving self-destructively, you may find it all but impossible not to start prescribing what's good for him or her and in other ways trying to change his or her behavior.

There is, however, this sobering reality with which Christians must reckon: God has given us prodigious freedom in *not* forcing us to do his will. If God puts that high a premium on freedom, we should think long and hard before limiting someone else's. This is not an argument in favor of passivity. It is, rather, an attempt to suggest that we restrain our impulses to intrude. Genuine Christian love—agape—is by its nature far more freeing than it is stifling.

SELF-ASSESSMENT

To get a quick sense of how much you may rely on this Default Style, ask yourself the following questions. Although these questions do not constitute a test, they may give you a rough idea of where you stand. Please consult www.relationaldynamics.com for information about more sophisticated methods of assessment.

1. Do you often insist on helping others, even when they say that they do not want help?

2. Are you inclined to tell others that without you they'll fail or end up in trouble?

---

3. Do you give to others and then feel entitled to show up uninvited on their doorstep?

ANTIDOTES TO TOXICITY

I am now going to provide you with two sets of suggestions. The first may help you reduce any tendency you find in yourself to operate in the Default Style we have discussed in this chapter. Before trying out any of these suggestions, it would be wise to read Part Four of this book, particularly Chapter Fifteen, on myths about behavior change. The second set of suggestions may help you respond more effectively to others who relate to you through this Default Style. These suggestions are of necessity general and therefore may not work with a specific individual. So use them wisely and judiciously, and above all, do not apply them mechanically or put yourself in danger. Although people with certain interpersonal styles tend to be more troublesome and combative than those who rely on other styles, it is best to err on the side of caution. When in doubt, consult those with publicly sanctioned expertise in personality disorders, such as mental health professionals.

If You Tend Toward Intruding . . .

Here are some suggestions that may help you reduce this tendency:

○ As hard as it may be at times, assume that the other person will be OK without your help. Focus on increasing, rather than decreasing, his or her freedom.

○ Wait to be invited. Don't assume that you automatically have a ticket. Find out how much the other person truly wants your company, perhaps by declining invitations until you verify that he or she is sincere.

○ Reverse the pursuer-avoider arrangement. The more one person pursues, the more the other person tends to avoid, and vice versa. Become, in a mild way, the avoider. This may result in your receiving more invitations that are genuine and prevent others from feeling that you are intruding, that they have to indulge or accommodate you even when they would prefer not to.

○ Give gifts without strings. Whether it is money, time, or expertise that you are donating, do not expect that in return you have a right to move to the center of the other person's life. Understand that when you give to those who genuinely need what you provide, it can become difficult for them to tell you honestly when they do not want your advice or company.

○ Stay away from playing the role of martyr. Statements such as "I'm only doing it for you" should tip you off to the possibility that you're moving into the martyr position. One problem with this is that others will resent you for it, because acting like a martyr is likely to leave them feeling beholden and guilty. Be a cheerful rather than an anguished "self-sacrificing" giver.

○ Recruit Anchors to help you (see Chapter Sixteen).

How to Respond to Intruding

If someone else is relating to you through Intruding, here are some potential countermeasures:

○ Assert your need for freedom, space, and privacy, even if this results in some hurt feelings. If you don't do this, you will probably build up a large reservoir of resentment, and resentment is like cancer. It can injure or destroy almost any relationship.

○ Establish limits sooner rather than later. As soon as you begin to feel uncomfortable, take action. This does not mean that you should be rude or insensitive. It does mean that you should not ignore your own psychological instincts. If you feel that you're being crowded, you probably are. Intruding is likely to increase steadily unless you put limits on it. Stop the pattern before it becomes ingrained.

○ Do not take handouts with strings attached. Or if you must take them, openly discuss your concerns about the strings. Giving and receiving gifts always involves an unwritten contract. Often the terms of this contract can be worked out much more rationally if you talk about them up front, before you accept the gift.

○ Be on guard against lapsing into dependence, which is a compatible position for someone who wants to give and advise all the time.

○ If the Intruding becomes a serious problem, confront it head-on. Talk about your feelings of emotional claustrophobia. And if you run into a wall of defensiveness, which is likely to happen with a heavy-handed Intruder who has only limited insight, don't let this deter you from expressing what you feel. Doing so may cost you. But I think it's better to choose autonomy and dignity than bondage and the loss of person-hood that comes with it.

10

FREELOADING

CLINGING AND DEPLETING

Keep away from [everyone] who is idle. . . . We were not idle
when we were with you, nor did we eat anyone's food without
paying for it. On the contrary, we worked night and day,
laboring and toiling so that we would not be a burden to any of
you. We did this . . . in order to make ourselves a model for you
to follow, [and] we gave you this rule: "If a man will not work,
he shall not eat." We . . . command and urge [such people]
in the Lord Jesus Christ to settle down and earn the bread they
eat. . . . If anyone does not obey our instructions in this letter,
take special note of him. Do not associate with him,
in order that he may feel ashamed. Yet do not regard him
as an enemy, but warn him as a brother.

—2 Thessalonians 3:6–15 [NIV]

FREELOADERS ARE FOREVER ON THE LOOKOUT for people who will
provide them with what they crave, which is an enormous amount of
time, energy, attention, resources, and nurturance. The more you give, the
more they want, and by such giving you increase rather than decrease the
size of their desires. If the Intruder is the toxic provider, the Freeloader is
the toxic receiver. The Freeloader's version of the Golden Rule is "Do for
me or I will perish." Exhibit 10.1 summarizes the principal features of the
Freeloader's personality.

Exhibit 10.1. Profile of the Freeloader.

Theme	"I'm desperate and need you to take care of me."
Self-Presentation	Emotionally hungry, amiable, and insecure; eager for someone else to take charge and make things OK; not self-reliant; states or implies that you are his or her only hope and that if you turn your back and walk away, he or she will somehow perish.
Additional Characteristics	Congenial, warm, friendly, and affectionate; responsive and easily persuaded; desperate and helpless; generally appreciative; superficially wholesome; unwilling to accept responsibility for his or her own welfare; may be flaky and unreliable; sometimes sexually demanding; often disappointed with past treatment by others; willing to attach and fold his or her identity into someone else's, in particular the benefactor's.
Responses Induced in Others	Generosity; nurturing and providing; if not all-consuming, will prompt caring, attending, indulging, compassion, and the desire to love and rescue; if excessively demanding, dependent, or unappreciative, may be abandoned.
Healthier (Milder) Version	Bonding, connecting, appreciating; offering loyalty and providing healthy companionship; forming friendships and building camaraderie.

Your first instinct, when you meet a Freeloader, will be to take care of him or her, especially because Freeloaders tend to be forthright about their needs and grateful for whatever attempts you make to meet these needs. You may be hooked strongly by the pull that he or she exerts on you to play the role of benevolent parent, invincible superhero, and personal savior. The Freeloader hangs on your every word, especially when your words convey comfort and protection. Because the Freeloader is engaging, you may develop a strong desire to help and find yourself deeply involved in the Freeloader's life.

Soon, however, you will discover that, like an octopus, the Freeloader entwines himself or herself around you, eventually prompting you to resent this continual clinging. You may feel as if you were stuck to flypaper or swimming in a pool of molasses. And at that point, you will probably want to back away.

The Freeloader's Script

The Freeloader's life pattern is to attach to an individual or a group of people who will take care of him or her. Once established, the Freeloader will do whatever it takes to maintain this attachment. He or she will remain docile as long as this source of supply continues to provide what the Freeloader wants or needs. Such provision routinely includes some form of indulgence, whether it be material giving, endless patience, massive attention, or unending emotional support.

○

Case 10.1

Within a week of their meeting, Perry proclaimed that he loved Rita, a senior vice president for a manufacturing company. Perry, who attended Rita's church, seemed to her like an affectionate puppy. He began to call her office twice a day and eagerly to wait for their evening telephone calls. Although she was drained by a high-pressure job that would have exhausted a professional athlete, she stayed up late listening to his problems. She reassured him that his faltering career as a radio announcer would turn out all right. After months of burning the candle at both ends, Rita complained that she wasn't getting enough sleep. Perry pleaded with her to stay on the phone just a little longer, and she listened to him that night until the sun came up. A few days later, she declined to take one of his calls at her office because she was late for a meeting. That evening, Perry complained that Rita never had enough time for him, and once again they talked for hours. Sleep-deprived, Rita got up the next morning and dragged herself off to work.

○

This case illustrates how toxic Freeloading can be. It also shows the need, often, to put a decisive stop to it.

Central to the Freeloader's strategy is the attempt to merge with the caregiver. The Freeloader wants to fuse his or her identify with the provider's so that the two become a single self. Although in marriage, two people become one flesh, married persons do not ordinarily lose their individual identity. They do not suddenly turn into nonpersons or give up all personal freedom and responsibility. The Freeloader is willing to do exactly that, in return for the indulgence provided by someone else.

Like the Intruder, the Freeloader seeks to establish a relationship of strong dependence. But whereas the Intruder endeavors to induce another person to depend on him or her, the Freeloader wants to become the one who does the depending. Whenever you interact with another person, you focus either on yourself or on that person. While the Intruder focuses mostly on someone else, the Freeloader focuses primarily on himself or herself.

If the caregiver fails to deliver what the Freeloader wants and expects, he or she may resort to any number of tactics designed to reopen the supply lines, from mild complaining to vociferous demanding. This may require the Freeloader, briefly, to act like a Humiliator (see Chapter Eleven) or even a Victimizer (see Chapter Thirteen). But because the Freeloader's fundamental interpersonal orientation is to move toward others, he or she will return to the Freeloader's comfort zone of deferential affiliation as soon as possible.

Benefits of the Behavior

As with most other interpersonal styles in their milder versions, moderate forms of the Freeloading style actually benefit society. Recall that this style involves moving one-down and toward. In its less extreme form, this amounts to Bonding, which is characterized by Connecting and Appreciating (see Figure 5.3). Dependent people contribute to social cohesion, usually get along well in organizations, and do not typically cause trouble. They are willing to do what is asked of them and find it rewarding simply to belong and, if in an employment setting, cash their paychecks.

It is only when the need to be taken care of is rigid and extreme that the person with a Freeloading style becomes troublesome. This is because, at that point, the person's inclination to bond takes on the character of overdependence and exploitation.

Justifications for the Style

The Freeloader will usually justify excessively dependent behavior in one of the following ways:

Depression. The Freeloader is feeling down and therefore needs you to take care of him or her. The help needed is, of course, temporary, which can mean anything from days to decades.

Need. The Freeloader is down on his or her luck and therefore needs money or some other form of assistance. He or she may ask you, against all odds, to believe that this neediness is temporary.

Morality. You have been blessed or lucky, while the Freeloader has been handed one bad deal after another. It is only right, therefore, that you share your good fortune.

Debt. Because the Freeloader loves you so much, you owe it to him or her to provide. Giving to the Freeloader will allow you to pay him or her back for all that love.

Desperation. If you don't help the Freeloader, no one will.

Blackmail. If you don't give the Freeloader what he or she wants, you will reveal yourself to be selfish and withholding. By refusing to help, you will demonstrate that you do not, in fact, have a Christian heart and think only of yourself.

Inadequacy. Because you have failed the Freeloader, perhaps as a parent, it is your everlasting duty to support him or her in all ways possible—even if the Freeloader makes no effort whatsoever at self-help.

As you can see, the Freeloader does not lack for excuses.

Psychology of the Freeloader

Freeloaders are often social and affectionate, sometimes to the point of being syrupy. Such pleasantness is partly designed to mask whatever anger they feel, since expressing negativity in any way could discourage potential donors. Because they combine friendliness with the desire to win favor, Freeloaders represent one of several ideal personality types in our culture, in this case the "popular" one. Most people therefore find them pleasant or even entertaining.

○

Case 10.2

Peter, a thirty-eight-year-old stockbroker, is polished and gracious. He met Kathy at church. Having been widowed two years earlier and feeling lonely, she fell in love with him, and he soon proposed marriage. When they began to discuss the wedding, Peter insisted that it be grand because she deserved a gala affair and suggested that they invite everyone from church. Thrilled by his gallant and generous mentality, she felt as if she were twenty years old again and pictured herself walking down the aisle in a flowing gown. They began to finalize the guest list, which at Peter's urging had grown to more than five hundred people.

She was shocked when they ordered engraved invitations and he instructed the saleswoman to send the bill to Kathy. The same thing happened with the caterer, who required a $5,000 deposit, and the florist, who asked for an advance of $1,700. Although they had not talked much about his business, Kathy noticed something she had somehow missed before—Peter played tennis every morning. "Don't you have to be at your office to execute orders when the market opens?" she asked, beginning to wonder about the man she was going to marry. He reassured her that his assistant, Virginia, "took care of all that." Then it dawned on Kathy that she had been doing everything for Peter, from making his lunch to washing his laundry, which he would bring over twice a week. When he suggested that they purchase a new Mercedes, she realized that she would probably end up paying for it.

○

Clearly, Kathy needs to deal head-on with this behavior (see the suggestions at the end of the chapter).

The Freeloader's principal defense mechanism is repression. He or she feels most secure, and least anxious, when someone else is taking care of things and everyone is on good terms. Because being liked is usually a precondition to getting another person to adopt you, the Freeloader is motivated to evoke positive reactions from others. The feel-good quotient and smile index are therefore of central importance to the Freeloader.

Most Freeloaders resent those who control them, which means that they are destined to resent their caregivers. Even the most docile Freeloader may shock you by occasional outbursts of rage. We all have a shadow side, aspects of ourselves that we would just as soon not be there, and these are of course at the core of our personal dispositions to sin. Because the Freeloader has such a strong interest in maintaining a façade of amicability, his or her shadow side can become like a caged animal, waiting for the right moment to pounce. There is often a deep ambivalence in the Freeloader, which is what may lead the Freeloader to punctuate his or her customary style of affectionate dependence with short bouts of hostile independence. The ambivalence is that the Freeloader wants to be cared for but does not truly want to suffer the loss of autonomy that this sometimes requires.

Consciously, the Freeloader views those who meet his or her needs as wonderful and cannot praise them enough. Just as the Freeloader represses negative thoughts and impulses, the Freeloader denies that providers have any either. But such a glow tends to fade because you could never give enough to meet the Freeloader's needs. Regardless of what you offer, you will be unable to satisfy his or her demands. Routinely, he or she will want more and become unhappy with you for not providing it.

Pervasive dependence in any human being tends to drive that person back to his or her roots. For the Freeloader, this often means returning to his or her parents' home. If the parents are still living, the Freeloader may attempt to get them to assume their earlier roles. Even when they agree to do so, of course, there will be tension because no matter what they give the Freeloader will find it insufficient. To the Freeloader, the entire world is doomed to come up short.

◦

Case 10.3

Arthur, now twenty-seven, attended an out-of-state college for three semesters and then dropped out because he found his classes boring. When he was nineteen, he moved back home. Arthur told his parents that he wanted to work for a while before returning to school. But he was never able to find the right job. Over the past eight years, he's been employed a total of five months, at seven different companies. He was fired twice, but the other five times he simply quit because he found the work meaningless. Besides, he told his parents, he was not about to work for anything near the minimum wage. When his parents ask about his plans, Arthur tells them that it is still his intention to return to college. When they ask when, he says that he is not quite ready but expects to be soon. This has gone on for years. He spends most of his time playing computer games, lying on the couch watching television, or bouncing around town with his friends.

◦

The spouse of a Freeloader may enter the relationship in the belief that the Freeloader will become the provider. But the whole arrangement is a set-up because, regardless of whatever promises the Freeloader makes, he or she is unlikely to care for anyone else in a sustained way. Even worse, the Freeloader may eventually turn the tables and conclude that the spouse is lazy, cold, unloving, stingy, self-centered, and mean.

A Freeloader makes a terrible bargain by trading individuality for the right to lean and rely on another person. Part of what the Freeloader gives up is the ability to *feel*. To maintain his or her position of dependence, the Freeloader has to at least try to remain pleasantly superficial, which makes it difficult to experience the full range of emotion. Despite occasional expressions of frustration and displeasure, the Freeloader must largely pretend, even to himself or herself, that everything is fine. This leads to a severe restriction of awareness, which in turn also guarantees that the Freeloader, like the Intruder, will lack insight. The Freeloader becomes a hollow shell, an imitation person, a mannequin going through the motions. In the language of the corporate world, the Freeloader becomes an empty suit.

The Freeloader is not inclined to engage in much self-exploration because, if introspection were to be embarked on seriously, the Freeloader might have to admit that his or her entire life is constructed around the avoidance of responsibility. Such avoidance is what leads the Freeloader to leech off others and, if they allow it, to drain their emotional and financial resources. The Freeloader is not, however, a sociopath. He or she is well socialized, has a conscience, and knows the difference between right and wrong. It is just that the Freeloader needs so much that he or she cannot refrain from asking and then asking some more.

Sometimes the other person does not respond with the kind of nurturance that the Freeloader desires, and when this happens he or she tends at first to become more ingratiating. If additional doses of deference and flattery do not maneuver the other person back into the role of provider, the Freeloader may throw tantrums, as noted earlier. And if that doesn't work, the Freeloader may eventually break off the relationship and resume his or her search for someone who is more understanding.

Freeloaders in the Bible

Although Judas Iscariot demonstrated many toxic styles, including that of Victimizer, he was also someone who freeloaded:

> Six days before the Passover, Jesus arrived at Bethany, where . . . a dinner was given in Jesus' honor. Martha served, while Lazarus was among those reclining at the table with him. Then Mary took about a pint of pure nard, an expensive perfume; she poured it on Jesus' feet and wiped his feet with her hair. And the house was filled with the fragrance of the perfume. But one of his disciples, Judas Iscariot, who was later to betray him, objected, "Why wasn't this perfume sold and the money given to the poor? It was worth a year's wages." He did not say this because he cared about the poor but because he was a thief; as keeper of the money bag, he used to help himself to what was put into it [John 12:1–6, NIV].

The same could be said of Ananias and Sapphira (Acts 5:1–11) because they were trying to "beat the system" by pretending to be one thing while in reality they were another. This, of course, is what some Freeloaders try to do. They pretend to be helpless when they are just lazy. As even a quick tour through Proverbs will demonstrate, the Bible expresses no fondness for those who refuse to pull their own weight.

The Arrangement Sought

The Freeloader wants, above all, to be taken care of by someone else. He or she is willing to trade freedom for security, as long as the other person will take on the responsibility of providing. In some instances, the Freeloader will settle for a Controller, someone who will be heavy on direction but light on nurturance, or even for a Humiliator or Victimizer, neither of whom is inclined to be at all nurturing. But the ideal person for the Freeloader to associate with is either a (conventional) Nurturer or, if necessary, a (toxic) Intruder (see Figure 6.9). What the Freeloader wants is a condition of infantile bliss, in which another person tends to pretty much all of his or her basic needs.

Payoffs for the Freeloader

A major benefit of relating to the world through the Freeloading style is that you can almost always count on someone to come along who will provide. This is especially true if you are an attractive person.

People who have supported themselves throughout adulthood sometimes fail to grasp just how gratifying it can be to define yourself as helpless and have someone else take care of you. As soon as you communicate that you are unable to fend for yourself, you become a supplicant—a humble beggar. While this may not sound appealing, it brings with it one enormous benefit. It lifts the responsibility for your life from your shoulders and places it squarely onto whoever is willing to sustain you. Doing this, of course, robs you of a certain amount of dignity and diminishes your personhood. But if you can accept such losses, you may be able to craft for yourself an unusually secure existence. Let the record show, however, that there is no security on earth apart from God. What feels like security today may become, in the face of a serious and newly discovered health problem, little more than a cruel joke that the world has played on you. "What does it profit them if they gain the whole world, but lose or forfeit themselves?" (Luke 9:25, NRSV).

You can be a grown-up baby if you adopt a strong Freeloading style. Your actual or surrogate parents will guide your life and ensure that your needs are met. Even better, you might be able to link up with someone with low needs to control but high needs to give, in which case you will obtain all the benefits of the Freeloading style but pay none of its usual costs; in other words, you can maintain your freedom of choice and, at the same time, have someone else shower you with whatever it is you need, such as time, attention, compliments, or money.

Freeloaders are not inclined to make waves or pick fights, except of course with those who are "supposed" to provide for them but, predictably, fail to do so adequately. Thus in addition to achieving practical or emotional security, the Freeloading style is almost certain to garner goodwill and acceptance. Because others see the Freeloader as friendly and cooperative, unless they have been bled dry others generally like the Freeloader.

Society rewards people roughly in proportion to some ambiguous combination of how much risk they take, how much responsibility they carry, and how much value they create. The entrepreneur who mortgages a house to fund a new venture will, if successful, be well compensated. The neurosurgeon who accepts the responsibility for operating on someone's brain will also be well paid. And the builder who transforms a barren stretch of land into a housing development will, under most circumstances, be handsomely rewarded too.

The Freeloader does none of this and yet lives as if he or she did— especially if the Freeloader is clever enough to link up with the entrepreneur, neurosurgeon, or real estate developer. By perfecting the triad of asking, accepting, and acquiescing, the Freeloader ensures that he or she prospers. If, however, the Freeloader is someone who is very hard to satisfy and who tends aggressively to complain about deprivation, the relationship may take a different turn, as illustrated in the following example.

———————————————— o ————————————————

Case 10.4

Maggie and Hank, both in their twenties, were married three years ago. She says that she loves Hank but complains endlessly about how ungiving he is. According to Maggie, he works too hard, has an income that barely allows them to make ends meet, doesn't send her flowers very often, forgets to empty the cat's litter box, fills his own glass first, rarely asks where she wants to go to dinner, doesn't take her out often enough in the first place, refuses to cuddle up on the couch, and so forth. In the judgment of their friends, Hank is more giving than most men, but that is not how Maggie sees it.

———————————————— o ————————————————

Notice that Maggie does a fair amount of whining and complaining (see Chapter Twelve, "Scurrying"). But as you can see from what is going on overall, this is not her predominant style. She is operating with a Freeloader Default Style because she puts most of the responsibilities they jointly share on Hank. And she puts him in no-win situations. For example, she complains that he works too hard but also complains that he does not make enough money. "Give me more and more" is the message.

What the Freeloader Avoids

Unless the Freeloader becomes massively frustrated, the Freeloader tries not to think ill of others, especially those who give to him or her. Well socialized as the Freeloader is, he or she wants life to be orderly, pleasant, and "nice," and anything that upsets this equilibrium will cause disturbance. The Freeloader has a strong positive bias, which causes him or her to see good where it doesn't exist and to ignore bad where it does. Thus the Freeloader credits others with more friendliness than they deserve and is also unrealistically optimistic.

Because of the Freeloader's need to follow the dictates of society, including its prescriptions about what is and is not OK to think, the Freeloader is unlikely to impress you with inventiveness or creativity. And because the Freeloader needs to restrict his or her attention to the more pleasant aspects of life, the Freeloader is not particularly empathic toward the downtrodden; the Freeloader does not want to think about the unpleasantness of their lives. The Freeloader's empathic capacities are further reduced by the tendency to focus on himself or herself rather than on others. The Freeloader's inclination is to be the taker rather than the giver, emotionally as well as materially.

The Freeloader will not spend much time or energy cultivating such thoughts as "I am the captain of my ship" because, in truth, the Freeloader is not. If he or she were to think along these lines, the Freeloader would have to own up to the fact that he or she lives as a kind of human parasite.

Freeloaders have difficulty admitting negative feelings, even to themselves. Because their approach to life works only if they can keep others involved with them, they try especially hard to avoid anger, since it can easily trigger expressions of aggression. They generally steer clear of any urge or impulse that might prompt them to move against anyone who might be good for a handout.

If and when Freeloaders allow themselves to become angry, they usually make every effort to hide it. The last thing in the world they want is to come across as ungrateful or rebellious because, if they did, it would give the appearance of not delivering the two things that providers typically expect and crave: affection and cooperation.

Any kind of strong statement by a Freeloader, especially if it expresses independence, runs the risk of making it seem as if the Freeloader is trying to change the rules of the game, as if the Freeloader is now striking out on his or her own. The Freeloader therefore tries to avoid saying or doing anything that directly or indirectly asserts individuality.

Breaking out is not part of the Freeloader's repertoire, and so you should not expect much that is wild or crazy. The Freeloader wants to remain in the land of the familiar, where life is predictable and he or she can be reasonably sure that the provider will continue to provide.

What the Freeloader Trains You to Feel and Do

The Freeloader teaches others to respond with nurturance and affection and to appreciate, accept, and approve of him or her. Other people will be inclined to offer compassion, understanding, and practical help. An accomplished Freeloader draws out of others a willingness, even an eagerness, to transform his or her responsibilities and problems into their duties and obligations. Parking tickets not paid? No problem. Rent late? No problem there either.

Many people find the Freeloader's bid for assistance irresistible because it leaves them feeling strong, competent, and one-up. The Freeloader's helplessness and ineptitude also induce in others a sense of privilege. They secretly thank God that they are not like the pitiful Freeloader and feel both guilty and responsible because of it. Add to this the sense of superiority one gets from being the magnanimous helper, and you have the makings of one person carrying the burdens of two. While the most powerful word in any language is *no,* the two most powerful words are *help me,* especially when prefaced with *please* and followed by *thank you.* Most of us find such a request seductive, a lesson the Freeloader has learned well and relies on routinely.

The sort of person most likely to swallow the bait offered by the Freeloader is one with strong Intruding tendencies. People who relate to others through dominance combined with intense affiliation find it hard to resist the temptation to become rescuers. They bask in their own strength and pride themselves on their ability to make things turn out right, whether it's tending to the boo-boo on little Henry's knee or turning around that failing business owned by Uncle Wilfred. They love to advise and prescribe.

While it may seem that the Freeloader is predatory, this is not his or her fundamental nature. Although the Freeloader engages in exploitation, he or she is more the dependent lamb than the ravenous wolf. Ironically, the Freeloader can therefore prove to be an easy mark for the unscrupulous. Not all who offer help to the Freeloader are honorable, and not all Freeloaders are after money. Most, in fact, are not. If they themselves have money, they are usually looking for someone to manage it and, in the process, tend to their emotional as well as financial needs. Con artists love to provide such assistance.

A potential downside of relating to others in a submissive manner is that it encourages them to be more dominant. If the submissiveness is friendly, as it is with the Freeloader, and the dominance hostile, as it is with the Victimizer or Humiliator, a sadistic game of cat-and-mouse may develop. The passivity shown by the Freeloader, together with his or her inability to express anger, makes the Freeloader an easy target for a bully. Victimizers and Humiliators, who are quickly turned off by sugary optimism, sometimes toy with Freeloaders as if doing so were an indoor sport. And the more the Freeloader allows this, the nastier the game becomes.

When the Arrangement Breaks Down

A close relationship with a Freeloader usually deteriorates because few people are willing to devote their lives to meeting limitless needs. The Freeloader takes until the other person can give no more and finally says so. Sometimes the giver just retreats to a club, withdraws into a hobby, or stays at the office until 10:00 P.M. every night. For some people, their escape from a Freeloader is to attend every church service they possibly can, which leaves little time for draining conversations.

Relationships with Freeloaders also break down because those who once accepted the role of the heroic provider discover that they cannot continue to play it. They face the reality that they've promised more than they can deliver and honestly conclude that the Freeloader's needs are too great to meet. The idyllic fantasy they shared, that one of them would be loved and cared for by a tireless saint, dissolves into mutual disappointment.

Finally, the relationship can deteriorate because the Freeloader was initially on good behavior. Although the Freeloader pretended to be friendly, even docile, he or she turns out to be chronically nasty and relentlessly demanding. In such instances, the Freeloader may move rapidly and unpredictably among three or four toxic styles: Freeloading, Controlling, Humiliating, and possibly Victimizing. The other person may also oscillate between two or more Default Styles. He or she may try hard to remain conventionally Nurturing but, out of frustration, degenerate into Humiliating or Victimizing (see Figure 6.9).

Life History

Freeloaders enter adult life with huge unmet needs and spend the bulk of their time and energy trying to get someone else to make up for what they never received as a child. Sometimes this pattern develops because the parents were so caught up in hostile combat that they had little left to give. The parents, in such cases, were simply not there for the child, in any meaningful way, during critical periods of development, when the child needed extra measures of love and attention. Other times, the Freeloading pattern emerges because the Freeloader, as a child, was moved from place to place. He or she rotated through a series of foster homes, was shipped off to relatives, or remained with the parents but, because they changed residences frequently, was never able to form lasting and fulfilling friendships.

Unmet needs, however, are not by themselves enough to stamp in the Freeloading style. The child must also learn to be dependent. Sometimes this comes about because even though the child is emotionally malnourished, a relative overindulges the child, anticipating his or her every material need before the child is even aware of it. But it can also result from being raised by an overbearing parent who communicates that the child is insufficient, incapable, and inadequate. Any attempt the child makes to fend for himself or herself, it is stated or implied, will prove unproductive, and so the main parental message becomes this: "The smartest thing you can do is find someone else like me to take care of you." Thus the child is set on the path of searching for and attaching to a substitute parent. The child thus develops an attitude of passivity and helplessness that is psychologically crippling.

Intimacy and the Freeloader

The Freeloader makes intimacy difficult, if not impossible, by being too "relational." Such relationality is an illusion, however, because the Freeloader is, in reality, hardly relational at all.

Like the Intruder, the Freeloader sacrifices genuine emotional closeness on the altar of enmeshment. The Intruder does this out of a need to dominate, whereas the Freeloader does it out of a need to be nourished—by hanging on. He or she sacrifices independence for the compulsive need to be directed and guided in a benevolent way. The other person cannot, therefore, relate to a full person but must settle for someone who suppresses individuality in an attempt to curry favor. Intimacy can exist only when there is mutuality. And to be genuine, mutuality requires two autonomous persons who voluntarily decide to open up emotionally to each other.

Spiritual and Moral Choices

As Paul insists in the passage quoted earlier from his second letter to the Christians at Thessalonica, it is wrong to take without giving, which is the essence of the Freeloading style. If, therefore, you find yourself inclined to do this, stop it, for such conduct does not please the Father. The Christian, if anything, is to give more than other people give and in this way glorify God.

Knowing how to respond to others who freeload is more difficult. This is because we can never know, for sure, whether a particular Freeloader is simply lazy and exploitative or, beneath the surface, truly lacks the wherewithal to get through life on his or her own.

SELF-ASSESSMENT

To get a quick sense of how much you may rely on this Default Style, ask yourself the following questions. Although these questions do not constitute a test, they may give you a rough idea of where you stand. Please consult www.relationaldynamics.com for information about more sophisticated methods of assessment.

1. Do you tend to rely excessively on others for material or other forms of support?

2. Are there people to whom you cling because you feel that they are your only hope?

3. When the check comes in a restaurant, do you wait until someone else reaches for it?

ANTIDOTES TO TOXICITY

I am now going to provide you with two sets of suggestions. The first may help you reduce any tendency you find in yourself to operate in the Default Style we have discussed in this chapter. Before trying out any of these suggestions, it would be wise to read Part Four of this book, particularly Chapter Fifteen, on myths about behavior

---

change. The second set of suggestions may help you respond more effectively to others who relate to you through this Default Style. These suggestions are of necessity general and therefore may not work with a specific individual. So use them wisely and judiciously, and above all do not apply them mechanically or put yourself in danger. Although people with certain interpersonal styles tend to be more troublesome and combative than those who rely on other styles, it is best to err on the side of caution. When in doubt, consult those with publicly sanctioned expertise in personality disorders, such as mental health professionals.

If You Tend Toward Freeloading . . .

Here are some suggestions that may help you reduce this tendency:

- Own up to the price you're paying—the loss of your freedom and perhaps of your dignity also.
- Refuse unending handouts. Although there is no virtue to refusing help when you truly need it, such help should be occasional rather than chronic.
- Assert your independence of thought and action. This will give you an opportunity to test whether you've fallen into the trap of being bought. Find out how much of a connection there may be between what the other person gives (offering) and what he or she expects in return (obligation).
- Move from a passive-dependent to an active-independent position, especially with anyone who is crowding and smothering you.
- Laziness does not please God. To the extent that you are dodging your responsibilities, do something about it. Put your shoulder to the wheel. Pull your own weight.
- Recruit Anchors to help you (see Chapter Sixteen).

How to Respond to Freeloading

If someone else is relating to you through Freeloading, here are some potential countermeasures:

- It is sometimes difficult to tell the difference between someone who truly needs help, perhaps for a legitimate reason, and someone who only wants a free ride. If you discover that another person is taking advantage of you, by settling into a position of lazy dependence, put a stop to it. Many people have unintentionally crippled others by fostering unnecessary dependence. This happens between parents and children, but it also occurs in other relationships.

- Not all contributions to another person's life are misguided. Such contributions can be worthwhile and sometimes even noble. If, for example, your parents need help, give it to them. They were there for you. Be there for them. If another relative or loved one needs help, perhaps because for psychiatric reasons he or she cannot make it alone, help that person also. Learn to distinguish between genuine need and Freeloading. Be generous with those who work diligently. These are not Freeloaders. Reinforce and support their industry.

- If you have been contributing heavily to someone else's life but now conclude this is counterproductive, begin the process of weaning. But don't cut the person off abruptly, because you have helped train him or her to be dependent. There are two errors you can easily fall into. One is to rush the weaning process, and the other is to delay it too long. Avoid both.

- Do not intrude into the lives of those you help. Establish and maintain the right interpersonal distance, and when in doubt slightly increase it.

- Ask those whom you help for help in return. They may not be able to give back the same thing that you give them— how could they?—but perhaps they can contribute something else. In this manner, you will be able to keep the relationship more one of equals and less that of superior and subordinate.

11

HUMILIATING

DEMEANING AND BELITTLING

---

*Now Sarai, Abram's wife, bore him no children. She had
an Egyptian slave-girl whose name was Hagar, and Sarai said to
Abram, "You see that the Lord has prevented me from bearing
children; go in to my slave-girl; it may be that I shall obtain
children by her." And Abram listened to the voice of Sarai.
So, after Abram had lived ten years in the land of Canaan, Sarai,
Abram's wife, took Hagar the Egyptian, her slave-girl, and
gave her to her husband Abram as a wife. He went in to Hagar,
and she conceived; and when she saw that she had conceived,
she looked with contempt on her mistress.*

—Genesis 16:1–4 [NRSV]

HUMILIATORS LIKE HAGAR thrive on interpersonal victories. It is not
enough for them to succeed. To feel satisfied, success has to come at the
expense of others. Unlike Victimizers (see Chapter Thirteen), who delight
in inflicting pain for its own sake, Humiliators are mainly interested in triumph. If, for example, you were running near the front of the pack in a
10-kilometer race, the Victimizer might intentionally trip you to enjoy seeing you scrape your elbows and knees on the pavement. The Humiliator,
by contrast, would trip you primarily to eliminate you from the race and
then watch you slink away in defeat. His or her version of the Golden

Rule is "I will win and leave you dejected." Exhibit 11.1 presents the distinctive characteristics of the Humiliator.

When you first encounter a Humiliator, you may not detect his or her agenda to attack. You might simply perceive the Humiliator as strong, confident, and capable and perhaps sense that he or she expects others to subordinate themselves. Armed only with this information, you may conclude that the Humiliator is the managerial sort, a leader (see Figure 4.3) who guides and advises others and who at worst may tend to be a Controller (see Chapter Seven). It may take you a while to realize that the Humiliator relishes putting others down, causing them to feel uneasy, and aggrandizing himself or herself at their expense. Humiliators are experts at psychological oppression.

Your personal reaction to the Humiliator may soon lead you to feel off balance, not quite centered or in possession of yourself. However he or she accomplishes it, the Humiliator is likely to let you know that he or she is a member of a club to which you do not belong. The Humiliator, you are to understand, is elite, while you are common, ordinary, and undistinguished. Your initial impulse may be to get on his or her good side, to convince the Humiliator that you are a person of quality and that he or she should accept and approve of you. Hoping that the Humiliator will no longer deem you inadequate, you may try harder and harder to win favor and to make the "A" list. Without realizing it, you may in this manner start down the path of appeasing, placating, and bargaining (see Chapter Twelve).

Unless you have a need to be humiliated or completely lack inner strength, you may put up with this for only so long. It will eventually dawn on you that being around the Humiliator is not pleasant, since he or she thrives on increasing your anxiety and decreasing your sense of self-worth. At this point, you may confront the Humiliator but also pull back markedly or end the relationship. Few of us are willing to accept oppression just to make someone else feel good. We do not like to be told, again and again, that we are flawed, stupid, weak, incompetent, ridiculous, undeserving, or in some other way unworthy.

The Humiliator's Script

The Humiliator's motif is to elevate himself or herself by stepping on the heads and hearts of others. As a specialist in social comparison—assessing worth by how one person stands in relation to others—he or she has an insatiable need for glory. The Humiliator's intention is to demonstrate that

Exhibit 11.1. Profile of the Humiliator.

Theme	"Look at me and feel inferior."
Self-Presentation	Competitive, bold, arrogant, independent, and self-sufficient; eager to display superiority and point out the weaknesses and defects of others; openly indicates that he or she expects to be admired, revered, and perhaps worshiped.
Additional Characteristics	Egocentric ("full of himself or herself") and socially insensitive; quick to dominate conversations and to correct, improve, and top what others say; often pedantic and ostentatious; feels best when others are anxious and depressed, especially about themselves and their lack of achievement, status, power, or success; perceives the world in win-lose terms and hence sees everyone as a potential competitor; conveys that he or she is wonderful and that most others, by comparison, are pathetic.
Responses Induced in Others	Anxiety, resentment, self-doubt, and insecurity; prompts others to disparage themselves, scurry, appease, and placate; if excessively harsh or humiliating, others may withdraw, rebel, or end up in despair.
Healthier (Milder) Version	Competing, striving, excelling, and working hard; innovations in art, science, and commerce; often winners of Nobel, Pulitzer, and other prizes; because individual and social benefits are often aligned, personal achievement motives often benefit society.

he or she is superior and others inferior by vanquishing them. Their losses are the Humiliator's gains, and without such losses he or she feels incomplete. Humiliators build up their self-esteem and reduce their anxiety by establishing preeminence through combat, whether economic, organizational, intellectual, verbal, or social. They are addicted to conquest.

The Humiliator's goal is to turn other people into envious and conquered rivals. To such a person, others are decaying stars that revolve around the Humiliator and thus exist in his or her firmament only to adorn the Humiliator's self-presentation. He or she may care little for or about them as persons.

○

Case 11.1

Eric, a thirty-eight-year-old computer scientist, graduated first in his class from a top-notch technical college and then attended a prestigious British university, where he picked up a business degree and mastered the art of debate. He loves to draw his colleagues into arguments and then tie them up in knots. With great relish, he points out their logical errors ("That's affirming the consequent") and corrects their facts ("The French Revolution occurred in 1789"). His fellow workers end up feeling stupid and, predictably, resent him. So does his wife, Madeline. Not a day goes by without Eric criticizing her for something. He says things like "Can't you do anything right?" and "What's wrong with you—don't you see that I'm busy?" The more Madeline tries to please him, the more he becomes unbearable. She knows that she is not as smart as he is and wishes that she could find a job that was fulfilling, something that would make her feel better about herself. When she brings this up, Eric says, "What's the matter now—don't I make enough money to keep you happy? All you ever want to do is buy things. Run up the charge cards. If you went to work, we'd end up even deeper in debt."

○

As you can see, much of what Eric does interpersonally has the result—the intended result—of aggressive domination. He thrives on making others feel bad about themselves.

Benefits of the Behavior

Because they are so competitive, Humiliators are often high achievers who contribute to society. Although social benevolence is rarely their primary goal, they can occasionally turn out to be great benefactors of humankind. Up close and personal, they prove to be less endearing, which is why the private lives of eminent scientists and business magnates are sometimes disastrous. Innovation, it has been said, is by nature an act of arrogance, and there is something to this. Creativity often hinges on believing that you can do something better than others have done it before. It is exactly such arrogance that lies at the root of the Humiliator's accomplishments and contributions.

While the Humiliating style often fuels the engine of technological and commercial advance, it does not necessarily promote moral progress. Humiliators are hardly models of altruism. Few exemplars of agape here!

Yet in an odd way, they sometimes foster such progress, especially if they are crusading for noble causes, such as children's welfare.

Justifications for the Style

If you challenge the Humiliator about arrogance, self-centeredness, or devaluing other people, he or she will be quick to offer up a defense. This may take the form of dismissing you ("What gives you the right . . . ?"), which is yet another attempt to dominate and thus win one more power struggle. The Humiliator may seize on your challenge as a welcome opportunity to establish superiority by verbal combat. Alternatively, the Humiliator may resort to one or more of the following justifications:

Excellence when compared to mere mortals. Others are, by definition, inferior, so it is only logical for the Humiliator to assert himself or herself and, by implication, the exceedingly fine nature of what he or she has to offer. You cannot be too hard on the Humiliator for valuing himself or herself in this manner and, as a matter of course, showing minor intolerance toward those of lesser quality.

Manifest destiny. It is clear to the Humiliator, and should be clear to you, that he or she has a responsibility to offer his or her ideas and opinions to society. If others take offense at this, so be it. Progress cannot be held up simply because a few malcontents are excessively sensitive or lack the capacity to appreciate the Humiliator's virtues.

Intrinsic nobility. Since the beginning of civilization, kings and queens have asserted their inherent superiority. Such superiority is, of course, the moral of the fairy tale "The Princess and the Pea." The true princess is revealed because only she has the refinement and sensitivity to detect a single pea placed under the lowest of many mattresses and is therefore unable to sleep soundly. The Humiliator is, by nature, better than others and requires no further evidence of nobility than this bold assertion.

Obvious superiority. Because of the Humiliator's remarkable insight, intelligence, wealth, achievement, status, education, connections, or pedigree, the Humiliator expects to be treated with honor or even reverence. If you do not so treat the Humiliator, you may be dismissed as a hopeless dolt who "just doesn't get it."

Simple denial. The Humiliator will debate your interpretation of reality, suggesting that your view of him or her as someone who demeans others is incorrect. Such a view may well be the result of some psychological hang-up that is distorting your perceptions: "Are you feeling OK? You're awfully touchy today. It might be wise to consult a specialist in psychological disorders."

Consider this case:

Case 11.2

Shelly is married to a successful executive and makes sure that everyone else knows it. She is forever telling her friends about her latest expensive vacation and where they stayed (for example, the Ritz-Carlton) or about the new car she intends to purchase (a Mercedes or Jaguar). Some listen politely until they can slip away, but many become entrapped in her game of try-to-top-this. They feel one-down and even more fed up with hearing Shelly imply that they, or others around them, are not quite up to snuff. One of her friends decided, a year ago, to talk with her about how she comes across. Shelly defensively justified herself and aggressively questioned why this friend was so sensitive to Shelly's innocent and well-intentioned sharing.

You can see from this case that it is rarely easy to get a true Humiliator to own up to what he or she is doing with and to others.

Psychology of the Humiliator

Humiliators present themselves as independent and self-sufficient. They neither ask for nor provide assistance. As they craft the self-centered dramas of their lives, others are useful principally as props. Other people also serve, of course, as members of an audience in whom Humiliators can induce jealousy. I once heard a comedian say, "What's the point of having a big house if no one envies it?" This brilliantly captures the psychology of the Humiliator, who is at root a show-off.

Packaging is important to Humiliators, and you will therefore find them devoting considerable time, energy, and money to self-presentation. If they are good-looking, they may attend meticulously to their grooming, and if they are not, they may make frequent visits to the cosmetic surgeon. If, instead of beauty, they rely on some other source of power, such as wealth or position, they will let you know, early on, about this instead. Yet they rarely express appreciation, much less admiration, for how others look or act or what others own or have accomplished. Even if Humiliators are seething inside with envy, they may conspicuously ignore such assets or achievements.

The word *supercilious* (meaning "haughty and disdainful") comes from the Latin word for "eyebrow." Raising or crunching up one's brows is a way to express scorn or doubt. With scarcely a moment's reflection, the Humiliator raises his or her eyebrows at nearly everyone. The Humiliator is smug, skeptical, critical, and sometimes overtly mocking. He or she is both egoistic (the world revolves around me) and egotistical (my greatness is incalculable). Here are some of the messages that the Humiliator sends out:

"You should be like me."

"You are without merit and therefore deserve to feel bad about yourself."

"I will constantly remind you of your deficiencies."

Most of all, the Humiliator conveys this: "Unless you publicly acknowledge your unworthiness, I will cause you to suffer." Those in positions of authority may cloak such messages in a mantle of self-righteousness, and when they do the guilt they induce may be considerable.

Few Humiliators are accused of showing warmth or compassion, although, when it suits them, they may make benevolent gestures. Unlike the Avoider (see Chapter Fourteen) who is rebelliously distant and genuinely aloof, the disdainful and sophisticated detachment of the Humiliator is something of a put-on. Contrary to appearances, the Humiliator cares about what others think, including those made to suffer. This is why Humiliators are inclined to wear designer clothes, flaunt expensive jewelry, live in exclusive neighborhoods, and join prestigious clubs, even if they can't afford such luxuries and are living beyond their means. Humiliators gravitate toward occupations that accommodate their needs for victory and acclaim, such as performance careers that give them visibility or jobs that allow them to wield power.

It does not take a psychoanalyst to figure out that Humiliators carry within them an abiding sense of inadequacy and that their flamboyant displays of haughtiness are defensive attempts to avoid coming to grips with a deep sense of inferiority. Humiliators appear to cherish, adore, and worship themselves but on closer inspection often turn out to be filled with self-loathing. They *seem* to love themselves when in truth they may silently despise everything they are or ever were. The irony is that the more they insist that others acknowledge their magnificence, the more they loathe themselves for needing such acclaim. Their need to conquer often stems from directing onto other people the anger and loathing they feel toward themselves. Whereas many self-destructive people redirect the anger they feel toward others inwardly, Humiliators redirect the anger they feel toward themselves outwardly.

Humiliators rely heavily on the defense mechanism of projection, which is perceiving characteristics of yourself in others that they do not, in fact, possess. Suppose that you are a jealous person but find it difficult to admit this to yourself. One way to protect your self-esteem is magically to foist your jealousy onto other people. It is not you who are jealous—they are! There is a moral element to projection, in that it serves as a wonderful way to avoid owning up to sin. You will find fascinating examples of projection in the story of the expulsion from the Garden of Eden (Genesis 3:1–13). When God asks Adam why he has eaten what God has specifically told him not even to touch, Adam blames the deed explicitly on Eve and implicitly on God: "The woman *you* provided gave me the fruit" (v. 12). Eve, in turn, blames the crime on the serpent and also on God (v. 13), since God has made all creatures.

The Humiliator is ambitious and avaricious but refuses to admit this and, as a result, attributes these qualities to others. Humiliators want fame, glory, wealth, eminence, talent, possessions, titles, offices—anything that allows them to extort the tribute they require. Because of projection, Humiliators view others as wanting to extort tribute from them and so tend to regard everyone else as a potential competitor. They detect hostility where it does not exist, which further impels them to humiliate others since, at any moment, someone in the crowd might attempt to topple them from their pedestal. Because anyone might, in theory, make the Humiliator feel small and insignificant, other people are enemies lying in wait who must be kept down, lest they rise up to challenge the Humiliator's preeminence.

Independence is important to the Humiliator, because he or she does not trust others but instead suspects them. Dependence on other people is therefore anxiety-producing. Unlike the Victimizer or the Avoider, who finds all closeness unpleasant, the Humiliator wants to maintain a connection with people, but to feel comfortable this connection must be based on power. One reason for the Humiliator's quest for external signs of status and prestige is the Humiliator's need to know and be reassured that he or she can, if need be, "put others in their place." Sometimes the Humiliator does this through the arbitrary infliction of pain, simply to remind others who's boss.

Humiliators despise the weak, yet weakness is precisely what Humiliators work hard to foster in others. We despise in others what we loathe or fear in ourselves, and so the Humiliator paradoxically becomes anxious around anyone who symbolizes vulnerability. This means that all the while enjoying making them feel weak and vulnerable, the Humiliator detests them once this has been achieved.

Some Humiliators are inclined to throw themselves into activities that threaten to result in what they most dread, which is loss of autonomy and power. Race car driving and motorcycle racing, for example, have put thousands of Humiliators permanently in wheelchairs. They like dangerous pastimes, in part because such activities inspire admiration and in part because these pursuits create opportunities for them to gain a sense of mastery over their fear of helplessness. It is not as if the Humiliator wakes up one morning and says, "Seems like a pleasant enough day, so I'll take up bungee-jumping or skydiving to convince myself that I'm invincible." This all happens unconsciously.

When Humiliators marry, they are likely to view their spouses as passive, defenseless, and inadequate. None of this should cause surprise.

○

Case 11.3

Bonnie was prom queen as well as a National Merit Scholar. Before she married Craig, she made it clear that her career as a business consultant came first and that he would have to accommodate himself to that. If her work required them to move from time to time, so be it. She also expected him to do the laundry, clean the house, and cook dinner. Craig, who always seemed marginally depressed, agreed to all of this. Bonnie would criticize Craig for everything from not dusting enough to forgetting to buy ice cream, and he would usually apologize. She treated him as she did her employees, as people who needed constant supervision. Bonnie was simply "raising the bar" and "improving his performance." At least twice a day, she said something to Craig that conveyed how, in her view, he was boring, dimwitted, and incompetent. And she wondered if he had even an ounce of empathy in his soul: "All you ever think about is yourself!"

○

Bonnie, in this case, is an accomplished Humiliator. And unless Craig does something to change the pattern, he is likely to feel more depressed as the years go by. The Humiliating style is clearly toxic. I alluded earlier to narcissism in the Humiliator. Since this is a central feature of the Humiliator's psychology, I want to spend a few moments to elaborate this.

When we say that someone is "narcissistic," we mean that the person is self-absorbed—preoccupied with his or her appearance, talent, wealth, intelligence, power, or what have you. Most of us have encountered the good-looking man ("male model") or stunning woman ("beauty queen") who constantly stares in the mirror. We have also seen the bodybuilder who is forever flexing, the entrepreneur who babbles on endlessly about financial cleverness, or the intellectual who pompously recites the date of the Norman Conquest, the year Nietzsche was born, or the atomic number of selenium. All of this suggests that the individual is self-satisfied.

The reality, as I have suggested, is quite the opposite. Conceit, self-centeredness, and preoccupation with one's appearance do not signify self-love. They are efforts to conceal the individual's deep sense of failure and, even more fundamentally, that he or she feels inherently unlovable. A person who cannot love others is also unable to love himself or herself. While narcissists demonstrate what appears to be abundant love for themselves, they are actually trying to compensate for a deficiency in self-love.

Most narcissistic people have an interpersonal style that falls somewhere in the range of the Controller or the Humiliator. The more the individual uses his or her gifts to demean others, the more the style will be Humiliating, and the more he or she uses them to enforce compliance, the more it will be Controlling. But there are plenty of narcissistic people who are Intruders, Freeloaders, Drifters, Scurriers, Avoiders, or Victimizers. Narcissism is therefore not restricted to a single Default Style. It is a psychospiritual defect, rooted in self-doubt and insecurity, that can intensify and rigidify any style. If there is a single psychological characteristic that shouts out a person's need for God's unconditional acceptance, it is narcissism.

The Humiliator, like the Victimizer, is inclined toward the sadistic, a subject to which we will return in Chapter Thirteen. Humiliators enjoy watching others squirm and, to some extent, suffer. But unlike the Victimizer, the Humiliator causes others to suffer primarily to dominate them. One way to think of the difference between them is that the Humiliator wants to win the battle and enjoy the spoils of war, while the Victimizer also wants to burn the villages and annihilate their inhabitants.

Like the Victimizer, the Humiliator tends to alternate between two kinds of behavior in personal relationships. Victimizers move back and forth between attack and displays of remorse. Humiliators, by contrast, alternate between inclusion and rejection. They condition others to escape or avoid ridicule and gain inclusion by these others acting submissively and resentfully and then reward them for doing so. The reward can be anything from a warm smile to designating them a probationary member of the inner circle.

Humiliators in the Bible

Among the best examples from scripture of a Humiliator is Goliath. As noted, Humiliators are often addicted to conquest, especially if it demeans and belittles others. The Philistines had gathered their forces of war at Socoh in Judah and had camped between Socoh and Azekah. Saul and the

Israelites were camped in the Valley of Elah. The battle line was drawn, with each army occupying a hill. Then this happened:

> A champion named Goliath, who was from Gath, came out of the Philistine camp. He was over nine feet tall. He had a bronze helmet on his head and wore a coat of scale armor of bronze weighing five thousand shekels; on his legs he wore bronze greaves, and a bronze javelin was slung on his back. His spear shaft was like a weaver's rod, and its iron point weighed six hundred shekels. His shield bearer went ahead of him. Goliath stood and shouted to the ranks of Israel, "Why do you come out and line up for battle? Am I not a Philistine, and are you not the servants of Saul? Choose a man and have him come down to me. If he is able to fight and kill me, we will become your subjects; but if I overcome him and kill him, you will become our subjects and serve us." Then the Philistine said, "This day I defy the ranks of Israel! Give me a man and let us fight each other." On hearing the Philistine's words, Saul and all the Israelites were dismayed and terrified [1 Samuel 17:4–11, NIV].

Goliath didn't just want to prevail in battle. He wanted to make his opponents suffer psychologically, which is at the core of the Humiliator's mentality.

The Arrangement Sought

Humiliators are forever searching for those individuals who are willing to be dominated, persecuted, and demeaned. They attract dependent people who have an unconscious need for abasement. The psychological qualities that draw another person toward a Humiliator, such as the willingness to grant others oppressive power and the need to suffer in silence, are the very same ones that make it more likely for the humiliation to increase.

If the Humiliator is not too oppressive in establishing superiority, the other person may respond with deferential scurrying, in which case the relationship may become stable. You may recall Edith Bunker's way of relating to her husband, Archie, in the 1970s TV series *All in the Family*. This kind of arrangement can be established, for example, between a Humiliator who is closer to being a Controller than a Victimizer and a Scurrier who is closer to being a Drifter than an Avoider. The Humiliator will conclude that he or she has found someone who truly appreciates his or her magnificence.

It is also possible for a stable relationship to be established on the basis of more aggressive humiliation. A Humiliator who is decidedly sadistic and a Scurrier who is fundamentally masochistic may be compatible. The former will do a good deal of berating, and the latter will spend a lot of energy trying to get the Humiliator to stop, but the relationship may still endure. Many people, both men and women, remain in relationships with partners on the borderline between Humiliating and Victimizing, not because they lack the strength to get away but because they have an unconscious need to be abused and degraded. Though they may *say*, and believe, that they remain because they are afraid to leave or to press for change, in reality they stay because they need to suffer.

The problem in some cases may be spiritual. Instead of falling on God's mercy to forgive and save them, they agonize in the unconscious hope that their suffering will atone for their sins. They are, in a sense, reenacting the crucifixion with themselves in the role of Jesus.

Payoffs for the Humiliator

Beyond the psychological payoffs discussed so far (foisting one's flaws onto others, warding off feelings of helplessness, defending against feelings of unworthiness, and so on), the Humiliating style allows one to feel important. It is easier to approve of and accept oneself if others are constantly admiring you for your competence, wisdom, intelligence, wealth, beauty, or social standing. When Humiliators do not inflict too much pain on others, they may be admired.

Like the Controller, the Humiliator may be put into a position of leadership and, in general, treated as special. Confident people, especially those who have an aggressive edge to them, are looked up to in our society. Because the Humiliator comes across as the embodiment of the competitive spirit, he or she is a kind of cultural ideal. Think of how often the heroes of adventure films, such as Ian Fleming's James Bond, are inclined to humiliate their opponents. Although we do not like humiliation inflicted on us, we may relish seeing it inflicted on others.

What the Humiliator Avoids

Humiliators do not like to think of themselves as ordinary because being so feels to them like becoming invisible or ceasing to exist. The Humiliator therefore avoids thinking of others as peers. Because the Humiliating stance is aggressive and arrogant, the Humiliator tends to regard others as "rabble."

As noted earlier, Humiliators are not inclined to trust, express admiration, or defer. They do not often allow themselves to feel weak or dependent. And they do not display vulnerability, since doing so brings the possibility that one's rivals may "do unto" the Humiliator what he or she is forever trying to do to them. Tenderness of any kind is also frightening because it could prompt the Humiliator to reveal something that could create a disadvantage. The Humiliating strategy rests squarely on keeping other people guessing and at a safe distance, where one can keep an eye on them.

What the Humiliator Trains You to Feel and Do

Unless Humiliators are compulsively belittling, their audiences may fawn over them, tell them how wonderful or talented they are, and stumble over themselves to act like sycophants—especially if the specific Humiliator is even a minor celebrity. Such homage is almost always given ambivalently, however, because resentment sours it. How could it be otherwise? Whether crassly or not, the Humiliator causes other people to feel bad about themselves. Resentment involves unexpressed aggression. Rather than pushing someone to the ground, you hope that he or she slips on an oil slick. Resentment is the desire for another person to suffer, coupled with the desire to avoid taking responsibility for inducing his or her suffering. Because Humiliators tend to be so skilled at inflicting pain, others are reluctant to express their aggression directly and hence often seethe with resentment. The Humiliator usually senses this resentment and, in response, punishes others all the more for feeling that way.

Vanquishing others typically prompts them to engage in toxic self-talk: "You're a loser who should have tried harder." It induces them to embark on the path of self-persecution, shame, and guilt. There is an important difference between guilt and shame. Guilt is *private*. You could feel guilty if you were alone on a desert island. Shame, however, is *public*. To feel shame, you must have a real or imagined audience. Guilt is punishment you inflict on yourself. Shame is punishment that others inflict on you.

When the Arrangement Breaks Down

The arrangement sometimes falls apart because the other person actually needs *more* vindictive persecution than the Humiliator provides; he or she is looking for a Victimizer. If the Humiliator begins to feel genuine love and affection (moves toward the right side of Figure 6.3), the other individual may conclude that the Humiliator is insufficiently interesting or exciting. It may also break down if the Humiliator becomes too aggressive (moves left in Figure 6.3). Finally, the arrangement may founder not because the Humiliator changes but because the other person does. Whether through a spiritual transformation or some other life-altering event, the individual may simply conclude that he or she has had enough and refuse to put up with the Humiliator's arrogance, criticism, blaming, disparagement, or abuse.

Life History

The parents of some Humiliators overestimated the worth of status, wealth, looks, or achievement and underestimated the value of kindness, generosity, empathy, and holiness. Reared in such an environment, children learn to regard themselves as their parents do, as privileged production machines, engineered to conquer the world and, along the way, to bring other people to their knees.

Other Humiliators were raised by parents who subjected them to substantial humiliations of their own. As they grew into adults, these children learned to do unto others as their parents did unto them. These Humiliators can be among the most narcissistic of all because they have gaping holes inside of them that no amount of human attention or earthly achievement could ever fill. Like all human beings, they need a living relationship with God.

Another group of Humiliators were raised by parents who scampered around to meet their needs and automatically deferred to them. Such parental conduct trained them in self-centeredness and, sometimes, massive insensitivity. Nearly all children will push the boundaries of behavior if limits are not maintained. Adolescents, as they strive to firm up who and what they are, frequently define their identities by pushing *against* other people, and weak parents are handy targets for such pushing. Because teenagers can be brutal to each other, adolescents often carry resentment toward their peers that they attempt to displace onto their parents. When they are permitted to do this, year after year, such adolescents become callous, tyrannical, and ready at a moment's notice to indulge the pathological lust for power that lurks within the human breast. This lust is closely related to pride and is therefore at the core of much sin.

Still other Humiliators had parents who either neglected them deliberately or were so withdrawn that they provided little nurturance. Children raised in such circumstances understandably grow up to view the world as emotionally barren. They are largely oblivious to the joys of intimacy and are therefore inclined to treat other people as objects.

Finally, some people who relate through the Humiliating style do so largely because they are in empty marriages in need of repair. They feel cheated by life and so demeaned by their spouses that they take their misery out on others by constantly putting them down.

Adult Humiliators tend to regard their parents in one of two ways. They either view them as heroes and models, whose ruthless but successful ways are to be emulated, or see them as cold, uncaring, and ineffective.

Intimacy and the Humiliator

The Humiliating style involves enhancing oneself to the relative exclusion of others. It is ideally suited, therefore, to thwart emotional closeness. Intimacy requires mutuality, and there can be no mutuality without the parties in a relationship attending to both themselves *and* each other. They must do this with the give-and-take of children playing cooperatively in a sandbox. Narcissism forces the parties into the posture of parallel play, simultaneously engaging in the same activities but not really doing them together. If and when the two start to have a conversation that might lead to intimacy, the Humiliator is likely to compete for airtime as if it were oxygen. Intimacy requires getting beyond such self-absorption. It is also difficult to get close to someone who constantly reminds you of your defects, imperfections, inadequacies, and deficiencies.

Intimacy with a Humiliator often turns out to be an illusion. The other person discovers that what he or she mistook for closeness was little more than a forbearing willingness to believe in the Humiliator and to pay tribute. Without knowing it, the individual was engaged in the worship of a hero, and sometimes a false god, who was revealed, at the end of the story, to be unwilling or unable to love.

Spiritual and Moral Choices

How you regard this kind of behavior should depend on whether you see it in yourself or others. Belittling and demeaning have no place in the life of a Christian.

There is, to be sure, sometimes a fine line between healthy competition and arrogant striving. And there are differences in how others may experience you in your more expansive moments. You may intend simply to share your joy over some bit of good news, while the other person may experience such sharing as a put-down. It is important to be sensitive to your audience. The true Humiliator's self-esteem is so impoverished that he or she cannot rejoice in others' blessings, which spark envy and further diminish feelings of self-worth.

When you notice that another person relies on the Humiliating Default Style, have compassion and, if you can find it within you, pray for that person. This can be difficult to do, especially if the person has singled you out as a target. Yet what looks on the surface like confidence and self-esteem in the Humiliator is in truth anything but.

SELF-ASSESSMENT

To get a quick sense of how much you may rely on this Default Style, ask yourself the following questions. Although these questions do not constitute a test, they may give you a rough idea of where you stand. Please consult www.relationaldynamics.com for information about more sophisticated methods of assessment.

1. To those less able or less fortunate, do you brag about your accomplishments or possessions?
2. Do you frequently point out to others their faults, weaknesses, or deficiencies?
3. Do you enjoy putting other people in their place and perhaps putting them down?

ANTIDOTES TO TOXICITY

I am now going to provide you with two sets of suggestions. The first may help you reduce any tendency you find in yourself to operate in the Default Style we have discussed in this chapter. Before trying out any of these suggestions, it would be wise to read Part Four of this book, particularly Chapter Fifteen, on myths about behavior change. The second set of suggestions may help you respond more effectively to others who relate to you through this Default Style. These suggestions are of necessity general and therefore may not work with a specific individual. So use them wisely and judiciously, and above all do not apply them mechanically or put yourself in danger. Although people with certain interpersonal styles tend to be more troublesome and combative than those who rely on other styles, it is best to err on the side of caution. When in doubt, consult those with publicly sanctioned expertise in personality disorders, such as mental health professionals.

If You Tend Toward Humiliating . . .

Here are some suggestions that may help you reduce this tendency:

- ○ Refrain from expansively telling others about what you've achieved or what you own. This is only likely to make more sensitive souls feel inadequate.

- ○ Draw attention to other people's accomplishments. Everyone has something that you can celebrate. Only do this sincerely, because insincerely celebrating someone else's accomplishments, if they detect what you're up to, will hurt them more than if you said nothing at all.

- ○ Watch out for hostile humor. Telling jokes at someone else's expense can be cruel and insensitive. If you find yourself wanting to tease another person with jokes of this sort, pause a moment. Ask yourself if you resent or despise this person for some reason you have not yet acknowledged.

- ○ Face the sin of pride to the extent that you detect it within yourself. It is easy to be prideful and arrogant, especially when things are going well and you're successful. Many people who have been abundantly blessed in life start to conclude, like the Pharisee in relation to the publican, that they are inherently superior: "God, I thank you that I am not like other men" (Luke 18:11, NIV). Actively *practice* humility. Make it a spiritual discipline.

- ○ Try to get your self-worth from the right source, God. In the film *Adaptation,* one of the main characters says to his twin, in essence, that he is not defined by who loves and esteems him but by those whom he loves. Christians are defined by the Creator who loves them, not by any human audience. Human acclaim is fleeting.

- ○ Recruit Anchors to help you (see Chapter Sixteen).

How to Respond to Humiliating

If someone else is relating to you through Humiliating, here are some potential countermeasures:

- Recognize the aggression in the other person's behavior. Do not stick your head in the mud by denying this. Putting other people down, however it's done, is moving against them. Know what you're dealing with. Recognize, however, that some people demean and belittle but do not even realize what they're doing. This does not mean that their behavior is not aggressive, just that their level of insight is low.

- Put the behavior on the road to extinction by not reinforcing it. When the other person attempts to put you down, you might say nothing, look away, make no eye contact, go to the restroom, anything that will prevent you from responding.

- Above all, stay far away from anything that resembles scurrying. Do not whine, bargain, appease, grovel—do nothing that reflects passive and hostile submission.

- If the other person continually needles you, talk about it. Express how you feel. Do this gently at first but, if that does not make a constructive impression, say straight out that you do not appreciate the needling. This may or may not work, but it is far superior to doing nothing.

- Do not be a "good sport" toward someone who is being nasty, especially if such nastiness is not a onetime event but a pattern over time. This would only reinforce the unwanted behavior.

- If all else fails, exercise contact control. Although God generally wants us to move toward rather than away or against other people, there is no point to making yourself into an object of chronic abuse.

12

SCURRYING

WHINING AND APPEASING

When they had kindled a fire in the middle of the courtyard and
sat down together, Peter sat among them. Then a servant-girl,
seeing him in the firelight, stared at him and said, "This man also
was with him." But he denied it, saying, "Woman, I do not
know him." A little later someone else, on seeing him, said,
"You also are one of them." But Peter said, "Man, I am not!"
Then about an hour later still another kept insisting, "Surely this
man also was with him; for he is a Galilean." But Peter said,
"Man, I do not know what you are talking about!" At that
moment, while he was still speaking, the cock crowed.
The Lord turned and looked at Peter [who] remembered. . . .
He went out and wept bitterly.

—Luke 22:55–62 [NRSV]

ALTHOUGH PETER WAS ORDINARILY BOLD and not given to Scurrying, this passage suggests that we are all capable of it. Scurriers are typically anxious and fearful. They continually scan the environment to see who might be getting ready to hurt them and whom, therefore, they must buy off by groveling. Convinced that the world is menacing, they try to placate and appease whoever might be inclined to injure them. Such placations and appeasements involve self-abasement and may degenerate into begging and pleading. The Scurrier's version of the Golden Rule is "I will do anything unto you . . . just grant me mercy."

Your first reaction to a Scurrier is likely to be an empathic attempt to reassure and comfort. You will want to convince the Scurrier to trust you and to relax in the knowledge that he or she is safe and that you care. But sooner or later, you will probably become uncomfortable with the Scurrier's self-effacing manner and resentful whining, and you may even begin to despise the Scurrier's fearfulness, especially when you notice that your efforts to assuage the Scurrier's anxiety go nowhere. The Scurrier remains as jittery as ever and continues to act as if you, and the rest of the world, were about to deliver a slap on the cheek. This "everyone is down on me" attitude will wear thin, and you may find yourself doing the very things to the Scurrier that he or she claims others do and that the Scurrier *says* he or she most fears. Yet the Scurrier proves that the best way to become a target for disrespect and humiliation is to play the role of the victim. Exhibit 12.1 summarizes the major characteristics of the Scurrier.

The Scurrier's Script

Whereas the script of the Drifter (see Chapter Eight) is to avoid rejection through compliance, the script of the Scurrier is to bribe his or her way out of trouble by putting on demonstrations of suffering, coupled with proclamations of unworthiness and *mea culpa* ("it's my fault"). Such maneuvers increase the likelihood that others will abuse the Scurrier and, beyond that, treat him or her as a kind of buffoon whose very existence can be ridiculed, dismissed, and made fun of. The Scurrier's occasional attempts to be a good sport only make things worse, particularly if he or she is up against others with sadistic tendencies (Victimizers and Humiliators).

The Scurrier attempts to induce other people to act mercifully by proving to them that he or she has suffered enough, a strategy based on three assumptions:

○ People are threatening and, unless appeased, will hurt you.

○ There is no point to resisting, and so it is best to give in, go along, and hope that the misery will go away.

○ Maliciousness in others can be reduced by displays of pain and suffering.

Scurriers try to disarm potential persecutors by doing to themselves what they believe others want and intend to do to them.

Exhibit 12.1. Profile of the Scurrier.

Theme	"Please don't hurt me—I'll do what you say."
Self-Presentation	Ruminative, passive, resentful, and preoccupied; tense, pessimistic, and cynical; self-doubting and vulnerable; weak and ineffective; a victim of cruel circumstance and ill will; highlights own inferiority and unworthiness.
Additional Characteristics	Willing to tolerate abuse; anxious and fretful; eager for peace at any price; if intelligent, tends toward the analytical and technical; may recount how the world has been unfair; relates stories of having been used, taken for granted, and abused; often concerned with own moral failings and inadequacies; quick to put self down; apologetic and obsequious; when not scanning for danger, focuses on self as opposed to others and is, in this sense, childlike.
Responses Induced in Others	Initial attempts to comfort and reassure; these may turn into contempt, disparagement, and oppression, since Scurrying behavior prompts disparagement and disrespect.
Healthier (Milder) Version	Conceding and capitulating; yielding when this is appropriate; being self-reflective about own faults and failings.

○

Case 12.1

Bruce is twenty-three and wants to marry Marie, who is not yet twenty-one. They recently went to dinner with Marie's parents specifically so that, if the mood was right, Bruce and Marie could raise the subject of marriage. During the first hour, Bruce made several statements that announced, in one way or another, that he was a loser. His report "I broke the axle on my truck last week, and that cost me two thousand dollars" had special significance for Marie's parents, who knew that Bruce had run his credit cards up so high that he could barely pay his bills. Then he said to Marie's father, "I ran that scooter you fixed for me into a curb and bent the frame." Next came "We done it . . . ," which was bound to irritate Marie's mother, who detested bad grammar.

○

Bruce shows the self-demeaning behavior that is characteristic of the Scurrier. The message he communicates constantly is "I'm a jerk and a loser." This only invites others to treat him like a jerk and a loser. Although this short case doesn't demonstrate it, Bruce is likely to put up with abuse from others and perhaps to make a joke of it in the hope that they will stop. Unlike the Drifter, who tries to win love through obedience, the Scurrier tries to avoid or escape punishment through self-effacement. Here's how the Scurrier's script tends to play out in real life:

1. The Scurrier subtly communicates that he or she is a defenseless victim.
2. Others begin to oppress and abuse the Scurrier.
3. The Scurrier oppresses and abuses himself or herself in the hope of fending off further persecution.
4. Others accept the Scurrier's definition of himself or herself, as someone worthy of mistreatment.
5. The humiliation increases until the Scurrier agonizes and writhes in pain.
6. Others may back off temporarily but will soon resume the harassment.

As noted in Chapter Eleven, the Scurrying style was poignantly depicted by Edith Bunker (played by Jean Stapleton) in the 1970s TV sitcom *All in the Family*. She ceaselessly scampered around to please her ignorant but self-inflated husband, Archie (played by Carroll O'Connor). While Archie showed the sort of affection toward Edith that one might feel for an old pair of pajamas, he constantly demeaned and diminished her. Because of her mental simplicity and good heart, Edith was able to deny the existence of most of Archie's punches, but occasionally one got through. And when it did, she would end up in tears, trying in vain to comprehend what was going on around her and why Archie was so mean.

Benefits of the Behavior

Like the Drifter, the Scurrier is more likely to defer to others than to start trouble or join in a battle. The Scurrier often comes across with a certain likable humility. This, of course, makes for smooth relationships. And the Scurrier is astonishingly skilled at apologizing.

The Scurrier can serve as an effective shock absorber for people who are nasty or vindictive, except that, as noted, the Scurrying style actually tends, over time, to intensify such behavior in others. Unlike people who are overtly sensitive or touchy, Scurriers tend on the surface to underreact to slights and provocations, even if beneath the surface they are writhing in emotional pain.

Justifications for the Style

If you criticize the Scurrier for his or her obsequious manner, and especially if you allude to his or her resentment, the Scurrier is likely, first, to agree automatically with your criticisms. Then he or she will fall back on one or more of the following defenses:

Helplessness. The Scurrier does not have the power to change, and if he or she attempted any kind of interpersonal repositioning, something terrible might happen. He or she might get fired, the spouse might leave, and so forth. For practical reasons, such as preserving the Scurrier's standard of living or keeping the family intact, the Scurrier *must* remain as he or she is.

Sabotaging counterarguments. The Scurrier may say yes to everything you say and then offer excuses for why he or she cannot implement your recommendations. He becomes an expert in the art of "yes but."

Pseudocompliance. The Scurrier will agree with you and express a firm intention to act on your wonderful advice. But nothing happens. Every time you provide counsel, the Scurrier will assent to its value and then not follow up.

Whining. The Scurrier will implicitly beg you to stop asking for behavioral change because he or she has already suffered enough.

All of these maneuvers are examples of passive-aggressive behavior. Such behavior is exactly what you would expect from a person who is invisibly angry and subtly hostile but cannot admit or come to terms with this.

Psychology of the Scurrier

Scurriers are unwilling or unable to take charge of their lives or circumstances. They render themselves powerless and then resent others for having done to them what, in essence, they have permitted and encouraged. Inclined to walk on eggshells lest they offend, Scurriers are quick to feel embarrassed. They are also sensitive to criticism. There is an inhibited, ineffective, and defeated quality to the Scurrier, which can result in others' viewing the Scurrier as helpless and pathetic. If you listen carefully to how the Scurrier talks, attending not only to the words but also to tone of voice and body language, you will quickly pick up the Scurrier's protesting manner, tendency to complain but not take action, and proclivity either to agonize over minor decisions or to make decisions impulsively to end some form of pain.

The Scurrier's social posture is insecure, unassertive, and often reserved. Although not as reclusive as the Avoider (see Chapter Fourteen), neither is the average Scurrier drawn to people. Recall that both interpersonal styles unite submission and hostility. Their styles reflect a fundamental refusal to compete and therefore a level of reticence that often leaves the Scurrier playing the part of the court jester or village idiot. Despite the Scurrier's angry feelings and hostile disposition, he or she is afraid to express anything that might come across as rebellion.

○

Case 12.2

Howard often works weekends for his overbearing and demanding boss, who unjustly criticizes Howard's work and, while dangling before him the carrot of promotion, has yet to come through with even a modest salary increase. His wife also demeans Howard, hurling at him such insults as "Don't you have any backbone?" "Why can't you make more money?" and "I've asked you a hundred times to take out the trash *before* you read the paper." His coworkers see Howard as a solid contributor who simply lacks the confidence to stand up for himself. Howard recently turned down a better job in another department because accepting it would have angered his boss. When others tease him at work, he smiles and tries to be a good sport, which only increases their taunting.

○

Howard actually trains others around him to take him for granted and, even worse, treat him as a nonperson. He invites abuse by not respecting himself enough to stand up and demand that others treat him with dignity. Although it is not obvious with Howard, it is impossible to understand the psychology of the Scurrier without grasping the extent to which he or she is often filled with resentment, a reality that is easy to miss because of the Scurrier's docile manner. The Scurrier often seethes with repressed anger, which can sometimes be detected in the biting and cynical quality of the Scurrier's humor. If you study professional comedians to determine which of the eight styles they tend most to demonstrate, you will discover that it is Scurrying. By listening carefully, you will find that their humor almost always drips with resentment. Their assaults are expressed from a one-down position, and they are therefore often passively hostile rather than actively aggressive.

The Scurrier may mistake the attention he or she derives from being persecuted for genuine affection, especially when taking on the role of buffoon, and the Scurrier often prefers to be an object of ridicule to remaining obscure and unnoticed. Low self-esteem may prompt the Scurrier to become the doormat that the Scurrier, deep down, believes that he or she *deserves* to be. And so the Scurrier encourages others to become abusive. Such provocation can occur in all sorts of ways, such as forgetting to lock the door before leaving the house, neglecting to balance the checkbook, refusing to pick up after himself or herself, failing to appear for an appointment, or, if all else fails, making snide remarks. Such remarks, when uttered by a powerless person like the Scurrier, are almost sure to elicit additional abuse.

Many people with a Scurrying style are unconsciously trying to recreate the persecution-appeasement pattern that they lived through with a punitive parent. Thus the Scurrier seeks to feel bad in order to feel good. Scurriers may abase themselves so that they can feel the imaginary comfort of a lost and unfulfilling childhood. As the following example demonstrates, Scurriers will sometimes go to extraordinarily lengths to maintain their sense of security.

○

Case 12.3

Charlene and Norman have been married for three years, and through this time he has increasingly called her frumpy, dull, and ill-informed. Several months ago, Charlene joined a gym and now works out vigorously, hoping that Norman will revise his opinion of her. She has also begun to read the *New York Times* from front to back so that she will have interesting things to say to him at dinner. Charlene recently discovered lipstick on Norman's handkerchief and, worried sick, asked if he were seeing another woman. "You know I have female friends," he answered, and added, "You don't expect me to sit around here bored for the rest of my life, do you?" He stomped off toward the liquor cabinet, drank himself into oblivion, and the next morning blamed her for his hangover: "If it weren't for you, I wouldn't drink at all." Charlene told her mother what had happened—this was not the first time—and became depressed when her mother suggested that she stand up for herself. "I could never do that," she insisted. Nor could she bring herself to ask Norman directly if he were having an affair, though she suspected he was.

○

By bending over backward in a self-demeaning manner, Charlene is only inviting Norman to abuse her. She is also running away from reality because she is afraid to confront him about the lipstick. So she just scurries along, allowing him to treat her abominably.

In addition to using self-persecution to disarm others, the Scurrier is inclined to rely on the defense mechanism of undoing. This involves saying or doing things that make up for the Scurrier's deficient behavior or, better still, make it seem as if the whole thing never happened. Whenever his or her anger leaks out, the Scurrier is quick to employ the word magic of "I'm sorry" and "I was only kidding." Alternatively, the Scurrier may offer gifts (for example, flowers or candy) to atone for alleged misdeeds.

Scurriers look for someone to confirm their self-concepts, people who will agree in one way or another that they deserve to suffer. The Scurrier has been taught that he or she is most lovable when proclaiming, through words or deeds, unlovability. Once this self-concept has been solidified, the Scurrier will go to great lengths to preserve, validate, and defend it. Having this self-concept threatened, even by someone with the noble intention of changing it for the better, feels to the Scurrier like perishing. Though Scurriers may *say* they want to change and often mean it, when they come face to face with how this will alter their ideas about themselves, their motivation wanes. We all feel most secure and least anxious when our ideas, opinions, and expectations, especially about ourselves, are supported. This drive for predictability and comfort can, of course, do great harm.

The Scurrier is unconsciously driven toward self-abasement in the hope that if he or she is deferential enough, others will finally deem the Scurrier lovable. But the more abased the Scurrier becomes, the less lovable the Scurrier is by his or her own definition. And *that* is the terrible trap in which the Scurrier is caught. The more the Scurrier tries to become lovable through suffering, the less lovable the Scurrier assumes himself or herself to be. A poignant example of self-abasement is portrayed in Joseph Conrad's 1915 novel, *Victory*. Jeffrey Meyers writes in *Joseph Conrad: A Biography*, "Lena's almost suicidal desire for self-sacrifice is at once an attempt to punish herself and . . . make herself worthy of love" (p. 286).

As with many toxic Default Styles, there is a paradox at work: The Scurrier unconsciously wants to atone for being a worthless person, but the more abuse he or she suffers, the less worthy the Scurrier feels and the more humiliation (atonement) he or she needs. This dooms the Scurrier to chronic unhappiness. Yet in this unhappiness the Scurrier finds security. The Scurrier feels most comfortable (secure) when interpersonally uncomfortable (oppressed). Whereas the Avoider is most likely to become the victim of a serious attack, the Scurrier is most likely to play the role of professional victim.

Of the eight toxic styles, Scurrying is the one most associated with feelings of guilt and shame. But there is a subtlety to the Scurrier's guilt that is important to understand. What many people, including and perhaps especially the Scurrier, experience consciously as guilt is, at a more basic level, the unconscious expectation that they are going to be whacked, that the world will get them back for something they did or failed to do. "I feel guilty" often means "I'm dreading the retaliation that's about to be inflicted on me." To the extent that the Scurrier's guilt is a thin veil for fear of punishment, it is a sign that he or she has assumed something of a paranoid position—a stance, by the way, that the Avoider is likely to assume with even more vigor. As psychoanalysts have pointed out, a wish and a fear are often two sides of the same coin. Thus the Scurrier may both wish and fear that others will hurt him or her, even when the thought of doing so has never entered their minds. All guilt cannot be interpreted as a symptom of fear; some of it is simply self-persecution, internal oppression of the self. Still, for the Scurrier, guilt is largely saturated with dread and self-oppression.

Many Scurriers are analytic and restrained and therefore tend to think carefully before they speak. Often they think too much, with the result that speech becomes stiff and stilted. Other Scurriers are just the opposite. They are loud, boisterous, and inclined to draw attention to themselves as misfits and failures.

Scurriers in the Bible

Abraham provides a poignant example of Scurrying. He claims that his wife, Sarah, is his sister, with the result that King Abimelech sends for her. But God warns Abimelech in a dream that he will die if he touches her because Sarah is a married woman. God further tells the king to return Sarah to her husband, who is a prophet: "So Abimelech rose early in the morning, . . . called Abraham, and said to him, 'What have you done to us? . . . What were you thinking . . . ?' Abraham said, 'I did it because I thought, There is no fear of God at all in this place, and they will kill me because of my wife'" (Genesis 20:8–11, NRSV). Abraham was resorting to Scurrying.

King Saul did the same. When he was in his thirties, he scurried, with tragic consequences. The Philistines had put together a formidable army and were about to attack Israel. The men of Israel were so terrified that they hid out in caves, bushes, rocks, pits—anywhere they could to avoid having to fight the Philistines. The prophet Samuel was supposed to come and help Saul, who waited for him a full seven days. But Samuel did not appear. Out of desperation, Saul asked that the burnt offering be brought to him, whereupon he offered it up. Then Samuel arrived and, shocked by Saul's impertinence, asked him to explain his actions. Saul said, "When I saw that the men were scattering . . . I felt compelled [to seek the Lord's favor]," to which Samuel replied, "You acted foolishly [and] have not kept the command the Lord your God gave you. . . . Now your kingdom will not endure; the Lord has sought out a man after his own heart" (1 Samuel 13:11–14, NIV).

The Arrangement Sought

Scurriers tend to link up with friends and spouses who are aggressive and critical, the sorts of people who are chronically dissatisfied with others. Such persons are strong, assertive, and not afraid to take charge. Although the Scurrier may be unaware of it, he or she feels most comfortable when someone else acts toward him or her in an aggressively dominant manner. Often the Scurrier feels best of all when this person is mildly sadistic.

The Scurrier wants, therefore, to find and connect with someone who will assume an oppressive one-up position, in part because the Scurrier finds normal relationships strange and unfulfilling. It just wouldn't feel natural for the Scurrier to establish a relationship with someone who related warmly. Nor would the Scurrier feel good to be treated as an equal. The Scurrier suffers *least* when suffering most. If the Scurrier can convince others to act oppressively, he or she feels less worried and more at home. It may not be fun to suffer, but it is less fun to be flooded with anxiety.

Thus the ideal arrangement is for the other person to criticize and demean the Scurrier and for the Scurrier to be able to writhe in pain as an unfairly persecuted victim. Such an arrangement allows the Scurrier to cling like a pit bull to passive resentment and so not have to take action or accept responsibility for his or her unhappiness. The arrangement validates the Scurrier's "ain't it awful" worldview and allows the Scurrier to continue in the role of unloved child, who has every right to feel self-pity and every right to whine and complain.

Payoffs for the Scurrier

The emotional rewards of Scurrying behavior could fill volumes, and so I will mention only a few of them. Most significant, perhaps, is that inviting persecution allows the Scurrier to work off guilt. As we have seen, however, whatever expiation the Scurrier feels is temporary, since a by-product of humiliation is that he or she feels worse and thus in need of still more humiliation.

On a still subtler level, the Scurrier may derive pleasure from watching guilt develop in his or her persecutors. If they have a conscience at all, they may begin to feel bad about their victimizing of the Scurrier, never realizing that the Scurrier has set them up to feel this way. This is the same sort of passive aggression that a child sometimes expresses to a parent after being punished: "You'll be sorry." This, of course, means that the child intends the parent to feel guilty. Adult Scurriers are more likely to induce guilt in a slightly more sophisticated way: "You'll be sorry when I'm gone."

The social rewards of the Scurrying style include the security that comes from knowing that others will not view one as a threat. And as we have seen, it helps disarm others. Unless they have been trained by the Scurrier to play the role of Humiliator or Victimizer or are naturally inclined to play one of these roles themselves, many people are reluctant to attack someone who is already suffering.

Finally, there is the sense of mastery that comes from being able to decide when one is, and is not, going to be persecuted. The Scurrier can turn appeasement and placation on and off, seemingly at will, and this provides the Scurrier with the comforting illusion that an otherwise unpleasant and unpredictable reality (random punishment) is now a predictable and controllable one. What makes this an illusion is that the Scurrier cannot, in fact, turn off self-abasing conduct because it pops up instantly and without forethought, as an interpersonal reflex.

What the Scurrier Avoids

Scurriers do not want to think of themselves as bold or assertive because such ideas might prove dangerous, especially if others detected that the Scurrier is thinking about rising up. Nor do Scurriers want to conceive of themselves as competent, worthy, or expansive. If they conveyed such a self-concept to those around them, they might be impressed into a position of leadership, and leadership, by definition, means taking risks. Such thoughts and possibilities move Scurriers away from their comfort zones and threaten to saddle them with unwanted responsibility. Many Scurriers are conscientious in every area of existence *except* when it comes to taking charge of their own lives and what happens to them. As far as the Scurrier is concerned, it is the world that does things *to* him or her, not the Scurrier who actively helps create his or her pain.

Many Scurriers harbor a pessimism that they cherish and protect. To view the world in optimistic terms or to see other people as nourishing and helpful would leave them feeling defenseless and vulnerable. Scurriers are convinced that the planet is filled with people who at any moment might hurt them and so are unwilling to entertain any naïve fantasies about the value of sticking their necks out.

Self-control and self-constriction are important to Scurriers, and so they are not given to spontaneity or impulsiveness. Scurriers often experience high levels of anxiety, since they are struggling to make sense of the world and to figure out how best to remain safe in it. And like Avoiders, Scurriers are inclined toward depression.

What the Scurrier Trains You to Feel and Do

By examining Figures 6.7 and 6.8, you will see that Scurriers are likely to prompt other people to act as their betters. They train others to be aggressively dominant. Unless these others are uncommonly kind, they will almost inevitably become arrogant, disparaging, and contemptuous. Once trained in this manner, others will patronize Scurriers, treat them with little respect, subtly or overtly turn them into objects of scorn and derision, and perhaps taunt and tease them. Other people will tend, in general, to communicate to Scurriers that they are neither a force to be reckoned with nor persons to be taken seriously. Scurriers will, in short, be rejected and depersonalized. Sometimes Scurriers even manage to teach otherwise kind people to become experts in insensitivity.

If those with whom Scurriers interact already demonstrate a Humiliating or Victimizing style, they can be counted on to pick up the vulnerable scent of the Scurrier and, having done this, to show him or her no mercy. The Scurrier will be maligned, depreciated, needled, blamed, and in other ways demeaned.

When the Arrangement Breaks Down

The arrangement with a Scurrier will break down if, for whatever reason, the Scurrier decides that he or she is tired of being put down. This sometimes happens because the Scurrier consults a therapist who is able to identify and nudge the Scurrier out of a self-defeating stance. Other times, going to school or church expands the Scurrier's psychological horizons. And if the Scurrier has a personal encounter with God and, as a result, grasps the significance of Christ's work on earth, he or she may stop trying to make peace with the cosmos through personal suffering.

If and when the Scurrier changes, interpersonal relationships are certain to suffer a strain. Many people in the Scurrier's life have learned to mistreat him or her. Like the Scurrier, they have grown comfortable with the roles they have worked out over the years. And now, suddenly, the Scurrier starts to speak up, stops the self-persecution, and, worse, announces that he or she has had enough of other people's abuse. When the Scurrier's spouse is a Humiliator or a Victimizer, the couple may find themselves in court, battling for custody or venomously dividing property.

The arrangement may also dissolve if the Scurrier becomes significantly depressed. Although a sadistic spouse may be more than happy to watch a mildly depressed partner scurry around in an attempt to please, the same spouse may take quite another view if the partner sits in a chair all evening and cries. For the arrangement to continue, the partner *has* to be able to react, grovel, whine, plead, beg, protest, and agonize. People who develop a serious mood disorder are often unable to do any of these things. Note that depression often follows oppression. Many people become depressed because, first, others oppress them, and then they learn to oppress themselves.

Finally, the arrangement may hit some rough spots if the Scurrier becomes more loving. This can happen if there is a spiritual awakening within the Scurrier. The Scurrier's self-esteem may or may not change, but the tendencies to placate and appease will. This is because the Scurrier begins to focus on others rather than on himself or herself. When this happens, the other person will be baffled and conclude that the Scurrier is acting strangely.

Life History

Many Scurriers were raised by harsh parents who were not inclined to spare the rod. Such parents may have been physically abusive. Once the child has been trained to suffer and, beyond this, has been taught that he or she will be loved most when suffering, a self-sabotaging template has been engraved on the child's heart.

Having learned that suffering is the key to getting attention and that self-abasement is the way to get others to deem him or her worthy of love, the Scurrier learns to advertise that he or she is, in fact, unworthy. If, in such a family, the parents toss the child even a morsel of affection, they are likely to be viewed as magnanimous benefactors who, despite the fact that the Scurrier is still regarded as an unworthy sniveler, "love" the child. The parents, as generous dispensers of grace, are granting the child what he or she doesn't deserve.

The Scurrier may try to please and get close to an aggressive parent by provoking the parent and then enduring whatever pain results. It can prove especially gratifying to a budding Scurrier for the parent to become violent and then, tearfully, voice remorse (see Chapter Thirteen). What could be more wonderful—or more reinforcing of the need to scurry—than to watch an all-powerful parent, who has caused you to suffer, inflict pain on himself or herself?

Over the past thirty years, the role of siblings in development has finally begun to receive the attention it deserves. It used to be thought that only parents could significantly affect a child's development, but that assumption is no longer tenable. Brothers and sisters, as well as stepsiblings and stepparents, can play a powerful role in shaping the child. If, for example, the child has an older sibling with a strong need to persecute, this may be enough to turn the child into a lifetime Scurrier. Often the parents allow this because they are oblivious to what's going on or are simply incompetent to stop it.

Intimacy and the Scurrier

The Scurrier may, at first, seem like the ideal candidate for intimacy. He or she is deferential, less contentious than most people, and quick to confess sins and own up to faults. But the avowed Scurrier is far from ideal because it is difficult to establish intimacy with someone who refuses to be your peer. How can the Scurrier be anyone's peer when he or she relates to others in a one-down, self-incriminating, and apologetic fashion?

The Scurrier may also thwart intimacy through distrust and accuse you of not respecting him or her when in fact the Scurrier has demanded, all along, to be taken for granted (for example, "Don't worry about me"). It is difficult to move closer to someone who makes you out to be the enemy.

You may also find yourself pulling away from the Scurrier because you get tired of hearing endless statements of unworthiness. The Scurrier's need to make such statements may crowd out the free-and-easy exchange of thoughts and feelings that intimacy requires. Everything for the Scurrier is serious, heavy, and of great importance, from buying groceries to ordering paper clips. You are likely to find yourself advising the Scurrier to lighten up and stop worrying. Heaviness makes intimacy more difficult.

Finally, you may tire of being cast in the role of a parent. You may become exasperated with the Scurrier's endless attempts to solicit your reassurance, especially when nothing you say does any good and the Scurrier continues to fret. If you are sadistic, of course, the Scurrier may be just your cup of tea. But if you are not, you may become exasperated with the Scurrier's need to worry.

Spiritual and Moral Choices

Among the greatest challenges for a Christian is to avoid the temptation to oblige a Scurrier who just about begs you to become scornful. It is just as important, however, to avoid the opposite pitfall of attempting to talk the Scurrier out of putting himself or herself down. Such self-abasement is what brings the Scurrier a sense of safety and security. To the Scurrier, such tactics feel like a lifeline, and few people are willing to give up what they believe sustains them. Like all persons, Scurriers need to experience God's grace and, in their case, become persuaded that they no longer need to buy off the world's anger by Scurrying.

To the extent that you are inclined toward Scurrying yourself, it is important to become clear about the following realities:

○ Scripture is filled with examples of people whom God loved in spite of their enormous defects and deficiencies. The message of the Gospel is not simply that God loves you but that He loves you *anyway.* No matter what you have done or failed to do, and regardless of how unworthy you are, there is no need to suffer for your sins. Jesus already did that for you.

○ You are just as worthwhile in God's eyes as anyone else on earth, from the worst sinner to the greatest saint. God made you the steward of your life. You are to value the person you are and not relate to others in a way that devalues what God has lovingly created.

○ If you relate to others in a way that rewards them for mistreating you, they will often do so. Because God loves you, quite aside from whether or not you love yourself, it is a failure of responsibility as a Christian to sell yourself short. Groveling is not the same thing as serving. Appeasing and placating those who should not be appeased and placated has no spiritual worth. Such behavior is, in fact, a form of sin.

SELF-ASSESSMENT

To get a quick sense of how much you may rely on this Default Style, ask yourself the following questions. Although these questions do not constitute a test, they may give you a rough idea of where you stand. Please consult www.relationaldynamics.com for information about more sophisticated methods of assessment.

1. Do you frequently find yourself writhing in pain because of how others treat you?

2. Are you quick to tell other people that you're inadequate, inferior, or unworthy?

3. Are you quick to apologize, placate, or act warmly toward someone who is needling you?

ANTIDOTES TO TOXICITY

I am now going to provide you with two sets of suggestions. The first may help you reduce any tendency you find in yourself to operate in the Default Style we have discussed in this chapter. Before trying out any of these suggestions, it would be wise to read Part Four of this book, particularly Chapter Fifteen, on myths about behavior change. The second set of suggestions may help you respond more effectively to others who relate to you through this Default Style. These suggestions are of necessity general and therefore may not work with a specific individual. So use them wisely and judiciously, and above all do not apply them mechanically or put yourself in danger. Although people with certain interpersonal styles tend to be more troublesome and combative than those who rely on other styles, it is best to err on the side of caution. When in doubt, consult those with publicly sanctioned expertise in personality disorders, such as mental health professionals.

If You Tend Toward Scurrying . . .

Here are some suggestions that may help you reduce this tendency:

- Face the fear and anxiety within yourself that prompts you to engage in Scurrying. And recognize that we've all done our share of Scurrying from time to time, whether in relation to parents, teachers, bosses, or other people who had power over us.

○ Practice courage. Do this by taking small steps in the direction of boldness. Instead of repeatedly smiling at someone who gives you a hard time, as if it didn't bother you, look that person squarely in the eye and say nothing that is warm or complimentary. You are unlikely to get a bully to stop picking on you by being nice.

○ Refrain from all bargaining, whining, placating, appeasing, groveling, and otherwise acting like a person who is unworthy of respect. People tend to accept you at your own definition of yourself.

○ Do not say things in response to others' nastiness that you don't mean. "That's OK" may be a self-destructive lie.

○ If someone is making your life miserable, tell the person to stop it. This may involve risk, and, depending on the circumstance, you may not be able prudently to do it. But you might be surprised at how often a person seethes inside and yet never directly expresses this to the person who is responsible for his or her suffering.

○ Recruit Anchors to help you (see Chapter Sixteen).

How to Respond to Scurrying

If someone else is relating to you through Scurrying, here are some potential countermeasures:

○ Avoid trying to reassure the Scurrier. This rarely works. Remember that the Scurrier is expecting to be punished. To ward off punishment, the Scurrier attempts to disarm potential attackers by self-demeaning behavior. You are unlikely to change this by telling the Scurrier that he or she is OK. The Scurrier is not so much worried that he or she is not OK but that others are not OK—that they are menacing.

○ Still, anything you can do to build up the self-esteem of a Scurrier is to the good. Comment on the person's competencies and virtues. Be warm and accepting.

○ Though you may find it difficult to respect the continual Scurrier, resist the temptation to criticize. Scurriers certainly do not need this. Refuse to play the compatible role of Humiliator. Relate to the Scurrier graciously. And pray that God will so work in this person's life that the Scurrier will no longer feel the need to engage in Scurrying. Scurriers, perhaps more than most people, need to *experience* God's grace.

○ Keep in mind that most Scurriers carry around a considerable amount of resentment. Often what the Scurrier complains about is *not* the real source of his or her resentment, which may be buried deep within. If and when the Scurrier begins to complain from a one-down position, as though the Scurrier were one of life's special victims, do not try to reason him or her out of such a view; this will only waste your time and further solidify the Scurrier's perception. But don't commiserate endlessly either, because that, too, reinforces passivity and whining.

○ Try to move into a friendly submissive role. Depend on the Scurrier. Ask for help. Do anything that will move the Scurrier to a friendly one-up position.

○ When the Scurrier expresses a deep feeling of any kind, pay attention to it and perhaps repeat back the essence of what the person has communicated. Scurriers tend to be long on intellectualization and short on emotional expression.

13

VICTIMIZING

INJURING AND EXPLOITING

But when his brothers saw that their father loved [Joseph] more
than all his brothers, they hated him. Once Joseph had a dream,
and when he told his brothers, they hated him even more. . . . "Are
you indeed to reign over us?" . . . He had another dream. . . .
"Shall we indeed come . . . and bow to the ground before you?"
. . . They saw him from a distance, and . . . conspired to kill him.

—Genesis 37:4–18 [NRSV]

EVERY ONE OF THE SCRIPTURE PASSAGES that we will refer to in this chapter depicts victimization. Joseph's brothers plotted to kill him and, had it not been for Reuben, would have. Cain, out of jealousy, murdered Abel. Jacob, himself a schemer, was outdone by Laban, who extracted from him an additional seven years of labor. Delilah manipulated Samson into revealing the secret of his strength and, having obtained it, caused him to come to a bad end. And Herod, in a ruthless attempt to eliminate all potential rivals, tried to kill the Savior of the World and, in the process, had thousands of infants slaughtered. We still have such madmen with us today, and their destructive capacity is enormous.

Victimizers—people who injure and exploit—specialize in hurting others. They take advantage of people and are quick to intimidate them. Often they do things that make them look exciting and captivating, but their underlying behavior patterns turn out to be menacing and dangerous. The Victimizer's version of the Golden Rule is "I'll do unto you what you might do to me if you had the chance—only I'll do it first." Exhibit 13.1 summarizes the basic characteristics of the Victimizer.

Crude and unsophisticated Victimizers often look, and act, like criminals. They are easy to spot, and as a result most of us steer clear of them. Prisons are filled with people who relate to the world in the Victimizing style, which is why society has found it necessary to lock them up. They prey on the vulnerable.

Yet many Victimizers are smooth, charming, and well versed in the ways of polite society. They are likely to impress you as interesting, even intriguing, especially if you are fascinated with the dashing, the adventurous, and the unconventional. You will soon find out, however, that such individuals are long on style but short on character. They may seem, at first, to be upstanding citizens but in truth have never internalized even the basic values of Christianity. These include truthfulness and candor, a commitment to honorability and fair play, and a willingness to accept the faults of others. For most of us, if another person has wronged us, we grant them grace and, when necessary, forgiveness. Not so with the Victimizer, whose first reflex is to take no prisoners, give no ground, and show no mercy. Such a person enjoys taking advantage of others and then looks for opportunities to justify predatory conduct.

Victimizers are overtly or covertly cold, insensitive, and often brutal. Their stance toward others, especially people close to them, is "Watch out—I can and will hurt you." Such persons are mistrustful, critical, and quick to draw negative conclusions. They can be cutting and sarcastic. And they tend to express their disgust and contempt openly.

The Victimizer's Script

Victimizers have no firm sense of boundaries and thus feel entitled to whatever they can take by force or persuasion. Right or wrong has little to do with it. People with this style care only about their own well-being and advantage and are quick to justify their ruthless and opportunistic actions. Viewing the world as a jungle in which survival of the fittest is the only enduring principle, Victimizers cannot afford the luxury of loyalty or other emotional distractions. Their script is to get what they can from others and, to the extent possible, inflict pain on them along the way.

○

Case 13.1
Lewis and Shannon met at a church party seven months ago. They had dated for less than three weeks when they had their first big argument.

Exhibit 13.1. Profile of the Victimizer.

Theme	"I'll use you and hurt you."
Self-Presentation	Strong, independent, and able to survive; uninhibited, nonconforming, and defiant of social customs and conventions; bold and willing to start or become embroiled in conflicts, arguments, or fights.
Additional Characteristics	Cold-hearted, calculating, and manipulative; spontaneous, impulsive, and short-tempered; tough and relatively fearless; intimidating and abusive; self-centered, irritable, and intolerant; high levels of anger and rage; adventurous and drawn to risk, thrills, and danger; often, but not always, superficially charming, debonair, attractive, and engaging; quick to turn violent and vindictive; inclined to retaliate rather than forgive.
Responses Induced in Others	Fear, agitation, and pain; avoidance, resentment, and rebellion; initial attraction and fascination, if present, may continue but become colored by uncertainly, foreboding, and physical or emotional suffering.
Healthier (Milder) Version	Opposing and confronting; challenging injustices and other wrongs; standing up for the weak and protecting the underdog; fighting for noble and worthy goals in a socially approved manner.

That was when Shannon discovered how volatile her new boyfriend could be. He yelled at her, called her names, and even threatened to hit her. Although she was rattled and told herself that it might be best to find another boyfriend, Shannon found Lewis attractive and was reluctant to put an end to an exciting romance.

Then she discovered, through a friend at work, that Lewis was married. When she confronted him, he said that he'd been separated for months and that, since obtaining a divorce was a mere technicality, he hadn't seen any reason to mention that he was married "on paper." God, he assured her, understood his heart and knew that Lewis was completely committed to Shannon. In God's eyes, Lewis insisted, they were already married.

A few weeks later, Lewis didn't show up for dinner at a restaurant where they had agreed to meet. After waiting for an hour, Shannon drove by his "ex-wife's" house and noticed his car parked in the driveway. She waited for thirty-five minutes until the front door finally opened and, after a warm embrace and a lingering kiss, Lewis bid the woman good-bye.

Shannon, who had parked down the street, drove back to her apartment. Lewis showed up five minutes later. She asked where he'd been and why he'd missed their dinner appointment. He replied that he'd had to stay at the office to finish some work. When Shannon confronted Lewis about his lies, he became enraged, called her an obscene name—not the first time—and slapped her.

○

There is no question that Lewis is Victimizing Shannon. To the extent that she tolerates such abuse, Shannon is actually inviting and rewarding it. Stopping the abuse of a serious Victimizer is not easy, and I will have more to say about this at the end of the chapter.

We noted in Chapter Eleven that Humiliators tend to be sadistic. What the Humiliator engages in as a sideline, the Victimizer turns into a profession. Of the eight Default Styles, Victimizing is the one most saturated with causing pain in others for the sheer pleasure of it.

Benefits of the Behavior

If you are threatened late at night in an alley, you might be glad to have someone at your side who is not afraid to express aggression—unless, of course, he or she decides to throw you at the crowd to eke out a few more seconds to run away. People with a Victimizing style make good bodyguards and, as you might predict, sometimes fine actors. They can also be effective disciplinarians, although they have an inclination to get carried away. And they can be strong advocates of "righteousness." Here is an example of someone who is able to use Victimizing behavior in a more or less socially acceptable fashion—which is not, however, to say that this use is desirable:

○

Case 13.2

Bonnie, an experienced nursing supervisor, delights in catching her subordinates doing something wrong or making a mistake, so much so that they call her "Nurse Ratchet." She seems to take joy in torturing those who cross her (for example, by threatening to recommend that they be dismissed from the hospital), and she mercilessly lectures anyone who does not show up with a perfectly pressed uniform. Sometimes she screams at the offender until tears flow.

○

Bonnie is lying in wait for someone to Victimize and, because people are human and make mistakes, she does not lack opportunities. She engages endlessly in the game of "caught you!"

Justifications for the Style

Few people are more passionately convinced of the rightness of their actions than Victimizers. Such persons can come up with an endless assortment of explanations to account for their misdeeds.

Rationalization. Rationalizations are plausible but irrelevant reasons to excuse antisocial behavior. The Victimizer misbehaved only because someone else made him or her do it. A person insulted the Victimizer, for example, which is why he or she beat the person half to death. As to why the Victimizer "borrowed" someone's car, well, its owner left it unlocked and running and thus put an irresistible temptation in the Victimizer's path, a "temptation no one could resist."

Ignorance. The Victimizer may also claim ignorance—he or she did not know that the behavior was wrong or inappropriate. When, for example, she used her boyfriend's credit card without permission to buy herself a new wardrobe—signing his name of course—she "assumed" that he would approve. Now, having spent several thousand dollars, she is flabbergasted over why he is angry, and she professes great embarrassment—though not enough to return the clothes.

Minimization. Often the Victimizer doesn't understand why you, or anyone else, would want to make such a "big deal" out of whatever it was that he or she did, which could have been anything from gambling away your life savings to walloping the daylights out of your new Irish setter—which he or she was "only trying to train."

Moral Debate. If all else fails, the Victimizer may simply deny that he or she did anything wrong.

As noted earlier, Victimizers are accomplished self-justifiers. If none of the excuses on this list work, they are sure to come up with others.

Psychology of the Victimizer

Although many people with a Victimizing style do not do physical harm to others, all Victimizers have the potential to explode. They demonstrate what missile experts call a "fast rise time": they are highly reactive and move quickly from docility to aggression. And when they do, they can be terrifying.

Victimizers try to make it impossible for anyone else to take advantage of them. And if they conclude that this has occurred, they become consumed with the notion of retaliation, which can turn them markedly dangerous, especially if they are at all paranoid. To the degree that Victimizers are suspicious, they will perceive slights and insults where these do not exist (for example, "Why were you looking at me like that?"), imagine the worst about others, and go to war with astonishing speed.

The Victimizer is frightened by tenderness and weakness because both have become associated with vulnerability and pain. Someone with this style therefore tends systematically to root softness out of other people through punishment. For the Victimizer, this has the happy consequence of increasing the distance from others and thereby reducing the probability of suffering harm or disappointment.

Victimizers do to others what they are afraid others will do to them, and in their eyes the best defense is always a good offense. Ironically, as the other person becomes weaker in the face of abuse, the Victimizer often becomes more aggressive. It is sometimes this growing weakness in the victim that fuels the escalation of violence in abusive relationships. The escalation is also accelerated by the major surge of adrenaline that the Victimizer routinely experiences when engaged in conflict. If forced to choose between fight and flight, the Victimizer attacks without hesitation.

○

Case 13.3

Whitaker is merciless to his wife, Janet. They have gone to see their pastor, but nothing has changed. He tells her she's stupid, makes fun of how she talks, and routinely yells at her when he comes home from work. When this happens, Janet begins to whimper, and the more she cries, the angrier he gets. It is as if her suffering spurs him on to further aggression. He always feels bad about what he's done—until the next time, when the cycle starts again.

○

Whitaker is a major-league verbal abuser. And the more Janet pouts and whimpers, the more she is going to get abused. Victimizers are sharks who become even more predatory when others bleed.

A Victimizer's dual aim is to keep others at bay and, if necessary, to punish their aggression. Victimizers are most at ease when on the attack, and although they can be warm and personable for short periods of time, they are unable to sustain this and invariably turn close relationships nasty.

Sexuality in the Victimizer can range from the mildly exotic to the flagrantly perverse. Many Victimizers are willing to do almost anything in the bedroom, or at least to push the envelope further than most people would. But instead of carrying on their activities *with* others (for example, spouses), they tend to do things *to* them. The Victimizer's sexual conduct can thus be both unusual and impersonal.

Victimizers carry around inside of them substantial reservoirs of pain, which they insulate themselves from with aggression. Rather than experiencing and working through the pain, which would require feeling vulnerable, they drain off the tension it produces by attacking and then making excuses for having done so. Often their aggression is directed toward someone other than the person who caused the pain in the first place, and so Victimizers also resort to the defense mechanism of displacement: taking things out on somebody else. They are also prone toward projection: they may perceive aggression where it doesn't exist, which greatly increases their reactivity to potential aggression in others.

The Victimizer is impulsive. It is, at times, as if he or she were an animal, with little forethought or self-control. This impulsivity goes hand in hand with an underdeveloped conscience, a core characteristic of the Victimizer, which makes many Victimizers capable of the most ruthless violence.

Victimizers vary tremendously in how violent they become. Some prefer simply to prey on others emotionally or financially. They can be verbally abusive and decidedly larcenous but refrain from doing physical harm. Others are cauldrons of rage who can turn homicidal in seconds.

I remember a retired navy Commander who was a patient at a rehabilitation facility where I worked in my early twenties. He made the mistake of attempting to break up a dice game near his ship while he was wearing civilian clothes instead of his uniform. One of the offended sailors dealt him a ferocious blow to the side of the head with a beer bottle. When I met the Commander, he had a one-inch indentation in his left temple, and his abstract reasoning capacities were impaired. That's the sort of wanton and unrelenting violence of which Victimizers are capable.

Like Humiliators (see Chapter Eleven), Victimizers can wrap their aggressiveness in a cloak of morality and become anything from a sociopathic clergyperson to a racial bigot. But unlike Humiliators, who are primarily interested in status, Victimizers derive gratification mostly from the infliction of suffering. They make excellent inquisitors and prison camp guards. Some people who use their Victimizing behaviors for a "noble" cause, such as fanatically ridding the congregation of all women with the hems of their skirts above the ankles, are in fact highly attracted to the very thing that they condemn, only they can't admit it, even to themselves. In such instances, they are using the defense mechanism of reaction formation: consciously experiencing the opposite of what one, on a deeper level, truly experiences. The more such a person is tempted, the more violently he or she will advance the cause, and woe to you if you get in the way or, worse, become suspect.

When others respond to them harshly, Victimizers may feel strangely reassured. They are most comforted when others attack and, in fact, tend to provoke such attacks, even when this results in their own injury. The Victimizer is most at ease when there is strife.

Victimizers in the Bible

The Bible is filled with Victimizers, beginning with Cain: "The Lord looked with favor on Abel and his offering, but on Cain and his offering he did not look with favor. So Cain was very angry. . . . Now Cain said to his brother Abel, 'Let's go out into the field.' And while they were in the field, Cain attacked his brother Abel and killed him" (Genesis 4:4–8, NIV).

As noted, Victimizers are prone to justify their predatory behavior. Jacob was himself a scoundrel, as evidenced by how he managed to obtain the birthright and blessing that rightfully belonged to his older brother, Esau (Genesis 25–27). But Laban made Jacob look like an amateur at the game of Victimizing: "'This is not done in our country. . . . We will give you the other [daughter] also in return for serving me another seven years.' . . . So Jacob . . . called Rachel and Leah . . . and said to them . . . , 'You know that I have served your father [Laban] with all my strength; yet your father has cheated me and changed my wages ten times'" (Genesis 29: 26–27; 31:4–6, NRSV).

While Delilah had multiple motives for what she did, there is a chilling callousness to her version of Victimizing: "[Delilah said to Samson,] 'How can you say, "I love you," when your heart is not with me?' . . . Finally after she had nagged him with her words day after day . . . he told her his whole secret. . . . She let him fall asleep in her lap . . . called a man . . . and had him shave off the seven locks [of hair]. . . . [Samson] began to weaken, and his strength left him" (Judges 16:15, NRSV).

And when it came to Victimizing, King Herod was among the best, because he had no scruples whatsoever: "When [the Magi from the east] had gone, an angel of the Lord appeared to Joseph in a dream. 'Get up,' he said, 'take the child and his mother and escape to Egypt. Stay there until I tell you, for Herod is going to search for the child to kill him'" (Matthew 2:13, NIV).

The Arrangement Sought

Victimizers seek out those who will take whatever punishment they dish out. They want others to shrink back psychologically but not physically. Victimizers need their victims to remain accessible and, in extreme cases, to experience so much pain that they curl up in a cocoon of despair. The accomplished Victimizer wants to see fear in the other person's eyes and still know that the arrangement will continue. How else can the Victimizer be assured of the opportunity to inflict more pain? There has to be a target available for the discharge of anger and rage and also for occasional exploitation (for example, stealing, defrauding, or cheating).

Because the Default Styles of Humiliator and Victimizer are neighbors on the circle (see Figure 6.10), they can blend into each other. It is therefore commonplace to find the Victimizer also engaging in a fair amount of demeaning and belittling. Similarly, there is no stone wall between the Default Styles of Scurrier (see Chapter Twelve) and Avoider (see Chapter Fourteen), and as a result people with either style may link up with the Victimizer. You will find that those who remain involved with Victimizers tend to use the tactics of both; that is, they tend to withdraw and rebel (as Avoiders do) but also to whine and appease (like Scurriers).

Victimizers sometimes attract people with a strong need to make contact with their own "shadow" sides, aspects of themselves that, until now, they have refused to acknowledge. These aspects usually have to do with forbidden impulses and may involve a certain fascination with sin (see Romans 7). Most of us have witnessed, at some time or other, a wholesome young woman who, despite having been raised in a strong Christian family, becomes strangely enamored of, and deeply involved with, a rogue or a scoundrel.

Due to their usual differences in size and strength, men physically abuse women more often than women abuse men. But assault and battery is not the only form of victimization. Verbal degradation can be as lethal to the soul as physical injury is to the body. A cold and critical spouse of either sex ("Can't you get a better job?" or "You're as fat as a horse") can inflict a massive amount of psychological and spiritual damage. There is, of course, sometimes a fine line between Humiliation (see Chapter Eleven) and Victimizing. The difference is that Victimizers are more intent on hurting you, while Humiliators are more intent on dominating you in an aggressive manner.

Payoffs for the Victimizer

Emotionally, the big payoff of the Victimizing style comes when Victimizers can indulge their need to hurt others and thus temporarily delude themselves into thinking that they are winning a private war with the cosmos. Adopting the posture of the renegade enables Victimizers to feel emotionally free. They declare, through their actions, that *they* do not have to follow the rules laid down by society and can, in this manner, become their own gods. Most important of all, they can bask in the false sense of security that comes from keeping people away.

The social rewards of the Victimizing style are modest because Victimizers tend to be outcasts. But they enjoy at least two advantages. The first is that unless they are overtly vicious, other people usually like them on initial contact. Victimizers are often *interesting* and therefore become the center of attention.

The second social advantage is power. Other people are usually reluctant to challenge or confront Victimizers because it is more or less clear that if they do, they'll get hurt. Victimizers show little restraint and are always ready to escalate conflicts; they are quick to resort to violence, whether verbal or physical, and everyone knows it. Contrary to what you might expect, some Victimizers rarely have to flex their muscles to get their way, and their lives, therefore, can be surprisingly and paradoxically free of combat. Street brawlers are a good example of this. They rarely get into fights because, on those rare occasions when they do, they show no mercy and ruthlessly inflict a great deal of unnecessary damage on people foolish enough to challenge their supremacy.

What the Victimizer Avoids

Victimizers rarely, if ever, believe that they are in the wrong. Regardless of what they say, they do not typically entertain such thoughts as "I'm sorry for what I did." Nor do they make conciliatory statements in the face of impending battles. They may voice sentiments of right and wrong, but remorse to them is largely unknown. Victimizers simply do not accept the idea that they are accountable for their actions or that they have any responsibility for what happens to other people as a result of their Victimizing behavior.

They avoid feelings of tenderness and, even as children, may react strongly against anything sentimental. Expressions of love, except in the service of manipulation (for example, seduction), feel alien to them. Victimizers are not disposed to experience fear either, and they become aggressive whenever it begins to afflict them. They avoid backing away from confrontation because doing so, to them, feels like weakness. Such people generally stay away from engaging in any behavior that reflects softness rather than toughness, vulnerability rather than strength, passivity rather than assertiveness, and affection rather than distance.

Finally, they do allow themselves to feel dependent and so will sometimes suffer rather than accept help. Forcing others to help—for example, pressuring an aging relative to dole out money—may be fine, but accepting aid from someone they do not dominate is threatening to them because it smacks of establishing an emotional connection (bonding).

What the Victimizer Trains You to Feel and Do

Once others get past whatever veneer of charm the Victimizer presents, they typically start to feel tense. And when they finally realize their vulnerability because of the Victimizer's readiness to hurt them, they become fearful and, as a result, may try to reason with him or her. They offer advice as to why the Victimizer should do this and not that. Such talk rarely does any good, however, and may make matters worse. The Victimizer's desire to injure and exploit are driven by anger (rage) and have nothing to do with reason.

When others discover that reason is getting them nowhere, they either attempt to end the relationship or take on the characteristics of an Avoider. They may at first pull back just a little and later move to an all-out retreat. People on whom Victimizers prey tend, as noted earlier, both to avoid and to scurry. Typically, they attempt initially to rebel, and to the extent that they express resentment and defiance they fuel the Victimizer's anger. Then they withdraw, detach, and try to escape. And when none of this works, they resort to placation and appeasement—in other words, to further submission (see Figures 6.2, 6.3, 6.4). Eventually, they crawl into a shell of detachment, insulation, and numbness in a desperate effort to wall off and protect themselves.

Although Victimizers train other individuals to cower, they provoke society at large to punish them. The social system does not back away from its fight with Victimizers and can be every bit as aggressive as they can—from suspending their driver's licenses to executing them. This is also what happens when Victimizers tangle with other Victimizers, such as in gang wars. People get hurt and sometimes killed.

When the Arrangement Breaks Down

If a woman, for example, becomes involved with a Victimizer and then discovers that he is explosive, she may try to back away. If all goes well, she may succeed in breaking off the relationship. Typically, this occurs only after several bouts of abuse have convinced her that the potential benefits of continuing in it are outweighed by the risks.

But some Victimizers become psychologically locked on and refuse to allow others to leave. These are the ones who become stalkers. They are dangerous and have demonstrated, time and again, that they can be lethal.

Life History

Most, though not all, Victimizers have themselves been victimized as children. Their adult conduct accomplishes two things.

First, it protects them from additional injury. It is difficult to hurt the feelings of someone who is angry or to physically injure someone who is ready to injure you first. Second, it gets back at the world for all that has gone wrong. Victimizers can symbolically even the score by hurting, sometimes destroying, anyone who resembles those who originally hurt them. People tend to do unto others what has been done unto them. Often Victimizers have been so emotionally damaged that they have little self-respect and view the world as filled with people who may further injure and berate them. But abuse alone is probably not enough to cause a person to develop the Victimizing style. In many cases, the Victimizer has also been punished for gentleness.

Such punishment is not always direct. It is not as if the parent waits for the child to say or feel something tender and then whacks him or her. The process is subtler. Just about any child will, from time to time, experience and express softness. He or she may try, for example, to cuddle up to a parent. If life within the family is chaotic and violent, such softening will usually be followed by getting hit or yelled at. Warmth will lead, even if coincidentally, to explosiveness. Moreover, if one of the parents detests or even hates the child—and this occurs more often than you might think— this parent will have a motive, albeit unconscious, for stamping out of the child all signs of love. This is because it is awkward and uncomfortable for most people to have someone they despise bond to them.

The typical Victimizer's parents have been poor role models, whom the Victimizer regards as ineffective, weak, and unloving. Victimizers commonly report that the home was an unpredictable war zone, that their parents were unable to mete out discipline in a sensible manner, and that they felt as if they were living in an asylum.

Intimacy and the Victimizer

There can be little or no intimacy with someone whose Victimizing style is extreme and inflexible. This is because, as we have seen, emotional closeness frightens the Victimizer, who will do everything possible to disrupt it. Regardless of how things look on the surface, Victimizers are emotionally terrified and are therefore, in one sense, emotional cowards—only I recommend that you refrain from saying this to them. They are running from the goblins of warmth and the specters of helplessness.

What is especially perverse about some Victimizers is that they will start an argument precisely when you begin to let down your guard and tenderness begins to develop. At the very moment when you conclude that the two of you are about to reach a wonderful new plateau of closeness— when you have finally been able to put out of your mind the last horrendous fight and are once again entering the hypnotic trance of trust—the Victimizer will pull the rug out from under you.

The typical Victimizer shows a decided lack of empathy and so simply cannot imagine what another person might be feeling. And even if the Victimizer can imagine it, he or she often doesn't care.

Spiritual and Moral Choices

A danger in analyzing the psychology of toxic Default Styles, especially this one, is that such analysis almost invites one to explain away all spiritual and moral frailty. This, of course, is exactly what the Victimizer wants: "I'm not responsible for what I do. Blame it on bad genes, inadequate parents, faulty education, lack of money, or anything else that strikes your fancy. It's my psychodynamics. Surely you understand that I have no control over them and therefore no accountability for anything they cause me to do." Yet to state that there are psychological causes for something—say, bad behavior—doesn't mean that such causes completely account for it.

Free will is surely limited. The real question here has to do with just how limited. Only God knows to what extent anyone's bad conduct is the result of free moral choice versus having been programmed by life to engage in it. Although, as humans, we will never be able fully to answer the question of accountability, it is important to bear in mind that human beings almost always have some degree of choice. If we blame everything a person does on something else, true accountability goes up in smoke. Two important points remain to be made.

First, we tend to regard faults in ourselves as temporary (accidental) and faults in others as permanent (dispositional). The bad thing I did yesterday was only because I had an off day, when I wasn't completely myself, but the bad thing you did was because you're by nature a terrible person. Christian charity suggests that even if we don't turn this inside out, we at least try to grant others the same measure of grace that we grant ourselves.

Second, even if a Victimizer is not responsible for his or her behavior, you still have a duty to protect yourself from mistreatment. A person's violent outbursts may be due to an undiagnosed brain tumor, but you must still exercise stewardship over your own life, the wonderful and precious gift that God has given you. There are occasions when a Christian ought to suffer for the Kingdom. Inviting or even allowing prolonged toxicity and chronic abuse is not ordinarily going to be one of them.

SELF-ASSESSMENT

To get a quick sense of how much you may rely on this Default Style, ask yourself the following questions. Although these questions do not constitute a test, they may give you a rough idea of where you stand. Please consult www.relationaldynamics.com for information about more sophisticated methods of assessment.

1. Are you quick to punish others, and when they get out of line do you show them little mercy?

2. Do others insist that you are quick to fly into a rage or to torment and abuse them?

3. Do you often cause others to suffer or writhe in physical or emotional pain?

ANTIDOTES TO TOXICITY

I am now going to provide you with two sets of suggestions. The first may help you reduce any tendency you find in yourself to operate in the Default Style we have discussed in this chapter. Before trying out any of these suggestions, it would be wise to read Part Four of this book, particularly Chapter Fifteen, on myths about behavior change. The second set of suggestions may help you respond more effectively to others who relate to you through this Default Style. These suggestions are of necessity general and therefore may not work with a specific individual. So use them wisely and judiciously, and above all do not apply them mechanically or put yourself in danger. Although people with certain interpersonal styles tend to be more troublesome and combative than those who rely on other styles, it is best to err on the side of caution. When in doubt, consult those with publicly sanctioned expertise in personality disorders, such as mental health professionals.

If You Tend Toward Victimizing . . .

Here are some suggestions that may help you reduce this tendency:

- Do whatever is necessary to ferret out and let go of the anger within. There is no question that people have failed you. Nor is there any doubt that they have hurt you. They did the same to Jesus, only worse. Get on your knees and ask God to remove from your heart whatever bitterness, even fury, you feel. It may take years for this to occur, but there's no time like the present to get started.

- Avail yourself of outside help. We all need it. No one can make it in life alone. Talk to a pastor. See a therapist. Consult a counselor. If it takes you the rest of your life to work through your angry feelings, so be it. What better way could you spend your time and energy? Don't lie to yourself about the anger. It's there. Just do something constructive about it.

- Reckon with God's command to love your neighbor as yourself. Not to love your neighbor is to refuse to love Christ. Get with the program!

○ Learn to reframe (reinterpret) emotional frustrations as intellectual puzzles to solve. When you become angry, turn the situation you face into a game. Ask yourself what might be best to do now.

○ Recruit Anchors to help you (see Chapter Sixteen).

How to Respond to Victimizing

If someone else is relating to you through Victimizing, here are some potential countermeasures:

○ Avoid defiance or resentful rebellion. Both of these are likely only to increase the passion of the Victimizer.

○ Do not play into the abuser-repentance paradigm (pattern). If someone abuses you and then voices remorse, over and over, something is wrong. And if you accept apologies each time, you are an integral part of what's wrong.

○ Use social systems to thwart further abuse. This can be anything from your church group to the police. I have often told women that if a man hits them, once is one time too many. Far too many people are slow to take action in the face of victimization. The time to do something about it is the first time it happens, not the umpteenth. Recognize that of all eight types of Default Styles, and by implication types of people that we have considered, the Victimizer is the most likely to hurt you. Taking action can therefore be risky. But not taking action can be riskier still. Use your own judgment. Listen to your instincts. Consult qualified advisers. And above all, don't be passive.

○ Trying to close off from a Victimizer is only likely to inflame the situation. This does not mean that you should stay around someone who is trying or threatening to hurt you. There is certainly merit in getting away, which is why "safe houses" exist for battered spouses. Just recognize that if you wall off emotionally and try to disengage psychologically while remaining physically present, you are likely to infuriate the Victimizer, who may have a strong need to *see* you suffer.

○ If you try to back away, a serious Victimizer may turn into a stalker. Such people are potentially dangerous, especially if they have a suspicious edge. Do not underestimate this. Ever.

○ Sometimes the best way to put an end to victimization is to meet it head on and, in the process, win the dominance struggle. This is almost impossible to do with a confirmed Victimizer, so don't try it unless you are relatively sure that you can win.

14

AVOIDING

WITHDRAWING AND REBELLING

Now the word of the Lord came to Jonah . . . saying, "Go at once to Nineveh . . . and cry out against it; for their wickedness has come up before me." But Jonah set out to flee. . . . Jonah prayed to the Lord his God from the belly of the fish . . . so Jonah set out and went to Nineveh . . . and cried out . . . and the people of Nineveh believed God. . . . When God saw what they did, how they turned from their evil ways, God changed his mind about the calamity that he had said he would bring upon them. . . . But this was very displeasing to Jonah.

—Jonah 1:1–3; 2:1; 3:3–5, 10; 4:1 [NRSV]

WHEREAS THE SCURRIER (see Chapter Twelve) primarily fears humiliation and other forms of emotional anguish, the Avoider is on guard against both physical and psychological injury. Most of all, Avoiders fear annihilation—being destroyed—and unconsciously believe that, if they allow others to get too close, this is the fate that awaits them. Their version of the Golden Rule is "I won't do unto you, and you certainly won't get the chance to do unto me either." It is important to keep in mind that, regardless of how gracious or innocent an Avoider may appear on the surface, the Avoiding style is fundamentally hostile and misanthropic: hateful, contemptuous, and distrustful.

I want to emphasize that we are not, in this chapter, referring to people who simply refuse to discuss interpersonal problems or who would not know how to express a feeling if one reared up and hit them in the face. Many men in our society have what I think of as emotional aphasia (a loss of the capacity to use or understand language). Although such incapacity can be troubling, even infuriating, by itself it does not make the person an Avoider. Jonah was, by this definition, not a full-blown Avoider, although he does illustrate some rather dramatic escape behavior.

The genuine Avoider does not want to transact with the world and prefers to lead an existence that does not require having to interact closely with people. The Avoiding style can perhaps be captured in the words "I will not!" Tending strongly toward the reclusive, the Avoider may turn into a fine wilderness explorer or forest ranger but does not make a good partner, friend, or spouse—except perhaps for those whose social skills and emotional capacities are similarly dwarfed and who therefore have little need for intimacy. Exhibit 14.1 presents the major characteristics of the Avoider.

Avoiders can be among the most frustrating people on earth. This is because they make it so difficult, if not impossible, to connect with them. They stubbornly refuse to engage, and on those rare occasions when they do, they interact in a sullen, sour, pessimistic, resentful, rebellious, and defiant manner. Avoiders are experts at inducing anger in other people, which is one reason why they are often victimized (see Figures 6.7 and 6.8).

While Avoiders may initially impress other people as having great depth, they do not connect on anything but a superficial level, talk mostly to themselves (inside their heads and, in some instances, overtly), and are either unable or unwilling to provide love. While some Avoiders are promiscuous and approach sex with a chilling objectivity, most either find it distasteful or, less commonly, transform it into something perverse. They may make frustrating spouses, border on the bizarre when it comes to deciding what is good for their children, and starve anyone who depends on them for nurturance. Avoiders are often failures who have trouble coping with everyday life and spend their time retreating into fantasy. They may be smart and creative but are nevertheless markedly inadequate.

It is crucial to keep in mind, when dealing with an Avoider, that he or she is as spiteful as the typical Victimizer (see Chapter Thirteen), a reality that is not obvious. Whereas the Victimizer expresses anger directly, actively, and dominantly, the Avoider expresses it indirectly, passively, and submissively. But the Avoider's anger is every bit as intense as the Victimizer's (see Figure 6.3). This is exceedingly difficult for most people to comprehend, especially if the Avoider smiles a lot and comes across, as is often

Exhibit 14.1. Profile of the Avoider.

Theme	"Leave me alone—I refuse to conform or to engage."
Self-Presentation	Shy, quiet, aloof; in a world of his or her own; off in space; different and eccentric; incapable of dealing effectively with practical matters; speaks little or in short, confusing, and hard-to-understand phrases; may be superficially pleasant and seem emotionally benign.
Additional Characteristics	Unconventional and defiant; loner; lost in a dream world; few if any close relationships; socially ill-at-ease and noticeably insecure; reluctant or unwilling to attend social functions or to entertain; may openly voice disdain for humanity; often heavily invested in the care of animals or in solitary hobbies; confused and chronically given to breakdowns in communication, such as getting directions wrong or misunderstanding verbal agreements; does not "close" and therefore fails to complete simple tasks or assignments; impoverished or bizarre mental life.
Responses Induced in Others	Coolness, criticism, humiliation, and victimization; in compassionate souls, may initially prompt a desire to protect, as if the Avoider were a wounded bird; some early fascination with the Avoider's "mysterious mind"; others who have naively chosen to rely on Avoiders for emotional sustenance may eventually go on the attack when they realize that Avoiders refuse to nourish them.
Healthier (Milder) Version	Functional skepticism and a refusal to be taken in by those majoring in flimflam; willing to resist trends and movements that have no substance but are simply stylish and in vogue; gives others constructive solitude and needed personal space.

the case, as soft, gentle, and harmless. The Avoider is anything but these things, and although most people will focus on his or her remoteness and reluctance to share thoughts and feelings, the Avoider's two most defining characteristics are cold impersonality and pervasive hostility.

Avoiders are quietly but rigidly rebellious. If their behavior were to be summed up in a single word, it would have to be *no*. As noted earlier, *no* is the most powerful word in the English language, and so the Avoider is more powerful than you might think. Avoiders refuse and reject just about everything, including people, norms, customs, and conventions, which makes them seem odd and typically invites ridicule.

Like the Scurrier (see Chapter Twelve), only more so, the Avoider frequently becomes a target of persecution, with people at large taking on the role of Victimizer. Society does not look kindly on those who spurn its values, and the Western world places a premium on extraversion. The core components of extraversion are warmth and assertiveness, and as you can see from Figure 6.3 the Avoider is low on both. Those who impress others as weird, cold, and preoccupied quickly define themselves as deviants who disdain the easy sociability that most people in our society value. Such sociability has to do with the ability to move smoothly among people, to engage comfortably in dialogue, and to hold one's own in a conversation.

When you are with a confirmed Avoider, you may feel strangely spaced out, as if what's going on around you were not real. This is an intriguing feature of the Avoider's effect on other people. His or her spaciness is psychologically contagious. Around an Avoider, you may soon feel as if you've lost your way. You may also find yourself intrigued with what you take to be the Avoider's subtlety, especially if you are psychologically minded or philosophically inclined. You may conclude that there's something deep going on here—and you would be right. But what's going on is the opposite of what you think.

The Avoider's noncommunicativeness, instead of reflecting depth of thought, mirrors the fact that he or she has few thoughts or that these thoughts are strange. If you become involved with such a person, you will eventually discover that what at first you found interesting turns out to be distressing. Try as you might, the Avoider has a fortress mentality and will not allow you into the castle of his or her mental life. And if the Avoider does share anything of substance, it will be to communicate a warped view of the world. This view defines other people as malicious, dangerous, and unworthy. It may come as a surprise to realize that the Avoider perceives you, since you are part of the human race, as a potential enemy and believes that your ability to nourish him or her is insignificant when compared to your capacity to do harm. The follow case illustrates the Avoider's basic style:

○

Case 14.1

Roy was a dental student when he met Beatrice, a biology major who loved animals but was uncomfortable around people. He was intrigued by her quietness and impressed by all the books she had read. No matter what he did, however, he could not get her to talk about any of them. She was bright and had the grades to prove it, but Beatrice was either unable or unwilling to engage in meaningful discussion. Her reticence to open up in this way only made her seem more mysterious and challenging. A few months after they started dating, Roy concluded that Beatrice had been emotionally injured as a child and therefore needed someone to treat her with patience and kindness. This he was able to do for quite a while—well into their marriage—but eventually his emotional needs caught up with him. Roy began to resent how one-sided their relationship seemed and how much he did for Beatrice, who did almost nothing for him. She refused to do the laundry or clean the house, and when their first child was born it was Roy who got up in the middle of the night to warm a bottle and feed the baby. Nor would Beatrice attend social functions, not even parties with his fellow dental students. They have never once invited another couple for dinner.

○

No matter what, Beatrice refuses to engage. She will give very little, if anything, to Roy emotionally. There will be no real interpersonal communication and therefore little communion between them. Notice that this has nothing to do with a lack of intelligence. Beatrice seems to be smart in the usual sense. It does, however, have a great deal to do with the person's general stance toward humankind.

The Avoider's Script

The Avoider's motif is to keep others so far away emotionally that they could not possibly cause pain or injury. Any kind of warmth or closeness brings acute discomfort and, if prolonged, an anxiety attack. The distance that the Avoider establishes allows him or her to refuse the obligations that routinely come with social relationships. Thus the Avoider, and only the Avoider, decides what he or she will do and when he or she will do it, whether "it" refers to writing a check, taking out the trash, or having sexual relations with a spouse.

This arm's-length style prevents others from meddling in the Avoider's life or interfering with the Avoider's freedom. And so, more than most of us, the Avoider can be his or her own person. This need for self-determination is massive because lurking at the edges of the Avoider's consciousness is a horrendous fear of being engulfed. To become close to another person would be, for the Avoider, to cease to exist as an individual. Similarly, to give emotionally to the other would not enrich but deplete the Avoider. The other's gain would be his or her loss. Such giving would also aggravate the Avoider's interpersonal claustrophobia. The Avoider's style of life ensures that he or she cannot develop soft or tender feelings, which, if left unchecked, might lead the Avoider to do something impulsive, such as opening up and becoming vulnerable. Why take the chance when you don't find much in people that you like?

---

o

Case 14.2

Regardless of what Gretchen tried, she could not convince Keith to discuss their marital problems. It seemed to her that the more she asked him to talk, the quieter he became. "Don't you care?" she would ask in desperation. "Yeah," he'd say. "Is that all?" she would follow up. "What else do you want me to say?" Keith would counter. And so it went until, utterly exasperated, she insisted that they see a marriage therapist. When the therapist asked what had prompted them to seek consultation, Gretchen poured out her agony for twenty minutes, ending with "He sometimes goes to the store and comes home hours later with no explanation. And when he finally does get home, he goes into the garage and works on his models. We sit for hours, and he doesn't say a word. I can't even pick a good fight with him. I'd like some romance in my life. Sex is mechanical. We don't talk; we just go into the bedroom." The therapist turned to Keith and said, "Your wife has a lot of feelings." After a long minute of silence, Keith answered, "Guess so." And so it went, for the rest of the hour. Keith had little to say, and Gretchen continued to writhe in pain.

---

o

It is worth noting that this is another example of the Pursuer-Avoider paradigm that we discussed in Chapter Nine. The only way out of this impasse—a way that is by no means certain in this case—is for Gretchen to reverse the pattern, to back away and try to turn Keith into the Pursuer.

Benefits of the Behavior

Because they have a unique capacity for objectivity, Avoiders make good critics. They are relatively uninfluenced by personal loyalties and so can be counted on to render dispassionate judgments in art or science, for example. This is also, in part, what makes them good artists and scientists themselves. Their existence is built around insulating themselves from other people, and as a result they can demonstrate an unusual amount of independence and resistance to public opinion. While it is primarily the Controllers (see Chapter Seven) who move civilization, it is sometimes the Avoiders, working by themselves, who provide the Controllers with the innovations to do so.

Avoiders also have other virtues. Because they are by nature skeptical, it is not easy to dupe them, and they show an uncanny ability to detect duplicity, hypocrisy, and manipulation. They are capable of noticing the foibles and follies that the rest of us miss, especially in the areas of customs and conventions. And because they expect little from the world, other than to be left alone, they can prove enormously resilient in the face of social adversity. Even if they cannot always manage to clean their homes or balance a checkbook, they will often persevere in their chosen specialty (for example, art, math, or science) long after others have thrown up their hands in despair.

Justifications for the Style

When challenged about their emotional inaccessibility, Avoiders often do what they have done all along, which is to refuse to engage. If pushed enough, they may fall back on one or more of the following justifications for their detachment:

Take it or leave it. This hard-boiled response usually assumes the form of "That's just the way I am, and I can't change it." What is missing, of course, is the unspoken statement, "I don't want to change." At root, it means, "That's just tough—like it or lump it."

Everyone's different. The unexpressed premise here is that there is absolutely nothing wrong with withholding or refusing to relate to other people emotionally. It's all a matter of individual preferences, and no value judgment should be attached to these preferences. Taken to extremes, such reasoning could be stretched to justify the actions of Genghis Khan or Adolf Hitler.

I'm doing the best I can. This attempt at justification subtly shifts the responsibility away from the individual and blames it on genes, development, lack of opportunity, environment, or what-have-you. What it really means is, "I don't intend to do anything differently."

Your demands are harsh, unreasonable, and excessive. This accusation puts the focus on the other person, thus moving it away from the Avoider, and suggests that there is something psychologically or morally wrong with wanting to be nurtured. It is not the Avoider who has the problem but the other person.

All of these defenses are exactly that: defenses. There is little honesty in them, little coming to terms with the person's anger at the human race.

Psychology of the Avoider

Avoiders are negative, pessimistic, and cynical and consequently tend to magnify whatever aggression, hostility, or duplicity they perceive. They craft their lives around detachment, resistance, and resentment and are ever on their guard, lest someone dangerous move in on them. Avoiders strive to retain emotional disconnectedness and thus autonomy. They are intentionally (strategically) indifferent to the opinions of others, reject most social customs and conventions, and are stubbornly resistant to going along with anyone else's program, regardless of what it might be. Such rebelliousness lies close to the surface and can be made overt by pressing Avoiders to conform. If and when you try this, you may find out that someone you thought was harmless turns out to have fangs like a Siberian tiger.

Because the Avoider is a social outcast who may be ostracized and ridiculed, the Avoider is acutely attuned to menacing behavior. He or she has a superb, if overly sensitive, detection apparatus for picking up criticism, hostility, and rejection. Such sensitivity is heightened by the large amount of resentment that Avoiders carry around within. They suffer as much from resentment as Scurriers do—sometimes even more—and are filled with suppressed anger and sometimes rage.

There is a tragic sadness to this rage, which is often self-directed. Avoiders loathe who and what they are almost as much as they loathe other people. Unlike Victimizers, who primarily turn their anger outward, Avoiders aim it at both themselves and others. The average Avoider is bitter, dissatisfied, unhappy, frustrated, jaded, and convinced by experience that people cannot be trusted. If the Avoider has married, he or she is routinely disappointed in the spouse, whom the Avoider typically perceives as having betrayed him or her. The spouse is usually even more disappointed because of how little emotional nurturance has come with the marriage.

Psychologists use the term *autism* to refer to the condition of living in a world of one's own making. The autistic individual is self-absorbed and trapped in daydreams, fantasies, delusions (fixed bizarre beliefs) or, in extreme cases, hallucinations (perceiving things that aren't there, such as voices). While all-out autism signifies a profound mental disorder, all of us are at least a little autistic. We occasionally believe things that aren't true, draw conclusions that are ill-founded, and misperceive how others act toward us.

Communication with other people is the antidote to such autism. Without the corrections that come as a result of sharing thoughts and feelings with others, autism grows. This is precisely what happens to the Avoider. Because he or she is so cut off from significant person-to-person communication, the Avoider thinks strange thoughts and does odd things. The Avoider may, for example, fill the front yard with used automobile tires in the belief that someday these will be worth money. Or the Avoider may acquire yet another animal when he or she can barely afford to feed the ones already in the house. Through all of this, the message the Avoider sends is "I'm different."

The psychology of the Avoider is based on the premise that, to avoid injury, he or she must keep other people from getting close. This allows the Avoider to focus on himself or herself, which is the essence of narcissism. Although the Humiliator and the Victimizer are both overt in their self-centeredness, the Avoider is subtler in the expression of narcissism. In Cases 14.1 and 14.2, how could Roy accuse Beatrice or Gretchen accuse Keith of "narcissism"? Yet both Beatrice and Keith were so self-absorbed that, in effect, they cared little for what was good for their partners.

When the Avoider provokes ridicule or other forms of aggression from others, this has the perverse benefit of confirming his or her distrust of people. We are all comforted when our beliefs are supported. There is an insidious process at work here. Often the Avoider continues to act weirdly in the hope that either of two opposite things will happen. And either way, the Avoider wins.

If, on the one hand, in response to his or her strangeness, other people increasingly victimize the Avoider, the Avoider paradoxically wins by losing. He or she can enjoy the comfort that comes from being able to predict that the world will deem him or her unlovable. Losing is, in this way, winning.

If, on the other hand, the Avoider actually manages to find someone— some rare human being—who will love and accept the Avoider as he or she is, the Avoider wins also. He or she will not, however, be able to stand the love—all that bright sunlight!—and will only feel comforted when he or she is, once again, at odds with humanity. And so the Avoider will sabotage the relationship.

The principal defense mechanisms used by the Avoider are depersonalization, alienation, and isolation. Depersonalization and alienation involve the sense that one is not quite oneself and that the surrounding world is not quite real. The Avoider feels like a spectator, uninvolved in his or her own actions. Isolation is the separation of emotion from ideas and, like depersonalization, is closely related to the detachment on which the Avoider relies.

Avoiders in the Bible

In looking through the Bible for Avoiders, it is important to remember that Avoiders are, first and foremost, rebels. Their rebellion is passive and submissive, rather than active and dominant, but it is rebellion nonetheless. Anyone in scripture, therefore, who turns away from God, especially with angry defiance, is relying on the Avoiding style. A case could be made that Avoiding is the essence of refusing to come to faith in a God who has made Himself known.

Those who instigated the crucifixion of Jesus were, in this sense, Avoiders, although certainly they were also Victimizers; note that these two Default Styles are next to each other in Figure 6.4. So were the many people to whom Paul refers, throughout his epistles, as resisting the Gospel and sometimes as advancing a substitute one of their own. And Pilate's infamous question, "What is truth?" (John 18:38), is another example of refusing to engage—which is the essence of this Default Style.

The Arrangement Sought

The Avoider often attracts, and is attracted by, those who combine dominance with aggression—Victimizers and Humiliators. This is partly because Avoiders are most comfortable in relationships that guarantee impersonality and distance and confirm their worldview. Nothing, of course, achieves these results as quickly or as dramatically as physical or psychological aggression, arenas in which Victimizers and Humiliators are accomplished performers.

Avoiders also form relationships with managerial people, whether these are outright Controllers or simply Leaders (see Figure 6.9). Such people are often from the health care professions and are smitten with the naïve possibility of healing the Avoider through patience, love, and understanding. It is the strength within such persons that attracts the Avoider. But it is almost certain that the Avoider will eventually move these Good Samaritans to the left side of Figure 6.2. Anyone with even a minimal need for intimacy will find the Avoider's rebellious detachment punishing. In such cases, the Avoider, who is ordinarily the victim, turns out ironically to be the persecutor.

Recall that the Avoiding style is fundamentally hostile. If you examine Figure 6.3, you will see that it is even more saturated with "against" sentiments than the Humiliating style. Avoiders actually seek out and link up with people they can provoke and who may even poignantly validate their misanthropic view of the world by injuring them.

Payoffs for the Avoider

You cannot hurt the feelings of a person who doesn't care, and so one benefit of the Avoider's detachment is immunity from emotional pain. You cannot emotionally injure someone who has turned numb. With the Avoiding style also comes the pleasure of refusing to allow others to intrude on one's life and thus use up one's time and energy. There is also the perverse satisfaction of defiance and rebellion that comes from rejecting society's rules.

By adopting an Avoiding style, one can become an undercover social criminal and largely get away with it. Such a posture is especially appealing if you view society as the embodiment of, and symbol for, all that has hurt you in the past. By thumbing your nose at society, however covertly, you can "get even" for everything anyone ever did to you.

There are few social rewards that derive from the Avoiding Default Style because, as we have discussed, this way of life runs counter to some of society's most cherished values. If, however, the Avoider achieves eminence in a particular field—say, literature or physics—society may overlook his or her idiosyncrasies.

What the Avoider Avoids

There are many ideas that, if the Avoider embraced them, would threaten to undermine his or her entire project of existence. Any idea that expresses or implies that human beings are, to a significant degree, benevolent or trustworthy will be threatening, and the Avoider will go to great lengths to avoid thinking it. The Avoider *must* continue to believe that people are dangerous and despicable in order to justify a fundamental loathing of them. With respect to the cosmos at large, the Avoider is inclined to maintain that it is cruel, impersonal, and the result of ice-cold random forces that show no mercy to anything or anybody.

The Avoider steers clear not only of people but of most tender sentiments as well. For the Avoider, love is psychologically tied to pain. The Avoider is fearful of closeness because it signals impending injury. So do all emotions that might prompt the Avoider to trust another person fully. Like the Victimizer, the Avoider finds emotional softness frightening and therefore aversive. Note the folly of trying to fix this with warmth and affection. The more you love an Avoider, the more frightened the Avoider becomes.

It is not the Avoider's way to express much of his or her inner self, least of all highly personal thoughts and feelings. The Avoider is not, for example, likely to tell you about his or her dreams. Nor will the Avoider make statements that convey optimism. He or she avoids expressing positive sentiments, offers precious little in the way of personal affirmation, and verbalizes love and commitment only with great effort.

The Avoider refuses to act sociably unless he or she is certain of being among people who will keep their distances. While the Avoider may have friends, these are likely to be odd birds themselves and to make little or no demands on the Avoider for closeness. Because the Avoider is a loner, he or she shies away from serving on committees, which is a good thing, because Avoiders are not always conscientious or reliable. And while the Avoider may be capable of sexuality, it will be more or less mechanical, since the Avoider is motivated to avoid the vulnerability that comes with an open exchange of feelings.

What the Avoider Trains You to Feel and Do

Avoiders tend to provoke criticism, frustration, and anger in others. Through their general incompetence and reluctance to improve their day-to-day practical performance, they train others, first to become irritated and exasperated, then to become impatient and intolerant of their ineptness, and finally to hold them in the same sort of contempt that they hold the rest of world. Others will conclude that they cannot rely on the Avoider, who may let them down and fail to come through at important moments. Other people will thus judge the Avoider as untrustworthy. This, of course, is precisely what the Avoider accuses *them* of being.

The Avoider will almost always be rejected and marginalized. And like the Scurrier, the Avoider may be disparaged, ridiculed, and made to writhe in pain. Others will do to the Avoider exactly what the Avoider has always feared—and what the Avoider's withholding and resentful manner has incited them to do. Social crimes provoke social punishments and, in this instance, mounting victimization. Many Avoiders are both detached and depressed, and they induce others to treat them in ways that deepen their depression.

When the Arrangement Breaks Down

Relationships with Avoiders often break down, and when they do, the end can be stormy. When the hurricane finally hits, the Avoider will be massively aggrieved, fail to understand what he or she did wrong, and become even more embittered. The Avoider will allege that the other person is unreasonable, unloving, and self-centered, thinking only of his or her own emotional needs.

Some of the most abusive and most enduring relationships on earth exist between Avoiders and Victimizers, especially when they are, respectively, masochistic and sadistic. However much the Avoider may protest and complain, he or she *needs* to suffer. And however much the Victimizer may repent of dishing out abuse and regale the world with heartfelt outpourings of remorse, he or she *needs* to cause suffering. Should the needs of either change, the relationship will become destabilized. It may appear to be less stormy, and such indeed may be the case, but it will also be less enduring. Some people require storms to make the voyage interesting.

Life History

It is almost always the case that people with strong Avoiding styles have suffered devastating rejection by parents or other caregivers. The Avoider's needs for love and tenderness have been frustrated to such an extent that he or she has given up all hope of finding nurturance. And since the Avoider has never been given nurturance, he or she does not know how to provide it for others. Even if the Avoider did know how to nurture, he or she would not want to. The Avoider is just too filled with pain and resentment.

○

Case 14.3

Claudette came to America, at the age of eight, from France with her mother, who immediately put her into a boarding school run by a stern religious order. The nuns at her new academy were as scholastically demanding as they were emotionally austere. Although Claudette was allowed to go home on weekends, she rarely did. By the time she was twelve, she had developed a passionate interest in zoology and botany but was largely unable to express affection. Other people would sometimes describe her as stiff or distant. She married a man with promise, but the relationship was strained from the beginning. Claudette found him too emotionally demanding, and he, in turn, found her cold and unloving.

○

This is a relationship with a poor prognosis because it would be difficult for Claudette, in any sudden way, to become comfortable with emotions and difficult for her husband to live without emotional contact. But if she sees what's missing in her life and truly wants to change it, she might be able to do so with consistent effort (see the suggestions at the end of the chapter).

I have pointed several times to the Avoider's tendency to experience tenderness as painful, a characteristic that the Avoider shares with the Victimizer. Because this characteristic is so central to the psychology of both, I want to describe how it develops.

If your needs for gentleness are routinely ignored or punished, you come to expect that this will always happen. And so whenever you begin to feel tenderness, you will be inclined to stiffen and to behave in a defensive or threatening manner. Such behavior, when expressed toward people who might otherwise be kind, induces them to *confirm* your expectations. They will not like you and will not treat you kindly. Psychologists call this malevolent (hateful) transformation, a term coined by Harry Stack Sullivan; what most people experience as nourishing (tenderness) is experienced as toxic.

This sometimes occurs when the parents are strongly narcissistic and so self-absorbed that they scarcely notice the child. No matter what he or she tries, the child is not going to get his or her needs for tenderness and intimacy met. The child may even be chided, if not ridiculed, for having them in the first place. It is easy to imagine this happening in show business families, and it sometimes does, but the parents do not have to be performers for the child to experience profound emotional neglect. The message communicated to the child is something akin to "Your feelings don't matter," often coupled with "but mine do."

In the history of many Avoiders, as with Victimizers, there has been both emotional and physical abuse. And frequently, there has also been a fair amount of "double binding": placing the child in a position in which the child loses no matter what he or she does. The classic example of a double bind is the child who does not know how to act toward the mother. If the child fails to hug her, she will say, "Don't you love your mother . . . after all I've gone through?" If, however, the child takes the initiative and hugs her, she may tighten up and refuse to embrace the child. Not all instances of double binds are as dramatic, but whatever their natures they all have a way of teaching the child to fear closeness and eventually to hate people for not having provided it when it was most needed.

Intimacy and the Avoider

The Avoider, more than any other type of person except the Victimizer, has no interest in emotional closeness and therefore no interest in intimacy. The Avoider may actually think that he or she wants intimacy and may lead you to think so too, but when put to the test it is never intimacy that the Avoider desires. The Avoider cannot tolerate it.

However much the Avoider may say that he or she would like nothing more than to find someone with whom to share a gentle, serene, and tender life, what the Avoider actually wants is for the other person to remain at a safe distance. The Avoider, at the most, wants someone to "be there" and perhaps take care of the practical things in life—and sometimes doesn't even want that. The key requirement is that the other person make no emotional or physical demands on the Avoider; in this sense, the Avoider wants a sort of preadolescent relationship, if even that. And how could it be any other way? The Avoider's capacity for intimacy is as undeveloped as the refrigeration industry at the North Pole.

Spiritual and Moral Choices

As I have stressed throughout this book, we always have at least some degree of choice. It is hard for me, therefore, to excuse an extreme Avoiding style on the basis of upbringing. Although, as we have seen, certain families routinely punish all needs for tenderness in the child, Christians are called to love others, and we cannot do this if we harbor in our hearts a hatred for humankind. Perfect love casts out fear. There is a pronounced coldness to the Avoider that, in my view, is the antithesis of Christian charity. And as with the Victimizer, there is ruthlessness. I have seen Avoiders do some terrible things to their children and then express little or no remorse. There are many ways to kill the spirit, and emotional starvation is one of them.

SELF-ASSESSMENT

To get a quick sense of how much you may rely on this Default Style, ask yourself the following questions. Although these questions do not constitute a test, they may give you a rough idea of where you stand. Please consult www.relationaldynamics.com for information about more sophisticated methods of assessment.

1. Do you find, in general, that you resent other people and what they stand for?

2. Do you shy away from close relationships because others seem likely to hurt you?

3. Would people describe you as detached, withdrawn, and hard to connect with?

ANTIDOTES TO TOXICITY

I am now going to provide you with two sets of suggestions. The first may help you reduce any tendency you find in yourself to operate in the Default Style we have discussed in this chapter. Before trying out any of these suggestions, it would be wise to read Part Four of this book, particularly Chapter Fifteen, on myths about behavior change. The second set of suggestions may help you respond more effectively to others who relate to you through this Default Style. These suggestions are of necessity general and therefore may not work with a specific individual. So use them wisely and judiciously, and above all do not apply them mechanically or put yourself in danger. Although people with certain interpersonal styles tend to be more troublesome and combative than those who rely on other styles, it is best to err on the side of caution. When in doubt, consult those with publicly sanctioned expertise in personality disorders, such as mental health professionals.

If You Tend Toward Avoiding . . .

Here are some suggestions that may help you reduce this tendency:

○ Avoiding and rebelling are closely related, so if you find yourself disengaging from people, ask yourself what it is that you're rebelling against.

○ Come to terms with the fact that silent rebellion is more hostile than it seems. Other people may look on avoidance of human involvement as a simple life preference, but it is almost always more than that. The Default Style of Avoidance is fundamentally misanthropic—antagonistic toward people.

○ Own up to your obligation as a Christian to engage. Involvement with other people is not optional. It is not as if God is saying take it or leave it. We have a profound spiritual and moral obligation to our neighbor—and that means everybody.

○ Understand, also, that avoidance is among the most powerful of interpersonal weapons. It makes use of contact control, of refusing to allow the other person an audience. You may be present physically but not emotionally. And this is sometimes worse than actually leaving. There is little in life that is more punishing that being with someone who, no matter what, will not engage or, if contact is established, will be hostile.

○ Monitor and try to rid yourself of passive aggression. If you are angry, admit it. As much as you can, express your resentments so that you don't carry them around inside of you, as a seething cauldron of unexpressed rage.

○ Recruit Anchors to help you (see Chapter Sixteen).

How to Respond to Avoiding

If someone else is relating to you through Avoiding, here are some potential countermeasures:

○ When you find that another person is avoiding you in a hostile manner, especially if expressing defiance and rebelliousness, the natural tendency is to punish the person. Don't, for that is not what God called you to do in Christ. As much as such a person might beg you to victimize him or her, resist the temptation.

○ Acknowledge that people who are committed Avoiders—those who routinely will not engage and express little emotion—are often a lot more psychologically troubled than you might at first think. Make allowances for this. Such people are emotionally crippled.

○ Recognize also the level of anger that sometimes underlies Avoiding. It can be considerable. Avoiders are passively rebellious people. They are often silently full of rage and have no use for people who might hurt them, which means just about anyone with whom they have to interact closely.

○ Try not to take it personally when an Avoider refuses to engage. Although it may be difficult not to personalize the aloofness of the Avoider, unless you can achieve this, you are likely to find yourself locked in mortal combat with a person who will not come out and fight fairly. Such a person is more inclined to throw boiling oil on you from above and then run away before you can look up to see who did it.

PART FOUR

TOWARD RELATIONAL HEALTH AND HOLINESS

THESE FINAL THREE CHAPTERS are intended to help you change behavior, in yourself or others. Chapter Fifteen briefly presents three myths about behavior change that have caused no end of misery to countless people. It is important to know what these are and, as much as possible, to avoid buying into them. Chapter Sixteen, which is considerably longer, presents nine strategies that you can use to increase your effectiveness. And the very brief Chapter Seventeen outlines some principles to keep in mind if you want to change the interpersonal behavior of another person.

15

THREE MYTHS ABOUT
BEHAVIOR CHANGE

*For the foolishness of God is wiser than man's wisdom, and the
weakness of God is stronger than man's strength.*

—1 Corinthians 1:25 [NIV]

BEFORE ADDRESSING THE SUBJECT of how to change behavior, either
your own or someone else's, I want to discuss in this short chapter how
behavior does *not* change. We all live in a society that bombards us, constantly, with one or another version of the three myths that we are about
to consider, which is why it is important to discuss them. These myths represent examples of how human wisdom—what we sometimes call common sense—can lead people astray.

Coming to faith in God through Christ can make an enormous difference in a person's life. Such a conversion (turning around) is about the
only thing, short of a major catastrophe or being marooned on an island,
that is likely to change us radically. I would therefore not regard as impossible *any* change in a person that might come about, in the power of
the Holy Spirit, as a product of transformation in Christ. But just as coming to faith does not guarantee physical health, neither does it guarantee
emotional health or the perfection of one's personality. Many times, we
have to strive for both of these, day by day, asking God for insight and
guidance: "If any of you is lacking in wisdom, ask God, who gives all
generously and ungrudgingly, and it will be given you" (James 1:5,
NRSV).

Many people cling steadfastly to naïve beliefs about how people change. Most of these beliefs are more or less harmless. Some young men, for example, believe that if they pump iron five times a week, they will automatically get to date a supermodel. Some women believe that if they drag their inattentive husbands off to romantic movies, these husbands will take on the mannerisms of a leading man. Such beliefs may cost a little time and money, but that's about all. Other beliefs, however, are more destructive.

The myths I'm about to discuss frequently generate misery because they leave people frustrated and demoralized. Frustration is the psychological state that sets in when we are unable to reach a highly desired goal. The more important the goal is, the more frustrated we become. The resulting turmoil is the gateway to misery because frustration often leads to anger, and we sometimes turn this anger on ourselves. Consider how disgusted you may become when you do not lose weight, manage your money better, or turn off the television. None of these may be a problem for you, but if not, something else probably is. We can experience the same sort of frustration and anger when we are trying to get others to change. And when they don't, we may be tempted to punish them. Instead of going about the business of change sensibly, we draw nasty conclusions, such as "He's lazy and just doesn't care."

Myth 1: Change Is Fast and Easy

As I've suggested, only two things bring about significant change in human personality. One is a dramatic life event that shakes an individual's foundations. This could be the loss of a loved one, a civil catastrophe such as losing one's possessions in a flood or a fire, or enduring the horrors of a prison camp. Such experiences are characteristically traumatic and cause a person to reevaluate his or her entire system of values.

The other cause of major personality change is Christian conversion and regeneration. Some people undergo spiritual transformations that fundamentally alter who they are and how they think. I know a man who, had he not come to faith in Christ many years ago, would almost certainly be serving a life sentence in prison. But God changed him, and he is indeed a new creation (2 Corinthians 5:17). Combative people *do* occasionally become gracious. Stingy people become generous. Selfish people become altruistic.

Yet as miraculous as new life in Christ can be, it is not necessarily going to change everything. The need to continue to develop ourselves, in cooperation with God's Spirit, is perhaps why Paul wrote this: "Therefore . . .

continue to work out your salvation with fear and trembling, for it is God who works in you" (Philippians 2:12–13, NIV).

You *can* change your behavior and, if you want, your personality. But you will probably not be able to do it in a weekend. Nor are you likely to be able to do it without help. Changing other people's behavior can be even harder. And if they do not want to behave in new and different ways, you may not be able to change them at all. As we noted in Part One, God has given all of us free will. Because we usually need others to help us change (see Chapter Sixteen), fellowship is both an essential and a powerful source of assistance.

The notion that we need help is not always pleasant. Neither is the idea that we have to change in the first place. Who among us really wants to face up to either of these realities? As for accomplishing significant change in a weekend, forget it. It took you decades to become the person you are. You have practiced your behaviors, good or bad, every day, incorporating them into your cells. There is instant-this and instant-that in the fast-food aisles of the supermarket, but there isn't any instant psychological change or maturity.

Myth 2: Change Results from the Simple Application of Willpower

We sometimes persecute ourselves for what we perceive to be a lack of willpower. Whenever we fail to achieve something we want, we tend to attribute this failure to an absence of fortitude. The reason we don't go to the gym three times a week, we say, is because we lack resolve. We don't read as many good books as we should for the same reason. Come to think of it, it must be deficient willpower that causes us to waste so much time—and perhaps why we spend too much money.

We draw the same conclusions about others. Harriet subscribes to too many magazines because she doesn't have the self-discipline to say no. Dick spends too much of his paycheck on recreation because he's too weak to resist. Sarah lets Sonny push her around because she doesn't have the gumption to put a stop to it.

The main problem with blaming our failings on lack of willpower is that, in doing so, we lose sight of the fact that willpower itself is a set of learned behaviors and a deeply ingrained set at that. Like all other behavior patterns that have been with a person for a long time, willpower resists change. It is not as if people can double or triple their willpower simply by deciding to do so.

In a life-threatening situation, such as getting caught in a blizzard, almost anyone will demonstrate extraordinary willpower, stemming from the desire to survive. In everyday life, however, when we face no lethal threats, willpower can turn to mush. A halfhearted jogger doesn't turn into a committed runner simply by deciding to try harder. Nor does the adolescent with a history of academic failure transform, on the spot, into a scholar because his father or mother delivers a lecture about the virtues of education. Strength of will comes partly from reinforced practice over a long period of time.

Consider the weight control industry. Millions of people spend their lives jumping on and off bathroom scales. They are elated if they lose a pound and discouraged, sometimes devastated, if they gain one. Off they go to diet doctors, fat farms, and motivational speakers, coughing up billions of dollars annually. They realize, on one hand, that willpower alone isn't the answer, which is why they seek outside help. On the other hand, they often persecute themselves for not having the willpower to lose weight.

Think also about the millions of individuals who misuse credit or purchase goods and services that they can ill afford. People who buy on impulse, which means all of us at one time or another, are not much helped by speeches about their lack of financial self-discipline. Willpower is an elusive thing, a kind of ghost, which by itself doesn't take us very far down the road to growth or maturity.

People sometimes demonstrate what looks like a dramatic increase in willpower, but if you look closely enough you will usually discover that something deeper is going on. Problem drinkers, for example, will often turn their lives around when they have reached what psychologists refer to as a point of clarity. Contrary to popular wisdom, they don't have to hit bottom, but they do need to snap out of their stupor long enough to see what alcohol is doing to them. The awareness comes first, not the willpower.

Myth 3: Insight Guarantees Change

People have insights all the time that result in major redirections of their lives. Judy discovers that her husband has been seeing another woman and confronts him about it. Matt finds out that his boss has been sabotaging him and resigns to work in another department. These are just two examples of people gaining insight into other people and taking action. Insight, either into yourself or others, can trigger change and, as noted earlier, is sometimes essential for change to occur. But insight does not make change inevitable.

Even more important than the insight we gain about others is the insight we develop about ourselves:

- A clergyman faces up to the fact that he has been leading a double life and leaves the ministry.

- A college student admits that she doesn't love her fiancé and breaks off their engagement.

- A writer comes to terms with the fact that he will never be a famous novelist and decides to spend more time with his family.

Insight into others requires social smarts. This is the kind of intelligence that prevents us from remaining clueless around people. Social intelligence enables us to sense what's going on inside of others. It helps us read their moods as well as the effects we're having on them. And this in turn enables us to have influence and empathy. A different kind of intelligence is required to have insight into ourselves. It is the kind that fosters self-awareness. It has been called psychological or emotional intelligence. It enables us to know ourselves as we truly are. Let me add that if a Christian is truly communing with God's Spirit, instead of pretending, his or her self-awareness is bound to increase. Even if it does, however, insight alone will not necessarily change behavior. As we will explore in Chapter Sixteen, more is usually needed.

When psychoanalysis emerged in the early 1900s, Freud believed that self-insight automatically produced change. All a psychoanalyst had to do was help the patient become aware of what was going on in his or her unconscious. Within a few decades, it became clear that insight by itself was not necessarily curative. Psychoanalysts then began to talk about an insight phase of treatment and a working-through phase. The latter was when insight began to make a difference in the person's everyday life. Psychoanalysts also started to make a distinction between intellectual and emotional insight.

Both of these developments were ways to try to reconcile their faith in the sufficiency of insight with the discovery that insight was often not enough. Some psychoanalysts resorted to circular reasoning, a form of intellectual cheating. What changes behavior? Insight. What qualifies as insight? Whatever changes behavior. If the patient's behavior didn't change, he or she had not developed deep enough (emotional) insight. Or he or she had not yet reached the working-through phases of analysis.

Another version of the insight myth centers on education. If only people were better educated, they would make better choices and act more admirably. You may recognize this as a form of utopianism (see Chapter

One). While education certainly expands the mind, it does not necessarily bring about improvement in the soul. Some very well educated people in our society are monsters.

Corporate training directors receive hundreds of calls every day from supervisors who want to find a workshop that will magically fix Mary or Willie. Wise trainers know that sending a problem employee off to a weekend seminar, however excellent, is unlikely to do the job. Instead of reaching for their course catalogues, savvy trainers find out what the real problem is and then coach the supervisor on how best to address it, which often involves, for the first time, candidly discussing it with the employee.

"Know thyself" is sound advice. But knowing yourself may or may not change you. Nor will insight necessarily change another person. Many people understand themselves quite well but continue to be ineffective or pathological. They can tell you all about their psychodynamics—what they do and why they do it—but this doesn't change them one bit.

16

GETTING OUT OF
YOUR OWN WAY

I can do all things through him who strengthens me.

—Philippians 4:13 [NRSV]

THIS CHAPTER IS BASED on more than three decades of experience as a practicing psychotherapist, research psychologist, doctoral-level professor for clinical psychologists in training, and front-line management consultant to some of the nation's most prestigious corporations. I was also the founder of *Clinician's Research Digest,* now owned and published by the American Psychological Association, and the years I spent editing that publication enabled me to survey a vast amount of psychological literature. In the pages of this chapter, I will share the best of what I've learned about behavior change.

Much of what you will read here is hard-hitting. But I assume that if you've made it this far, you're not in the market for mollycoddling and would prefer straight talk. It does no one any good, in the long run, to water down what should be provided at full strength.

You will encounter the word *success* many times in our discussion. Keep in mind that as a Christian you are likely to define success differently than many people, which is as it should be. In secular society, success usually means climbing a career ladder or accumulating possessions. As I have suggested throughout this book, success in any lasting sense has a lot more to do with the nature of one's relationships than the kind of car you drive or where you live. Always, when it comes to accumulation, there are these haunting words: "For what shall it profit a man, if he shall gain the whole world, and lose his own soul?" (Mark 8:36, KJV).

Jesus also gave us this stern warning about attending to our own faults before trying to correct anyone else's: "Why do you look at the speck of sawdust in your brother's eye and pay no attention to the plank in your own eye? How can you say to your brother, 'Brother, let me take the speck out of your eye,' when you yourself fail to see the plank in your own eye? You hypocrite, first take the plank out of your eye, and then you will see clearly to remove the speck from your brother's eye" (Luke 6:41–42, NIV).

Nine Strategies for Getting Out of Your Own Way

The nine strategies I am about to present are keys. If you use them prayerfully, they may help unlock your potential as a person and, more specifically, as a Christian. For these principles to do you any good, however, you must internalize and apply them. There is a huge difference between understanding something intellectually and making it part of you.

Strategy 1: Embrace the Responsibility for Your Own Life

We've all failed. You have, I have, and so has everyone else. No one has succeeded at everything. But often we may be tempted to engage in some form of "if only" thinking. If only I had started younger. If only God had given me more opportunities. If only I'd been born wealthier or attended a better school. "If only" is a cop-out, a way of refusing to own up. Instead of accepting responsibility for what we've done or not done, we pin it on someone or something else. Parents. Society. School. God. Or if we really get desperate, our genes. If only I had been born smarter or better-looking.

People rarely fail because they aren't smart enough, educated enough, or attractive enough. They fail because they *act* in ways that are self-defeating. What's worse, they never realize it, never figure out what's going wrong. They just keep doing the same counterproductive things. Stumbling around in the dark, they do more to sabotage themselves than everyone else put together. They never quite get it—never learn how to stop erecting barriers to their own effectiveness. You can't get out of your own way until you come to terms with the fact that you're in it.

As long as you indulge in the blame game, you define your life as out of your control. You get to cop out, but at the cost of living reactively instead of purposefully. And you put your life on psychological autopilot. If you want to reach your full potential, you have to take control of your life, and you can't do this if you define yourself as a victim of circumstance.

Whatever your shortcomings, stop blaming them on others. Give up all forms of whining. Put an end to making excuses and instead look inside for *reasons,* because failure is almost always an inside job. Sometimes this inside job can leave you stuck in a bad situation. But you still have choices, and if you allow such a situation to continue, the odds are you're probably not owning up to how you help perpetuate it.

Begin your journey toward greater joy by stepping up to life. Accept the sometimes frightening fact that you have more control than you may think. Don't resign yourself to life's adversities; confront them straight on. Sure, some things are out of your control. But there are more alternatives that you think there are. Start by getting on your knees and asking God to help you squarely face who and what you are.

Strategy 2: Accept the Fact That Behavior Is Difficult to Change

This relates to the first of the three myths we addressed in Chapter Fifteen, so I won't belabor it here. William James, the great nineteenth-century physician, philosopher, and psychologist, thought of habit as the great flywheel of society (see his *Principles of Psychology,* written in 1890). A flywheel is a heavy device for storing momentum. Once you get it going, its large mass will cause it to rotate for a long time. Your car has a flywheel because without one it would stop almost as soon as you lifted your foot from the accelerator.

Imagine what life would be like if you had to think about everything you did. A task as simple as brushing your teeth would prove overwhelming. You would have to decide first to use a toothbrush and then figure out where to find one. Then you would have to decide how to pick up the toothbrush, to run it under water, what to put on it, where to find toothpaste, how to make the paste come out of the tube, how to apply it to the brush, how to twist your hand to get the brush into your mouth, in what fashion to move the brush, and so forth. The amazing thing is that you manage to brush your teeth every morning without consciously thinking about any of this. Our days are moved along by countless habits, including some that keep us alive, such as stepping on the brake when a traffic light changes to red.

Default Styles, too, are constellations of powerful habits. They are the flywheels of relationships. And like other habits, they are resistant to change. How often have you tried to alter your own behavior, only to realize that you kept falling back into former patterns? You made resolutions and promises, to yourself and perhaps to God, but eventually gave up because the habits of a lifetime proved too much for you.

If you really want to grow, accept the fact that your Default Styles—reflected in how you live—can prove almost as resistant to change as the orbit of the earth. Default Styles are like giant boulders tumbling down the sides of mountains. They have enormous momentum and are exceedingly difficult to stop or redirect.

Changing behavior requires sustained effort. Instead of looking for the next ten-minute self-help gimmick, plant your feet firmly on the ground, look life squarely in the eye, and reconcile yourself to the fact that it takes time and effort, sometimes lots of it, to change. There are no shortcuts.

Strategy 3: Always Assume That It Can Be Done

With God, all things are possible. Pessimism is poisonous, especially when it reflects lack of faith. Once you conclude that something is impossible, it is. In drawing this conclusion you may take something away from yourself as well as from God—the opportunity to help you. If you think that God is too remote to care about helping you, get out your Bible and rediscover who He is.

No one ever accomplished anything by assuming that it couldn't be done. Such assumptions may rob you of your glory (2 Corinthians 4:17). Be audacious. Accept the fact that you will fail more often than you will succeed. When you get knocked down, get up again quickly. If one thing doesn't work, try something else. To succeed at anything, you have to believe that you can do it. The really good news is that many times you can. Edison tried almost a thousand filaments until he found one that would work in a light bulb. He failed repeatedly but never threw in the towel. The same has been said of Abraham Lincoln and of Winston Churchill. Their early lives were riddled with failure. "It can't be done" thinking protects your self-esteem by insulating you from failure, but it also prevents you from developing patience, fortitude, and confidence.

Allowing yourself to be optimistic, to believe in your partnership with God (see Romans 8:28), takes courage. If you indulge in optimism, you might try. And if you try, you might fail. Yet if you don't try, you've already failed. Winners lose more often than losers. Think about it. Suppose you were selling refrigerators and, on average, were able to sell one to every tenth person who came into the store. If you talked to one hundred people, you would fail ninety times, whereas if you talked to ten people, you would fail only nine times. Winners lose more because they try more. But because they try more, they succeed more. You are not doomed to repeat old patterns. It *is* possible to change, but you have to begin with hope and, if you're a Christian, with faith.

You may have to take bold steps. If you are shy, you will never learn to become comfortable around other people by staying home in front of the television. If you let others roll over you, merely thinking about it is not going to make you more assertive. And if you're afraid of emotional closeness, you will not get comfortable with intimacy simply by devouring self-help books in the comfort and safety of your parlor. You have to put yourself in circumstances that require you to stretch, to do something outside your zone of comfort. It may be necessary, and prudent, to take small risks at first, but large or small, you have to take them to grow. Many people are no further along, socially and emotionally, at age forty than they were at fourteen. This is often because when they encounter even the slightest setback, they give up. Don't be one of them. Your Heavenly Father wants more for you than that.

Strategy 4: *Systematically Chart Your Own Default Style or Styles*

Each of us has one or more Default Styles, patterns of behaviors toward which we naturally gravitate. These are not premeditated but automatic. We do not activate them on purpose. They are reflexive, built into us by our life experiences coupled with the choices we've made. Default Styles just seem to be there as part of us and, like all social behaviors, are more like conditioned responses than planned agendas. They may be functional or self-defeating.

Most people know very little about the impact they have on others or how others truly see them. It is as if, caught in a dense fog, they are endlessly trying to spot land through the wrong end of a telescope. They can make out the general contours far in the distance, but that's about it. I have often been struck by how the most sought-after commodity in any large corporation, and what employees seem most to long for, is candid feedback. People want information about themselves that they can use.

Your interpersonal behavior has an enormous influence on your relationships and therefore on how you do in life. Default Styles can make the difference between success and failure—and often do. Even more important, they can make the difference between a lonely existence and a life filled with intimacy.

To the extent that your Default Styles operate outside your awareness, they can hurt you and make it difficult to get out of your own way. Whatever your Default Styles, it is critical that you come to know them well. Consequently, the sooner you get on with the business of obtaining good feedback about your impact on others, the better. Throughout Part Three, I provided simplified tools, in the form of three-question self-assessments, to help you get a sense of how much you lapse into each of the eight toxic relational patterns. There are, of course, more sophisticated ways to do such an assessment, but they cannot be presented in a book. These methods include comparing how you see yourself with how others see you. Contact info@relationaldynamics.com for additional information.

Having such information will not, by itself, change you. You have to do something with it. But it is impossible to change what you are unaware of, which is why high-quality feedback is essential. As we have discussed in earlier chapters, our behavior communicates who we think we are, how we want other people to view us, and how we expect them to act toward us. Whenever we are with other people, there is no downtime, no muting of the microphone, no off-stage intermission, no utterance that doesn't count or is off the record. Only by coming to understand your impact on others will you be able to determine what's working and what's not.

Strategy 5: Get Beyond Defensiveness

Defense mechanisms are essentially evasions. They are mental devices we use to run from the truth about ourselves and sometimes the truth about others as well.

According to classical psychoanalysis, all defense mechanisms operate unconsciously. If you are aware that you're using it, it's not a real defense. Defense mechanisms often start out, however, as conscious attempts to come to terms with disturbing thoughts or feelings. What begins as *purposeful* behavior eventually becomes *automatic*. Among the more than twenty defense mechanisms that have been identified, three prove especially troublesome in everyday life and are, therefore, worthy of special attention:

1. *Projection* is perceiving in or attributing to others what we cannot accept in ourselves. To project is, at root, to blame. Whenever we hold others responsible for *our* mistakes and failures, we are using projection. By foisting accountability onto them, we shore up the walls of our own egos. The thinner these walls are, the more we tend to project.

> "It's not my fault that I've never been promoted—it's my supervisor's."
>
> "Our relationship would be perfect if you weren't so sensitive."
>
> "I'm not the selfish one—you are!"

2. *Rationalization* is making excuses for what we have done or explaining it away. The purpose of rationalization is to protect us from hav-

ing to reckon with our inconsistencies. To rationalize is to trump up reasons to justify thoughts, feelings, or actions that do not fit with our conscience or our ideal image of ourselves.

> "I had to lie to her because she wasn't being reasonable."

> "The reason I didn't pick up half of the check was I knew he'd feel better if he paid it."

> "I'd certainly return the suitcase I borrowed if I thought she'd need it again."

3. *Denial* is refusing to recognize something that is right in front of your nose. We've all met people who were so uncomfortable with conflict that they couldn't be insulted. If you told them to turn themselves into beggars, they'd thank you for the career advice.

> "I may use cocaine now and then, but I've never had a drug problem."

> "The lipstick on his collar every Thursday means nothing."

> "I have lots of close friends—I just never have time to see any of them."

The Chinese have a proverb: "Gain power by accepting reality." Many people spend their lives distorting reality rather than confronting it. Instead of facing what *is,* they behave according to what they *wish* could, should, or might be. You cannot thrive in a world of your own creation. Reckoning with reality is not an option. It is the only path to personal growth and psychological freedom. And as we noted in Part One, it is also the only path to God.

Facing the truth about ourselves, however painful it may be, allows us to get through life without suffering the side-effects of avoidance: emotional constriction, self-defeating behavior patterns, low levels of energy and focus, messed up relationships, lack of joy, disruptive mood states, impaired mental inefficiency, excessive conflict, and a host of other psychological afflictions.

Make learning the inner terrain of your feelings a central part of your mission in life so that you are sensitive to when and how you may be inclined to distort or hide from the truth. Although this is certainly easier said than done, there is no time like the present to begin. You cannot change what you will not acknowledge, especially about yourself, so be relentless.

Many people need a therapist or counselor to help them to understand themselves, while others are capable of considerable self-analysis. If you have the time and resources to explore your inner workings under the guidance of a wise and understanding professional, do it. But even if you don't, muster up the courage to look at your inner being. With a little effort and an earnest desire for self-knowledge, you may discover all sorts of things that you never imagined, and some of these things may be pleasant surprises.

Strategy 6: Enlist People Around You as Anchors

Few people avail themselves of the huge amount of *free* psychological assistance that lies at their fingertips. All around you are people who can and will help if you let them. Other people hold keys to our growth and progress because they often see clearly what we can make out only dimly. They have the power to help us shed self-destructive and self-imposed obstacles and sometimes, therefore, to catapult us toward spiritual and emotional growth.

To grasp our true impact on others requires that we get them to tell us what is inside their heads, that we convince them to share how they actually see us. Such sharing is *not* something the average person is comfortable doing. This is because the risk-reward ratio is usually unfavorable. People know from experience that requests for feedback are often disguised bids for reassurance. And so when we ask them to share their perceptions of us, they typically say whatever they think we want to hear. Getting beyond such niceties is critically important if you're ever going to soar into the stratosphere of high performance.

Most of us need people to play three roles in our lives: mentor, sponsor, and coach. *Mentors* are people who show us the ropes. Usually ten to twenty years older than we are, they teach us from their experience and so save us time, energy, and heartache. They stop us from making the same mistakes they did. *Sponsors* are people who promote us in one way or another. They value what we are, and they make sure we get an invitation or a seat at the table. *Coaches* are people who help us perceive what we might otherwise miss. They major in giving accurate feedback and, beyond this, suggesting ways to improve performance. Coaches say, in essence, "Not that way, this way," and do it in a manner that enables us to perform better.

The most helpful coaches are the ones I call Anchors, because they keep you from drifting into trouble. Anchors give you feedback about how you're coming across. And if they are knowledgeable about interpersonal dynamics, they may also provide you with wise counsel, such as how to handle others. People who become your Anchors will almost always become your sponsors also. They will promote you because they believe in you. And they will believe in you because they have helped make you what you are. While not everyone you meet will be capable of serving as an Anchor, there are probably more candidates for this than you think. Humble yourself and ask for their help. Pray that God will lead you to ask the right people.

Strategy 7: Prevent Other People from Holding You Back

We all need predictability, which can be a major problem. The world is easier to deal with when things turn out as we expect. Surprises are disconcerting. Though all of us need a certain amount of novelty to be happy, too much novelty can prove overwhelming. A totally unpredictable existence would soon put us in the asylum. We'd be crushed under the wheel of information bombardment. Unfortunately, other people's needs to be able to predict how we are going to act can be our undoing.

The effects of what psychologists call stimulus overload can be painfully evident in pilots, who sometimes find it impossible to process all of the data coming at them. They become what military psychologists call "task-saturated." When this happens, they make elementary errors that can cost them their lives. To thrive and sometimes just to survive, we have to be able to handle whatever life throws at us. The better our predictive powers, in general, the better we are able to cope. There is great value in knowing what will happen next, including what other people will do. We respond in one way to a friend walking toward us and in quite another to an angry teenager who is fast approaching us on the street.

We are all amateur scientists, forever coming up with theories that enable us to predict what other people will do: "Dottie is a nasty person, so I know that she'll be rude." Because it's reassuring to be able to predict how other people will act, we hold on tightly to our theories about them. And here's the insidious part: when they behave contrary to our expectations, we sometimes do whatever we have to do to drive them back into behaving in the way that is familiar to us. Once we conclude that Dottie is nasty, we will do things unconsciously to ensure that Dottie continues to be nasty. It is not so much that we don't want to give her a chance but that we do not want our theory of Dottie dismantled. Theories take time and energy to construct, and the less we have to revise them, the better.

If you try to change, the people around you will often attempt to push you back into your old patterns because they want *you* to be predictable. And they'll do this more or less without thinking. They won't realize they're doing it and would be horrified if you pointed it out. And even though they may sincerely tell you that they want you to change, as soon as you attempt to do so, they will try to mold you back into your former self. The sinister thing is that they will do this even if they don't especially like that self!

Strategy 8: Pull Your Weeds Quickly

If you're like I am, admitting that you're less than perfect is uncomfortable. When I have to do it, I take a deep breath. This is because I work hard at maintaining a concept of myself as competent and conscientious. When you try hard at anything, criticism is always painful, even when it's deserved. Once, when I was still teaching in a doctoral program, I asked one of my students a question. "Doug, you've spent years studying human behavior. Now that you're a month away from finishing your Ph.D., what do *you* think is at the heart of a good relationship?"

Soon-to-be Dr. Pepe thought for a moment and said, "Pulling weeds."

That was over twenty years ago, and I have yet to come up with a better answer. Unresolved resentments can accumulate until they kill a relationship. What starts out as a garden of graciousness turns into a thicket of tensions, and the good stuff, such as love and affection, gets choked out. It is easy to care for a well-tended garden. A weed here or there presents no special challenge. Allowed to multiply, however, these same weeds take over until you can't remove them without destroying everything else also.

What is true of relationships is also true of individuals. If you do not attend quickly to the weeds of your own personality, they will take hold, and you will have a tough time rooting them out. Sometimes the weeds become so much a part of who we are that we no longer recognize that they exist. Nasty cynicism that would have horrified us in our thirties may become a natural part of us in our sixties.

When we emerge from the womb, we are more or less innocent. Sure, we are born with genetically determined predispositions. Some of us are energetic and others lethargic, some bold and others timid. But that's about all there is to us in the beginning. We have no personalities to speak of. Almost immediately, however, experience begins to mold us. So do the choices we make. We are fed or frustrated, held or left alone in the crib, attended to or ignored. And we start to make primitive decisions. Eventually we become fully developed persons whose fundamental nature is to choose. We indulge ourselves or defer gratification. We help the accident victim or walk on by.

If we make wise choices, we pull every weed that threatens to ruin us, spiritually or emotionally, before it gains a foothold. We all know dozens of people who cannot manage to get out of their own way because they hang on to scores of behaviors that they should have discarded years ago. Root out your weeds, quickly, without looking back. If something is hurting you, face it honestly and change it, attacking it with the same ferocity you would an infection, for that is what it is.

Strategy 9: Judiciously Apply the Power of Reframing

We in the Western world pay far more attention to the external circumstances of life than to how we *interpret* these circumstances. Yet it is not always what happens to us that determines how we think and feel but the *meaning* we give to events.

Suppose you broke your leg and had to stay home for a few days or weeks. You could bemoan your fate: "I hate being cooped up like this." Or you could celebrate: "I can finally have some time to myself—maybe finish reading that book I just started."

I am not advocating that you live in fantasyland. Reckoning with reality is essential for health and well-being (see Strategy 5). But we also have tremendous latitude in how we make sense of facts, in what they mean. Changing this meaning is called reframing. As human beings, we are capable of creative thought. We can attach a wide range of meanings to any given event. It is not just that we select these meanings but rather that we create them. For a Christian, reframing should reflect how scripture reveals life to be, which is not always what we, in the flesh, assume.

When something occurs that sets you back or feels like it's causing you to take a dive into a cesspool, do not let it ruin your joy. I realize that this is not always easy to do, particularly in the face of tragedy. Some awful things happen to people, and at any point in time many of them could happen to you or me. But regardless of what befalls you, whether it's losing your job or discovering that your house went up in flames, find opportunity in it. Look for God's blessing.

This is not to say that you should relish suffering. It is, however, to recommend that you meet trials and tribulations with a certain inner resolve, the determination to turn responsibilities into privileges, obstacles into challenges, and setbacks into occasions for reassessing where you've been with God and where you're going.

17

SOME FINAL THOUGHTS ON CHANGING OTHERS

Make every effort to live in peace with all men and to be holy;
without holiness no one will see the Lord.

—Hebrews 12:14 [NIV]

AT THE END OF EACH CHAPTER in Part Three, I listed suggestions for how to counteract that specific Default Style in other people. In this final chapter, I want to share some additional ideas that you may find helpful.

Can People Change?

- Yes. But they can change their day-to-day behavior more easily than they can their underlying (long-term) personality.
- Change becomes harder with age. But it is a myth that people cannot change once they move past adolescence. People sometimes change well into middle age and beyond.
- Motivation is the key to change. Unless a person wants to change a toxic Default Style, it's going to be hard to alter it.
- Getting the other person to invest in making the change (for example, by paying for some kind of help) can move change along, but the person has to *want* to make the investment. If it is not voluntary, it can backfire. All you'll get for your effort is resentment.

- A person is more likely to change if he or she makes a public commitment to do so; church services are wonderful opportunities for this. But again, if the commitment is not voluntary, it won't do any good and may even do harm.

- Major emotional events are typically what cause people to make major changes. These are life experiences that often rock people to their foundations and therefore have lasting impact.

- There is no greater emotional event than repentance and conversion. So before you try to change anyone else, make sure that you are consistently praying for that person.

Are There Two Senses of Manipulation?

- There are two senses to the word *manipulation,* and even many psychologists confuse them.

- One is to maneuver people into positions that are not good for them, usually without their knowing that you're doing it. This is what unscrupulous salespeople and con artists do. It is not for us as Christians.

- The other sense is simply doing something that you know will have a predictable effect. When a surgeon makes an incision, he or she is manipulating tissue in a planned and constructive way. When a parent disciplines a child, he or she is also manipulating in this sense. What a good surgeon or a good parent does is noble.

- The line between the two kinds of manipulation is sometimes blurry. When does warm social skill, involving the free expression of appreciation, turn into flattery? Most of the time, however, the distinction between the two kinds of manipulation is clear.

What About Resolving Conflicts and Healing Resentments?

- There are no shortcuts to either of these. They both take time and energy, and sometimes lots of both.

- For resentments to be healed, they usually have to be expressed.

- The expression of resentment involves risk.

- Self-disclosure is absolutely necessary; you cannot work out what you don't reveal.

- You have to move *toward* the other person, without vacillation, and you have to be persistent.

- If you are dealing with someone who is very defensive, put the focus on you. Say things like, "I may be way off here, but I'd appreciate it if you'd listen to me while I say how I feel. Even if it makes no sense."

- If your efforts are unproductive, don't give up; bring in outside help and try again; this is one area where professional therapists and counselors can be of enormous benefit. You are far more likely to succeed if you have a skilled referee or arbitrator, someone who can clang the gong if anyone starts to make insulting and destructive statements. Having such a person with you is essential if you are trying to work out differences with someone who is volatile or otherwise predatory, such as a Victimizer or a Humiliator.

- People who are good at interpersonal relationships may become angry, just like anyone else, but they return to "finish the fight." They don't throw up their hands in despair and declare the situation unworkable. Such persistence, by the way, is what the Bible commends to Christians.

- If things get heated, take a brief timeout—just make sure that both of you are committed to resuming the conversation at a specific time and in a specific place.

What's the Role of Humility?

- Humility is not just spiritually desirable—it is also necessary when it comes to trying to change anyone else. Recall our prior discussions of how God has given all people free will.

- There are some things, and some people, that you cannot change. Accept this.

- Going about change humbly does not mean giving up easily. Nor does it mean ceasing to pray.

---

o

There is so much more that I would like to write, but it is time to bring this volume to a close, in part to keep it within manageable limits for the general reader. It is my sincere and heartfelt desire that, in the years to come, you will be able to use the information and insights contained in this book to lead a more fulfilling life and to glorify our Heavenly Father. May He bless you abundantly in all that you do.

SOURCES AND RECOMMENDED READING

THEOLOGY AND PHILOSOPHY

Boice, J. M. *Foundations of the Christian Faith.* (rev. ed.) Downers Grove, Ill.: InterVarsity Press, 1986.

Brown, C. B. (ed.). *The New International Dictionary of New Testament Theology.* Vols. 1–3. Grand Rapids, Mich.: Zondervan, 1978.

Jewett, P. K. *God, Creation, and Revelation.* Grand Rapids, Mich.: Eerdmans, 1991.

Jewett, P. K. *Who We Are: Our Dignity as Human* (M. Shuster, ed.). Grand Rapids, Mich.: Eerdmans, 1996.

Nygren, A. *Essence of Christianity.* Grand Rapids, Mich.: Eerdmans, 1960.

Popkin, R. H. (ed.). *Columbia History of Western Philosophy.* New York: MJF Books, 1999.

Stott, J. R. *Christian Beliefs: A Handbook for Beginnings, Beliefs, and Behaviour.* Grand Rapids, Mich.: Baker Books, 1991.

PSYCHOLOGY

Bales, R. F. *Personality and Interpersonal Behavior.* Austin, Tex.: Holt, Rinehart and Winston, 1970.

Beier, E. G., and Valens, E. G. *People-Reading: How We Control Others, How They Control Us.* New York: Warner Books, 1975.

Beier, E. G., and Young, D. M. *The Silent Language of Psychology.* (3rd ed.) Hawthorne, N.Y.: Aldine de Gruyter, 1998.

Benjamin, L. S. *Interpersonal Diagnosis and Treatment of Personality Disorders.* (2nd ed.) New York: Guilford Press, 1996.

Berne, E. *Games People Play: The Psychology of Human Relationships.* New York: Grove Press, 1964.

Carson, R. C. *Interaction Concepts of Personality.* Hawthorne, N.Y.: Aldine de Gruyter, 1969.

Goleman, D. *Emotional Intelligence.* New York: Bantam Books, 1995.

Heatherton, T. F., and Weinberger, J. L. (eds.). *Can Personality Change?* Washington, D.C.: American Psychological Association, 1994.

Jones, S. L., and Butman, R. E. *Modern Psychotherapies: A Comprehensive Christian Appraisal.* Downers Grove, Ill.: InterVarsity Press, 1991.

Kantor, M. *Diagnosis and Treatment of the Personality Disorders.* St. Louis, Mo.: Ishiyaku EuroAmerica, 1992.

Leary, T. *Interpersonal Diagnosis of Personality.* New York: Ronald Press, 1957.

Parrott, L. *High-Maintenance Relationships: How to Handle Impossible People.* Wheaton, Ill.: Tyndale House, 1996.

Plotchik, R., and Cote, H. R. (eds.). *Circumplex Models of Personality and Emotions.* Washington, D.C.: American Psychological Association, 1997.

Shafranske, E. P. (ed.). *Religion and the Clinical Practice of Psychology.* Washington, D.C.: American Psychological Association, 1996.

Wachtel, P. L. *Psychoanalysis, Behavior Therapy, and the Relational World.* Washington, D.C.: American Psychological Association, 1997.

SELECTED PUBLICATIONS BY THE AUTHOR

Brokaw, D. W., and McLemore, C. W. "Toward a More Rigorous Definition of Social Reinforcement." *Journal of Personality and Social Psychology,* 1983, *44,* 1014–1020.

Brokaw, D. W., and McLemore, C. W. "Interpersonal Models of Personality and Psychopathology." In D. G. Gilbert (ed.), *Personality, Social Skills, and Psychopathology: An Individual Differences Approach.* New York: Plenum, 1991.

McLemore, C. W. "Applications of Balance Theory to Family Relations." *Journal of Counseling Psychology,* 1973, *20,* 181–184.

McLemore, C. W. "Another Needed Kind of Clinical-Social Psychology." *Society for the Advancement of Social Psychology (SASP) Newsletter,* 1978, *4,* 6.

McLemore, C. W., and Benjamin, L. S. "Whatever Happened to Interpersonal Diagnosis?: A Psychosocial Alternative to DSM-III." *American Psychologist,* 1979, *34,* 17–34.

McLemore, C. W. and Brokaw, D. W. "Personality Disorders as Dysfunctional Interpersonal Behavior." *Journal of Personality Disorders,* 1987, *1,* 270–285.

McLemore, C. W., and Hart, P. P. "Relational Psychotherapy: The Clinical Facilitation of Intimacy." In J. C. Anchin and D. J. Kiesler (eds.), *Handbook of Interpersonal Psychotherapy.* New York: Pergamon, 1982.

Rudy, J. P., McLemore, C. W., and Gorsuch, R. L. "Interpersonal Behavior and Therapeutic Progress: Therapist and Patients Rate Themselves and Each Other." *Psychiatry,* 1985, *48,* 264–281.

THE AUTHOR

CLINTON W. MCLEMORE earned his Ph.D. in clinical psychology at the age of twenty-four from the University of Southern California. He has spent his career studying and working to improve relationships—as a nationally recognized psychotherapist, research psychologist, and management consultant.

McLemore taught for many years in a doctoral-level clinical psychology program where he used the principles in this book to educate scores of young therapists. While there, he founded and directed the Interaction Research Project, which yielded more than forty doctoral dissertations, professional articles, and research reports.

His writings on interpersonal psychology have been published in many leading journals, including the prestigious *American Psychologist,* whose editors described his work in interpersonal psychology as a "seminal contribution to the field." He has also written chapters in such books as the *Handbook of Interpersonal Psychotherapy* (1982) and *Personality, Social Skills, and Psychopathology* (1991). He has reviewed manuscripts for *American Psychologist* and the *Journal of Consulting and Clinical Psychology.*

A member of the Authors Guild, McLemore has written five previous books: *Clergyman's Psychological Handbook: Clinical Information for Pastoral Counseling* (1974), *The Scandal of Psychotherapy: A Guide to Resolving the Tensions Between Faith and Counseling* (1982), *Good Guys Finish First: Success Strategies for Business Men and Women* (1983), *Honest Christianity: Psychological Strategies for Spiritual Growth* (1984), and *Street-Smart Ethics: Succeeding in Business Without Selling Your Soul* (2003).

In 1980, he founded Relational Dynamics, Inc. (RDI), and since then has consulted for dozens of Fortune 500 corporations. He is the in-residence management and organizational psychologist for Sempra Energy, one of the country's premier energy companies, and for RAND, the nation's most revered think-tank. Often quoted, he has appeared on many radio and television shows. His ideas about behavior change have been written about in such publications as *Securities Industry Daily, Today's Leader,* and the highly esteemed *Harvard Business Review.*

McLemore founded, and for years edited, *Clinician's Research Digest,* now owned and published by the American Psychological Association.

INDEX

A

Abandonment
  Drifters and concerns about, 129
  Freeloaders and, 156
  painful, 15–16
Abel, 10, 208, 215
Abuse
  emotional, 238
  inviting or putting up with, 191–193,
    195–198, 211, 213, 221
  need to cause, 237
  physical, 202, 216, 238
  putting a stop to, 1,13, 20, 185, 189,
    202
  unconscious need for, 183, 237
Abuser-repentance paradigm, 223
Abusiveness, 78–79, 83, 97–98, 210,
    213–214, 219
Accountability
  free will and, 15, 221
  projection, defense mechanism of, and,
    256
  Victimizers and, 218, 220–221
Achieving and excelling, conventional
    tactics of, 60–61, 64–65, 78–79, 88
Acts, book of, 110, 162
Adam, 7, 35, 53, 179
Adaptation, 188
Affiliation, not synonymous with love, 84–85
Affiliative Dominance, toxic mode of,
    85–86, 89, 91–92
Agape, 84, 151, 175
Aggression
  active and initiating nature of, 85
  hostility as different from, 85
Aggressive Dominance, toxic mode of,
    85–86, 91–92, 101
Alienation, defense mechanism of, 234
All in the Family, 182, 193
Allport, Gordon W., 38
Ambiguity, moral, 16–17, 25–26
American Heritage College Dictionary, 73

American Psychological Association (APA),
    251
Ananias, 162
Anchors, value of enlisting other people as,
    258–259
Anger
  Avoiders and, 226, 232, 234, 236,
    241–242
  Cain and, 215
  Controllers and, 110
  Drifters and, 124, 126–129
  Freeloaders and, 159, 165, 167
  frustration and, 246
  handling, in good relationships, 264
  Humiliators and, 178
  Intruders and, 143, 145–149
  provocation stemming from, 98
  Scurriers and, 194–195, 197, 204
  sociopaths and, 145
  toxic relationships as causes of, 19
  Victimizers and, 210, 212, 215–216,
    218–219, 222–223, 226, 232
  See also Rage
Anxiety
  Avoiders and, 229
  central focus of psychologists and
    psychiatrists, 30
  Controllers and, 108, 111, 114
  Drifters and, 123–124, 127
  fear and, 30
  Humiliators and, 173–174, 179
  insecurity and, 30
  nature of, 30
  powerful motivation of, 30, 57
  reduction maneuvers as obstacles to
    closeness, 30
  Scurriers and, 191, 199, 201, 205
  some, inevitable, 30
  tension between, and faith and love,
    30
  See also Fear; Insecurity; Security,
    quest for

Aphasia, emotional, 226
Appearances versus realities of behavior, 46–47
Archie Bunker, 182, 193
Arrangements, interpersonal
    definitions of, 49–50
    metaphors for, 50
Arrogance
    Controllers and, 108
    Humiliators and, 174–176, 183, 185–186, 188
    Scurriers and, 201
Assert, meaning of, 39
Assertion, 34, 41, 44, 53–56, 63–65, 73, 76–77, 80, 85–86, 110, 176
Assertiveness, 75, 111, 218, 228
Atlas Shrugged, 109
Attaching, conventional strategy of, 34, 54–59, 64–65, 77, 80, 88
Attacking, toxic strategy of, 88–92, 94–95, 101
Autism, 21, 233
Avoiders
    antidotes to adopting the style of, 240–241
    arrangement sought by, 234–235
    in the Bible, 234
    cases illustrative of, 229–230, 237–238
    countermeasures to the maneuvers of, 241–242
    defense mechanisms of, 234
    intimacy in the lives of, 239
    life script of, 229–230
    payoffs for, 235
    profile of, 227
    psychology of, 232–234
    responses induced in others by, 227, 236–237
    self-presentation and characteristics of, 227
    spiritual and moral choices relating to, 239
    typical life history of, 237–239
    what, tend most to avoid, 235–236
    when the arrangement breaks down with, 237
Avoiding
    justifications offered for, 231–232
    potential benefits of, in mild form, 227, 231
    self-assessment for, 240

Awareness
    discipleship and, 8
    interpersonal, 8
Axes, primary, of interpersonal behavior, 38–40. *See also* Dimensions of interpersonal behavior

B

Bales, Robert, 42
Behavior, extreme. *See* Extreme behavior
Behavior, intense. *See* Intensity, interpersonal
Behavior, interpersonal, reflexive nature of, 57, 72–73
Behavior, rigid. *See* Rigidity
Behavioral implications of interpersonal postures, 40–41
Beliefs, corrections of by others, 29–30
Besting, conventional strategy of, 55–59, 64–65, 72, 77, 80
Biological and psychological connections, 28
Biological processes and human consciousness, 6
Bitterness
    Avoiders and, 232, 237
    Victimizers and, 222
Blame game, 252
Blocking and resisting, conventional tactics of, 61, 64–65, 78–79
Bond, James, 183
Bonding, conventional style of, 34, 56–59, 61–62, 64–65, 77–78, 96, 156, 158
Bonhoeffer, Dietrich, 13
Bossing and ordering, toxic tactics of, 90–91, 93. *See also* Chapter 7
Brain tumors, 21
Bunker, Archie, 182, 193
Bunker, Edith, 182, 193
Burns, Jack, 105

C

Cain, 10, 208, 215
Candor
    basic value of Christianity is, 209
    desire for, in corporations, 255
    fellowship, 12
    lack of in Drifters, 12
Caring, conventional strategy of, 34, 54–55, 57–59, 64–65, 77, 80, 88

Carson, Robert C., 86–87

Carson's simplified model of interpersonal behavior, 86–88

Categories versus dimensions of behavior, 43–44

Certainty
drive for in Drifters, 127
See also Predictability; Uncertainty

Challenging and confronting, conventional tactics of, 61, 64–65, 78–79

Change
neither fast nor easy, 246–247, 253–254
possibility of, 262–263
role of insight in, 248–250
willpower usually insufficient for, 247–248

Cheap grace and forgiveness, 12–13

Choice of interpersonal styles, determinants of, 58–60

Christ
mind of, 5, 27
new life in, 12, 22, 30, 246

Christianity, basic interpersonal nature of, 48

Churchill, Winston, 254

Circular model of interpersonal behavior, 73

Circumplex, basic nature of, 73

Clinging and depleting, toxic tactics of, 90. *See also* Chapter 10

Clinician's Research Digest, 251

Coaches, 62, 258

Cold Assertion, conventional mode of, 34, 53–55, 56, 63–65, 73, 77, 85

Cold Subordination, conventional mode of, 34, 53–55, 64–65, 73, 77, 85

Colossians, book of, 11, 12, 29

Commands, interpersonal, 48–49

Communion. *See* Fellowship

Community, church as, 10

Compatibility. *See* Interpersonal compatibility

Compensation, defense mechanism of, in Humiliators, 181

Competing, conventional style of, 56–62, 64–65, 77–78, 88, 96, 174

Complaints against others, 12

Complementarity. *See* Interpersonal complementarity

Condemning, 6, 12, 67, 215

Conditioning, 14–15, 58
rising above, 15

Conflict
Controllers and organizational, 111
denying, 257
Drifters and, 122
excessive, affliction of, 257
from incompatible behavioral styles, 41
inner, few people are free of, 21
Intruders and overt, 147
resolving, 263–264
Victimizers and, 210, 213, 217

Connectedness masquerading as affection, 102

Connecting and appreciating, conventional tactics of, 34, 61, 64–65, 77–79, 156, 158

Conrad, Joseph, 197

Conscious versus unconscious motivation, 58

Consciousness, states of, 5–6

Content versus process, 36–37

Continuous versus dichotomous scales, 43–44

Control
Avoiders and, 234, 241
contact, 38–39
Drifters and, 120–121, 125–126, 128–130, 134–135
Freeloaders and, 160, 163, 167
Humiliators and, 173, 181–182, 189
interpersonal postures and, 39, 41, 47, 54, 65, 70, 85, 98
Intruders and, 138, 141, 145, 147–148
Machiavellian, 47
taking, of your life, 252–253

Controllers
antidotes to adopting the style of, 116–117
arrangement sought by, 110
in the Bible, 109–110
cases illustrative of, 105–106, 109
countermeasures to the maneuvers of, 117–118
defense mechanisms of, 108–109
intimacy in the lives of, 114–115
life script of, 105–106
organizational conflict and, 111
payoffs for, 110–111
profile of, 104
psychology of, 108–109

Controllers, *continued*
   responses induced in others by, 104,
      112
   self-presentation and characteristics of,
      104
   spiritual and moral choices relating to,
      115
   typical life history of, 113–114
   what, tend most to avoid, 111
   when the arrangement breaks down
      with, 112–113
Controlling
   justifications offered for, 107
   potential benefits of, in mild form, 104,
      106–107
   self-assessment for, 116
Conventional and toxic styles, comparison
      of, 95–96
Conventional strategies, summary of,
      54–55
Conventional styles
   eight basic, 56–57
   social value of, 60–63
   summary of, 55–57
   tactics associated with, 60–61
Corrections of ideas, beliefs, and
      perceptions by others, 29–30
Correspondence, interpersonal, 76
Counseling, 18, 22, 24–25, 29, 135.
      See also Counselors; Psychotherapists;
      Psychotherapy
Counselors, 21, 25, 222, 257, 264. *See also*
      Counseling; Psychotherapists;
      Psychotherapy
Counterfeit salvation, 23–24
Courage, 62, 104, 132, 206, 254, 258
Creation
   God's purpose in, 8
   human beings as pinnacles of, 7
Creatures, fallen, 15, 28, 66
Criticism
   Avoiders and, 227, 232, 236
   Controllers and, 108, 112
   Drifters and, 122–123, 126
   drive to avoid, powerful, 57
   examples of, 88, 93–94
   Humiliators and, 175, 180, 185
   Intruders and, 137, 139
   inviting unwarranted, 69
   painful but often useful, 260
   Scurriers and, 194–195, 199, 207
Crowding and smothering, toxic tactics of,
      90–91, 113. *See also* Chapter 9

Cultures, embracing of different, 9
Cynicism
   Avoiders and, 232
   growing old and, 260
   living in silent, 14
   Scurriers and, 192, 196

D

Death, 10, 13–14, 20, 23, 82
Default modes and styles, definitions of,
      95–99
Default styles, importance of systematically
      charting, 255–256
Defensiveness, importance of getting
      beyond, 256–258
Delilah, 208, 215
Demeaning and belittling, toxic tactics of,
      88, 90–91, 93, 101, 113, 216. *See
      also* Chapter 11
Denial, defense mechanism of
   Humiliators and, 176
   Intruders and, 141, 147–148
   nature of, 124, 257
   Scurriers and, 193
   Victimizers and, 212
Depersonalization, defense mechanism of,
      234
Depression
   aggressive dominance as trigger for,
      75
   Avoiders and, 237
   Humiliators as inducers of, 174, 180
   Intruders and, 149
   psychopharmacology and, 25
   Scurriers and, 196, 201–202
   used as justification for Freeloading,
      158
Despair
   Avoiders and, 231
   Controllers and, 111
   giving up in, 264
   Humiliators and, 174
   Intruders and, 149
   Victimizers and, 216
   without God, 14
Desperation, lives of quiet, 14
Determinants of interpersonal styles, 58–60
Determinism, 14–15
*Diagnostic and Statistical Manual of
      Mental Disorders (DSM–IV)*, 21
Dichotomous versus continuous scales,
      43–44

Diet industry, 248

Differences, individual, God's appreciation of, 61

Dimensions of interpersonal behavior
  blending together of, 44–45
  categories versus, 43–44
  combining, 46
  meaning of, 40, 42–44, 63, 69
  primary, 38–40

Discernment, importance of, 67

Discipleship, 8, 10–11, 13

Disengaging, conventional strategy of, 55, 57, 59, 64–65, 72, 77, 88

Displacement, defense mechanism of
  Controllers and, 108–109
  nature of, 109
  Victimizers and, 214

Double binds, 238–239

Drifters
  antidotes to adopting the style of, 133–134
  arrangement sought by, 126–127
  in the Bible, 126
  cases illustrative of, 121–122, 124–125
  countermeasures to the maneuvers of, 134–135
  defense mechanisms of, 124
  intimacy in the lives of, 131–132
  life script of, 121–122
  payoffs for, 127
  profile of, 120
  psychology of, 123–126
  responses induced in others by, 120, 128–129
  self-presentation and characteristics of, 120
  spiritual and moral choices relating to, 132
  typical life history of, 131
  what, tend most to avoid, 127–128
  when the arrangement breaks down with, 129–131

Drifting
  justifications offered for, 122–123
  potential benefits of, in mild form, 120, 122
  self-assessment for, 133

Drinkers, problem, 248

DSM–IV, 21

Duty
  to care for others, 9, 13
  to care for ourselves, 9, 13, 221

  to endure toxicity, 19
  loving largely out of, 150
  making a religion of, 108
  manipulating others to do their, 159
  not to dominate others, 115
  to think, 35

Dysfunctional versus functional behavior, 52–53

E

Economics, 13–14, 16, 62, 175

Economists, 13

Eden, Garden of, 179. See also Adam

Edison, Thomas Alva, 254

Education, 1, 14, 16, 29, 82, 176, 220, 248–250

Elijah, 144

Embarrassment
  Intruders may use, 148
  motive to avoid, powerful, 57
  Scurriers and, 194
  Victimizers may feign, 212

Emotional aphasia, 226

Emotional health. See Psychological health

Emotional risk taking, sin, and fellowship, 10

Emotional scars, 15

Emperor Nero, 25

Engulfing, toxic strategy of, 88–92, 114

Enmeshed Submission, toxic mode of, 86, 89, 91–92

Envy, 114, 177, 186. See also Jealousy

Eros, 84

Esau, 215

Eternal significance, everything we do or say is of, 15

Eve, 7, 179

Evil
  allowing others to inflict, 83
  God's response to, 225
  human capacity for, 67
  potential subtlety of, 16
  private and hidden, 67
  psychological tension over, 21–22
  radically opposed to good, 16
  refusing to recognize, 83
  Rehoboam and, 126
  relational sin and, 6
  Solomon and, 119
  triumph over, 23
  See also Goodness

Extreme behavior
    Avoiders and, 231, 233, 239
    Controllers and, 105, 112, 115
    Drifters and, 123, 128
    Freeloaders and, 158
    Intruders and, 148
    toxicity and, 39, 63
    Victimizers and, 216, 220
    See also Intensity, interpersonal;
        Rigidity

F

Failure, life of, and faulty Default Styles,
    255–256
Failures
    accepting responsibility for own, 247,
        252–253, 256–257
    inevitable in life, 15, 254
    winners and, 254
Faith, interpersonal subtleties and, 2
Fall, the, 10
False religion, 23–24
Fanatic, 13, 21, 215
Fear
    anxiety and, 30
    Avoiders and, 225, 230, 236, 239
    Drifters and, 128, 132
    guilt, relationship to, 198
    Humiliators and, 179–180
    Intruders and, 145
    versus love, 30
    love as antidote to, 30
    nature of, 30
    relationship between punishment and,
        30
    Scurriers and, 190–191, 198, 205
    some, inevitable, 30
    tension between, and faith and love, 30
    Victimizers and, 210, 216, 218
    what not to, 82
    See also Anxiety; Insecurity; Security,
        quest for
Fellowship
    alienation from God and, 10
    candor and, 12
    caring and, 9
    communion and, 10
    emotional risks essential to, 10
    essence of, 3
    estrangement from God and, 10
    expensive nature of true, 10
    fostering genuine, 10

God as an eternal, 7
    human beings designed for, 7
    imitation or superficial, 10–11
    intimacy and, 4, 9, 18, 26
    life in the flesh and, 10
    marital status and, 26
    meaning of, 3, 9
    powerful and essential, 247
    relationship of, to behavioral change,
        247
    self-disclosure central to, 11, 27–28
    sharing and, 9
    spiritual beings hard-wired for, 14
    unique quality of Christian, 10
Fleming, Ian, 183
Flesh, meaning of living according to the,
    10
Flexibility in behavior, desirability of, 48,
    63, 84, 95, 129
Following, conventional style of, 56–59,
    61–65, 77–78, 88, 96, 120
Forfeiting and conceding, conventional
    tactics of, 61, 64–65, 78–79
Forgiveness, 12–13, 16, 140, 183, 209–210
Forster, E. M., 133–134
Fountainhead, The, 109
Four Loves, The, 84
Freedom
    human, 11, 14–15
    personal, 11, 49, 257
    responsibility and, 14–15
    versus determinism, 14–15
    versus legalism, 11
Freedom of choice
    Avoiders and, 230
    Controllers and, 113–114, 117
    Drifters and, 129
    Freeloaders and, 158, 163–164, 170
    Intruders and, 145, 149–153
Freeloaders
    antidotes to adopting the style of,
        169–170
    arrangement sought by, 163
    in the Bible, 162–163
    cases illustrative of, 157, 159–161, 164
    countermeasures to the maneuvers of,
        170–171
    defense mechanisms of, 160
    intimacy in the lives of, 168–169
    life script of, 157–158
    payoffs for, 163–165
    profile of, 156
    psychology of, 159–162

responses induced in others by, 156,
166–167
self-presentation and characteristics of,
156
spiritual and moral choices relating to,
169
typical life history of, 168
what, tend most to avoid, 165–166
when the arrangement breaks down
with, 167
Freeloading
justifications offered for, 158–159
potential benefits of, in mild form, 156,
158
self-assessment for, 169
Freud, Sigmund, 30, 249
Frustration
anger and, 246
Avoiders and, 232, 237
basic nature of, 246
experienced early in life, 260
Freeloaders and, 161, 165
how Avoiders prompt, 226, 236
how Controllers prompt, 111, 129
how Drifters prompt, 123, 129
how Freeloaders prompt, 167
how myths about change cause, 246
Intruders and, 143
in parent–adolescent interaction,
94–95
taking, out on others, 16, 108 (*See also*
Displacement)
Victimizers and, 223
Functional versus dysfunctional behavior,
52–53

G

Galatians, book of, 11
Garden of Eden, 179
Genesis, book of, 7, 35, 53, 83, 172, 179,
199, 206, 215
Glory, neurotic quest for, 173–174
Gnosticism, psychology as, 24
God
the Christian's proper stance toward,
64–65
as loving Father, 7, 10, 12–13, 18, 20,
28, 33, 65, 132, 169, 255, 264
relational nature of, 7
God's image, 6–7
Goliath, 181–182
Good news, 110. *See also* Gospel of Christ

Goodness
Avoiders and, 235
Controllers and, 109
Drifters and, 121
evil radically opposed to, 16
Freeloaders and, 165, 167
God and, 144
Good Samaritan as example of, 20
human potential for, 67
illusory, 17
Intruders and, 139–140, 146, 148, 151
knowing what is genuine, 5
love and, 20
practicing and ingraining, 247
simple, 193
simple-minded views of, 17
sometimes ambiguous, 16–17, 25
See also Evil
Gospel of Christ, 22, 204, 234. *See also*
Good news
Government, 14, 62
Grace, 12–13, 110, 203–204, 207, 209,
221
Greek philosophy, Jewish influence on, 23
n
Grievances, letting go of, 13
Guilt
can be oppressive, 24
fear often at the root of, 198
Freeloaders and induction of, 166, 178
Humiliators and induction of, 184
Intruders and use of, 137–138, 143,
147–148, 153
private nature of, 184
release from, 24–25
Scurriers and experience of, 198, 200
shame versus, 184
we all share, 6

H

Happiness, 2, 6, 72, 259
Health
holiness versus, 21–22
intersection of holiness with, 22
See also Psychological health
Heart, deceitful, 16–17
Hebrews, book of, 10, 28, 262
Hell, one definition of, 29
Herod, 208, 216
Holiness, 5, 9, 16, 18–24, 26–27, 245, 262
Holy Spirit, 7, 10, 19–20, 27, 110,
245–246, 249

Horney, Karen, 38–39
Hostile Submission, toxic mode of, 85–89,
    91–92, 96
Hostility
    aggression as different from, 85
    denial of in others by Drifters, 124
    detected where it does not exist by
        Humiliators, 179
    magnified by Avoiders, 232
    moving against others and, 85
    passive and reactive nature of, 40, 85
    pervasive, in Avoiders, 228
    Scurriers and, 195
    See also Aggression
Human beings
    biological, social, and spiritual in
        nature, 14
    regarded as pinnacles of creation, 7
Human moral judgment and God's image,
    7
Humans as spiritual beings and God's
    image, 7
Humiliating
    justifications offered for, 176–177
    potential benefits of, in mild form,
        174–176
    self-assessment for, 187
Humiliators
    antidotes to adopting the style of,
        187–188
    arrangement sought by, 182–183
    in the Bible, 181–182
    cases illustrative of, 175, 177, 180
    countermeasures to the maneuvers of,
        189
    defense mechanisms of, 176, 178–179,
        181
    intimacy in the lives of, 186
    life script of, 173–175
    payoffs for, 183
    profile of, 174
    psychology of, 177–181
    responses induced in others by, 174,
        184
    self-presentation and characteristics of,
        174
    spiritual and moral choices relating to,
        186–187
    typical life history of, 185–186
    what, tend most to avoid, 183–184
    when the arrangement breaks down
        with, 184–185

Humility, 8, 127–128, 188, 194, 259,
    264
Hypersensitivity in avoiders, 232

I

I Love Lucy, 46
Ideas, corrections of by others, 29–30
Identity, individual, and the Christian life,
    10–11
Idiosyncrasies, remedy for, 29–30
Image of God. See God's image
Immune system and stress, 28
Impact, importance of understanding your,
    2, 255–256, 258
Individual differences, God's appreciation
    of, 61
Individual identity and the Christian life,
    10–11
Infinite importance, everything we do or
    say is of, 15
Inflexibility, interpersonal. See Rigidity
Injuring and exploiting, toxic tactics of,
    90–91, 93. See also Chapter 13
Insecurity
    anxiety and, 30
    Drifters and, 121, 128
    hinders intimacy, 30
    Humiliators and, 174, 181
    Intruders and, 141
    See also Anxiety; Fear; Security, quest
        for
Insight
    asking God for, 245
    does not guarantee change, 248–250
    false, 24
    Humiliators and the pretense of, 176
    important interpersonal, 38–39, 68–69,
        75,
    limitations of, 248–250
    limited in Freeloaders, 162
    limited in Humiliators, 189
    limited in Intruders, 154
    into the power of God through Christ,
        68–69
    role of, in change, 248–250
    value of, 1
    See also Self-insight
Insights, fundamental, of relational
    psychology, 68–69
Inspiring and guiding, conventional tactics
    of, 34, 61, 64–65, 77, 79

Intellectual-emotional states and God's
        image, 7
Intensity, interpersonal
    Avoiders and, 226
    Controllers and, 104
    Freeloaders and, 166
    Humiliators and, 181
    Intruders and, 143, 148
    Scurriers and, 194
    toxicity and, 88, 96, 181
    See also Extreme behavior; Rigidity
Interpersonal arrangements, 49–50
Interpersonal behavior
    primary features of, 40
    reflexive nature of, 57, 72–73
    situational differences in, 45–46
    strategic nature of, 56–58
Interpersonal compatibility
    basic rules of in conventional behavior,
        76
    conventional behavior and, 75–81
    quest for, 80–81
    toxic behavior and, 90–95
Interpersonal complementarity, basic
        nature of, 76
Interpersonal correspondence principle,
        76
Interpersonal overtures, 73
Interpersonal postures, behavioral
        implications of, 40–41
Interpersonal reciprocity principle, 76
Interpersonal relationships
    and God's image, 7
    theology on, 3–31
Interpersonal sin, 6
Interpersonal strategy, nature of, 53–54
Interpersonal styles
    determinants of, 58–60
    difficult to alter, 68
    social value of specific, 60–63
Interpersonal tactics
    associated with specific styles, 60–61
    compatibility rules for, 77–79
Interpersonal toxicity, basic nature of,
        84
Interpersonal training, occurs continually
        and automatically, 69–72
Intimacy
    Avoiders and, 239
    becoming comfortable with, 255
    centrality of, to human existence,
        27–28

    Controllers and, 114–115
    emotional, 26–27
    fellowship and, 9–11, 18
    Freeloaders and, 168–169
    holy, 26
    Humiliators and, 186
    Drifters and, 131–132
    Intruders and, 150–151
    isolation versus, 29–30
    language and, 28–29
    loneliness versus, 29–30, 255
    moving toward or away from others
        and, 40
    mutuality and, 27, 114, 132, 150, 168,
        186
    nature of, 26–27
    Scurriers and, 203–204
    self-disclosure and, 11
    sexual, 26
    spiritual, 27
    Victimizers and, 220
Intruders
    antidotes to adopting the style of,
        152–153
    arrangement sought by, 145
    in the Bible, 143–144
    cases illustrative of, 138–142
    countermeasures to the maneuvers of,
        153–154
    defense mechanisms of, 141–142,
        147–149
    intimacy in the lives of, 150–151
    life script of, 105, 138–139
    payoffs for, 145–146
    profile of, 137
    psychology of, 141–143
    responses induced in others by, 137,
        147–148
    self-presentation and characteristics of,
        137
    spiritual and moral choices relating to,
        151
    typical life history of, 149–150
    what, tend most to avoid, 146–147
    when the arrangement breaks down
        with, 148–149
Intruding
    justifications offered for, 140–141
    potential benefits of, in mild form, 137,
        139–140
    self-assessment for, 151–152
Invitations, interpersonal, 48–49

Isolation
  defense mechanism of, 234
  trap of, 29–30

J

Jacob, 208, 215
James, William, 253
Jealousy, 10, 177, 179, 208. *See also* Envy
Jesus, death of, 8, 10, 13, 20, 183, 204, 234
Jewish influence on Greek philosophy, 23 n
Job, 25, 136, 143–144
Jonah, 225–226
Joseph, 208
Joseph Conrad: A Biography, 197
Judas Iscariot, 162
Judging, 12, 67

K

King Kong, 16
King Saul, 199

L

Laban, 208
Language, role of, in intimacy, 28–29
Lazarus, 162
Leading, conventional style of, 56–59, 61–62, 64–65, 77–78, 96, 104
Leah, 215
Legalism versus freedom, 11
Lewis, C. S., 84
Life
  meaning and shortness of, 14
  stewardship responsibility for, 6, 48, 204, 221
  worship as a way of, 5–6
Lincoln, Abraham, 254
Little Prince, The, 149
Logos, rationality and, 8
Loneliness
  versus intimacy, 29–30
  trap of isolation and, 29–30
Love
  Avoiders and, 226, 229, 233–234, 236–239
  caring as the core of, 9
  centrality of, in relationships, 84
  Christian, as freeing, 151
  Christian obligation to, 9

Controllers and, 110, 113
costly, 20
Drifters and, 193
duty to reflect and express God's, 20
emotional health and, 21–22
even our enemies, 20
fear versus love, 30
forsaking one's first, 132
Freeloaders and, 156–157, 159, 167–168
holiness and, 19
Humiliators and, 178, 181, 184, 186
Intruders and, 105, 141, 147, 149–151
misdirected toward the world system, 132
moving toward others and, 84
not an invitation to abuse, 1,20
not synonymous with affiliation, 84–85
Scurriers and, 105, 197, 200, 202–203
self-disclosure and, 11
sinners but not sin, 6
spiritual intimacy and God's, 27
tough, 1
turning sour, 250
types of, 84
unceasing, from God, 15, 20, 30, 204
Victimizers and, 218, 220, 222
voluntary nature of, 11
we are partly defined by whom we, 188
  See also Loving
Loving
  God with one's entire being, 1, 6
  other Christians, 19, 48
  our neighbors as ourselves, 1, 6, 9–10, 20, 48, 239
  sometimes difficult to be, 20
  voluntary by nature, 11
  See also Love
LSD, 21

M

Magic, moments of, 2
Malevolent transformation, 238
Maneuvering, recognizing when someone else is, 2
Manipulation
  allowing, not to be confused with love, 1
  Avoiders and detection of, 231
  Delilah and, 208

Drifters and, 128
Intruders and, 146
two senses of the word, 263
Victimizers and, 128, 210, 218
Marriage(s)
    abusive, 131
    Avoiders and, 226, 229–230, 232, 238
    Controllers and, 105–106, 113
    corrosive, 119
    defensive mechanism of displacement
        in, 109
    Drifters and, 125, 130–131
    fellowship and, 26
    frailties inevitable in, 15
    Freeloaders and, 159, 161, 164
    frustration in, 246
    Humiliators and, 177, 180, 182,
        185–186
    individual identities retained in, 157
    Intruders and, 140–141
    psychodynamics in some, 129
    satisfying, 29
    Scurriers and, 182, 193–196, 198–199,
        202
    toxic moments in, 19
    traumatic, 12
    Victimizers and, 209–211, 213–214,
        216–217, 223
Martha, 117, 162
Mary, 117, 162
Meaning of life, 14
Medicalization of behavior, 20–21
Meet the Parents, 105
Mentors, 62, 258
Metamessage, nature of, 150
Meyers, Jeffrey, 197
Mind of Christ, 5, 27
Misery, moments of, 2
Misunderstandings, tragic, 16
Modes, toxic, of relating, 85–88
Moments of magic and misery, 2
Money
    asking for, 97
    Avoiders and, 233
    Controllers and, 107
    Freeloaders and, 159, 162, 164–165,
        167
    giving away, 13
    Humiliators and, 175, 177
    Intruders and, 138, 153
    myths about change and, 246–247
    Scurriers and, 195

stored labor and, 13
Victimizers and, 218, 220
See also Wealth
Moral
    accusations used by Avoiders, 232
    appeals by Freeloaders, 159
    authority, appeal to by Controllers,
        107, 109
    built into existence, 16–17, 25–26
    choices and decisions, 115, 132, 151,
        169, 186–187, 204, 220–221, 239
    debate engaged in by Victimizers, 212
    duty to think, 35
    element in defense of projection, 179
    failings, particular concern of Scurriers,
        192
    guidance in the hands of secular
        professionals, 25–26
    judgments and God's image, 7
    obligation to be courageous, 132
    obligations to others, 241
    progress, not fueled by Humiliators,
        175
    purposes as disguise for aggression in
        Victimizers, 214
    reasoning, role of in everyday behavior,
        48
    responsibility and human freedom, 15
Moralistic rigidity, 16
Moralistic speeches, 109
Morality and psychiatry, fuzzy line
    between, 25–26
Moses, 144
Most powerful word in English, 166, 228
Moving against, 30, 38–39, 60, 85, 95. See
    also Chapters 11–14
Moving away, 30, 38–41, 43–44, 47–50,
    52, 55, 57, 60, 63, 74–75, 85, 95,
    98. See also Chapters 11–14
Moving one-down, 39–41, 43–45, 47,
    49–50, 57, 63, 74, 98. See also
    Chapters 8, 10, 12, 14
Moving one-up, 39–41, 43–44, 47, 49–50,
    52, 55, 57, 59, 71, 74, 84–85, 98.
    See also Chapters 7, 9, 11, 13
Moving toward, 30, 38–41, 43–45, 47–50,
    57, 59, 63, 74–75, 84, 98. See also
    Chapters 7–10
Mutuality
    Controllers and, 114
    Drifters and, 132
    Freeloaders and, 168

Humiliators and, 186
intimacy and, 27, 114, 132, 150, 168, 186
Intruders and, 150

N

Napoleon, 111
Narcissism
  Avoiders and, 233, 238
  can intensify any interpersonal style, 181
  Humiliators and, 180, 185–186
  meaning of, 180–181
Nazis, 13
Neighbor
  definition of, 20
  meeting the needs of our, 9
Nero, Emperor, 25
New life in Christ, 12, 22, 30, 246
Nietzsche, Friedrich, 181
Norman Conquest, 181
Nourishing (wholesome) versus toxic relationships, 18–19
Nurturing, conventional style of, 34, 56–59, 61–62, 64–65, 77–78, 88, 96, 137, 156, 167

O

Obeying and conforming, toxic tactics of, 88, 90–91, 93. See also Chapter 8
Obligations, relational, 9
O'Connor, Carroll, 193
Opposing, conventional style of, 56–62, 64–65, 77–78, 88, 96, 210
Oppression
  allowing, not the same as loving, 1
  Controllers and, 105
  depression resulting from, 202
  Drifters and, 121
  guilt can become, 24–25
  Humiliators as experts at, 173, 182
  legalism as source of, 11
  Scurriers and, 192–193, 198–199, 202
  self, 198
  social censure as source of, 11
Optimism, value of, 254–255
Organizational conflict and Controllers, 111

Other people, sometimes hindrances, 259–260
Overtures, interpersonal, 73

P

Pain, infliction of. See Punishment
Pascal's wager, 14
Passion of Ayn Rand, The, 109
Passive-aggressive behavior, 194
Pathos of life without Christ, 14
Paul, the Apostle, 5–7, 10, 22–24, 30, 67, 109–110, 169, 234, 246
PCP, 21
Peace
  Drifters and, 125, 127
  living at, with others, 52, 262
  Scurriers and, 192, 202
People as spiritual beings, 7
People reading, 29, 46–47, 67, 73, 249
Pepe, Douglas, 260
Perceptions, corrections of by others, 29–30
Personalities, obnoxious, tolerance of, 9
Personality and Interpersonal Behavior, 42
Personality disorders, 21. See also Chapters 7–14
Pessimism, poisonous, 254
Peter, the Apostle, 9, 144, 190
Pharisees, 103, 107, 109, 188
Philistines, 181–182, 199
Philosophy, 14, 23–24, 106, 109
Police officers, arguing with, 48
Postures, interpersonal, behavioral implications of, 40–41
Power
  Avoiders and, 228, 241
  contact control and, 38–39
  Controllers and, 104, 107–108, 110, 112–113
  of different interpersonal postures, 39, 41, 47, 56, 63, 65
  drawing on others', 258
  Drifters and, 119–121, 123, 127–128
  Freeloaders and, 166
  gaining by accepting reality, 257
  Humiliators and, 174, 176–180, 182, 185
  Intruders and, 137, 145–147
  of reframing, 261
  Scurriers and, 194, 196, 203, 206

struggles, 69, 80, 128, 147, 176
   Victimizers and, 217
Power struggles, 69
Predictability
   drive for, destructive potential of, 197,
      259
   normal need for, 48
Priests, secular, psychotherapists as, 25
"Princess and the Pea, The," 176
Principles of Psychology, 253
Prisons as centers of toxicity, 9
Process versus content, 36–37
Projection, defense mechanism of
   accountability and, 256
   Humiliators and, 179
   nature of, 179, 256
   sin and, 179
   Victimizers and, 214
Protecting and providing, conventional
      tactics of, 34, 61, 64–65, 77, 79
Psychiatry
   benefits and limitations of, 24–25
   and morality, fuzzy line between, 25–26
Psychological and biological connections,
      28
Psychological health
   holiness and, 21–22
   traditional definitions of, 20–21
   See also Flexibility
Psychological well-being. See Psychological
      health
Psychology
   destructive as religion, 23–25, 68–69
   Gnosticism and, 24
   helpful but insufficient, 22–23
Psychology, etymology of, 83
Psychopath, 13, 143. See also Sociopaths
Psychotherapists, 21, 25, 41, 135, 222,
      257, 264. See also Counseling;
      Counselors; Psychotherapy
Psychotherapy, 18, 24–25
   benefits and limitations of, 24–25
   See also Counseling; Counselors;
      Psychotherapists
Punishment
   avoidance of, powerful motive for,
      57–58
   Avoiders and, 235, 237–239, 241–242
   Controllers and, 112, 118
   Drifters and fear of, 127
   escape from, powerful motivation to,
      57–58

Humiliators as inflictors of, 184
Intruders capable of inflicting, 138
negative reinforcement different from,
   58
relationship between fear and, 30
Scurriers motivated to avoid or escape,
   193, 197–198, 200, 206
suffered often by seclusive people,
   29–30
value of detecting intent to inflict, 98
Victimizers and, 213–214, 216,
   218–219, 221
Purpose, strategic, meaning of, 53

                        R
Rachel, 215
Rage
   Avoiders and, 232, 241–242
   Drifters and, 129
   Freeloaders and, 160
   Victimizers and, 210, 214, 216, 218,
      221
Rand, Ayn, 109
Rationalization, defense mechanism of,
   212, 256
Reaction formation, defense mechanism of
   Controllers and, 108
   Intruders and, 142
   nature of, 108, 142
   Victimizers and, 215
Reading people, 29, 46–47, 67, 73, 249
Realities versus appearances of behavior,
   46–47
Reasoning, nature of human, 15
Reciprocity, interpersonal, 76
Reductionism, 14, 21–23
Reflexive nature of interpersonal behavior,
   57, 72–73
Reframing, judiciously applying the power
   of, 261
Regret. See Remorse
Reinforcement
   negative, different from punishment,
      58
   positive, 57–58
Relational Dynamics, Inc. (RDI), website
   for, 256
Relational obligations, 9
Relational psychology, fundamental
   insights from, 68–69
Relational sin, 6

Relationships
  bringing order out of chaos in, 34
  God and, fundamental questions about,
    3–4
  not optional, 33
  taxonomy foundational to, 35–36, 38
  theology of, 3–31
Religion
  etymology of, 23
  false, 23–24
  reconnection with God as true, 23
Remorse, 13, 181, 203, 217, 223, 237, 239
Repentance, 22–23, 263
Repression, defense mechanism of
  distinct from denial, 124
  Drifters and, 124
  Freeloaders and, 160
  Intruders and, 142, 148–149
  nature of, 124
  Scurriers and, 195
Requests, interpersonal, 48–49
Resentment
  Avoiders and, 226, 229, 232, 236–237,
    240–241
  compatibility may still breed, 80
  Controllers and, 105, 108, 110, 112
  Drifters and, 122, 129
  forgiveness and, 12
  Freeloaders and, 156, 160
  healing, 263–264
  Humiliators and, 174–175, 181,
    184–185, 188
  Intruders and, 137, 143, 147–148,
    153
  moving one-down and away and, 47
  Scurriers and, 191–192, 194–196, 199,
    207
  from trying to change others, 262
  unresolved, toxic nature of, 260
  Victimizers and, 210, 218, 223
  what, induces in others, 97–98
Responsibility
  for our actions, awesome, 15
  Avoiders and, 231
  Controllers and, 113–114, 116
  Drifters and, 123, 129, 132
  embracing, 252
  Freeloaders and, 156, 158, 162–164
  Humiliators and, 176, 184
  Intruders and, 149
  moral, 14–15
  moving one-up or one-down and, 39
  Scurriers and, 199, 201, 204

  for spiritual and moral guidance, 25
  stewardship, for your life, 6, 48, 204,
    221
  Victimizers and, 218
Retreating, toxic strategy of, 88–92, 94, 96
Reuben, 208
Revelation as God's self–disclosure, 11
Rigidity
  Avoiders and, 228
  can be an interpersonal fingerprint,
    96
  Controllers and, 103, 111, 115
  Drifters and, 123, 129
  examples of interpersonal, 71, 76
  Freeloaders and, 158
  Humiliators and, 181
  Intruders and, 143
  moralistic, 16
  narcissism as intensifying, 181
  psychological wholeness and, 48
  toxicity and, 31, 63, 84, 96
  Victimizers and, 220
  See also flexibility in behavior,
    desirability of
Risk taking
  Drifters and, 122, 126–127
  expression of resentment involves,
    263
  fellowship and, 10
  Freeloaders and, 164, 166
  growing through, 255
  Intruders and justification of, 140
  relationship to Opposing style, 62
  Scurriers and, 200, 206
  Victimizers and, 210, 219, 223
Roman Empire, accomplishments and
    limitations of, 23
Rome, ancient, 5

                    S

Sacrifice, life as holy, 5
Sadducees, 103
Saint-Exupéry, Antoine, 149
Salvation, counterfeit, 23–24
Samson, 208, 215
Samuel, 199
Sapphira, 162
Saul, King, 199
Scars, emotional, 15
Schizophrenia and biology, 21
Scripture, centrality of, 1–2, 6, 23, 33, 68,
    132, 204, 261

Scurriers
     antidotes to adopting the style of,
          205–206
     arrangement sought by, 199–200
     in the Bible, 198–199
     cases illustrative of, 192–193, 195–197
     countermeasures to the maneuvers of,
          206–207
     defense mechanisms of, 193, 195–198
     intimacy in the lives of, 203–204
     life script of, 105, 191–193
     payoffs for, 200
     profile of, 192
     psychology of, 194–198
     responses induced in others by, 192,
          201
     self-presentation and characteristics of,
          192
     spiritual and moral choices relating to,
          204
     typical life history of, 202–203
     what, tend most to avoid, 200–201
     when the arrangement breaks down
          with, 201–202
Scurrying
     justifications offered for, 194
     potential benefits of, in mild form,
          192–194
     self-assessment for, 205
Secrets, 28
Secular priests, psychotherapists as, 25
Security, quest for
     Controllers as satisfying the, 104
     Drifters and, 127
     false, apart from God, 163
     Freeloaders and, 163–164
     powerful motivational value of, 57
     Scurriers and, 196, 198, 200
     Victimizers and, 217
     See also Anxiety; Fear; Insecurity
Selection of interpersonal styles, deter-
     minants of, 58–60
Self, appropriately loving one's, 6, 9, 181
Self-awareness and God's image, 6
Self-destruction, 13, 39, 149
Self-esteem
     Controllers and, 108
     effects of arrogance on, 108
     falsely protecting, 254
     Humiliators and, 174, 179, 186
     misunderstanding the nature of, 23
     Scurriers and, 196, 202–206
     See also Self-respect; Self-worth

Self-insight
     Intruders and, 136, 156
     limitations of, 249
     See also Insight
Selfishness
     antithetical to fellowship
     life in the flesh and, 10
Self-respect
     Drifters and, 123
     Victimizers and, 219
     See also Self-esteem; Self-respect
Self-worth, feelings of
     Humiliators and, 186, 188
     Scurriers and, 197
     See also Self-esteem; Self-respect
Self-disclosure, 9–12, 26, 263
Sensory deprivation experiments as
     metaphor, 28
Seuss, Dr., 112
Sex, can be mechanical and impersonal,
     26
Shadow sides of ourselves and sin, 160,
     216
Shame
     difference between guilt and, 184
     Freeloaders and, 155
     Humiliators and, 184
     Scurriers and, 198
     social nature of, 184
Sin
     appeasing and placating aggressors as,
          204
     awkwardness of talking about, 16
     conscious and unconscious, 22
     fuzzy line between, and sickness, 25–26
     importance of distinguishing from
          sinner, 6
     important to take seriously, 23
     interpersonal, 6, 15–17
     interpersonal behavior and, 16–17
     issue of, always lurking around toxicity,
          25
     lust for power and, 185
     pride and, 188
     projection as no owning up to, 179
     shadow sides of ourselves and, 160,
          216
     sometimes inadvertently treated, 21
     tension between, and holiness, 30
     toxic relationships and, 18
Situational variations in behavior, 45–46
Social value of eight conventional styles,
     60–63

Society
    Avoiders and, 228, 235
    benefits of the eight conventional styles,
        62–63 (*See also* Exhibits)
    Christians to be fully part of, 11
    conflict and, 122
    Controllers and, 108, 139
    division of labor in, 61
    Drifters and, 122
    emergence of psychiatry good for, 20
    Freeloaders and, 158, 164–165
    habits the great flywheel of, 253
    Humiliators and, 174–175, 183
    instant-results nature of, 12
    Intruders and, 139, 147
    leaders and, 63
    men in, and emotional aphasia, 226
    myths about behavior change in, 245
    sin and, 16, 21
    spiritual and moral guidance in, 25–26
    status and rewards in, 111
    style of Competing and the advance of,
        62
    style of Following and, 63
    success and secular, 251
    values of secular, 132
    viable philosophical and religious
        options in, 14
    Victimizers and, 209, 217–218
    wealth in, 107
    withdrawal from, 25
Sociopaths, 145, 162. See also Chapter 13;
    Psychopath
Solomon, 119
Spirit, Holy. See Holy Spirit
Spiritual
    beings, people as, 7
    choices and decisions, 115, 132, 151,
        169, 186–187, 204, 220–221, 239
Sponsors, 62, 258
Stance toward God, the Christian's, 64–65
Stapleton, Jean, 190
Status
    Controllers and, 107, 110–112
    Drifters and, 120, 123
    Humiliators and, 174, 176, 179, 185
    interpersonal postures and, 39, 41, 57
    Intruders and, 147
    quest for, strong motivational value of
        the, 57
    rewards and, in society, 111
    Victimizers and, 215

Stonewalling, conventional style of, 56–59,
    61–62, 64–65, 77–78, 96
Strategic nature of interpersonal behavior,
    56–58
Strategic purpose, meaning of, 53
Strategies
    conventional, summary of, 54–55
    toxic, 88–89, 91
Strategy, interpersonal, nature of, 53–54
Stress and immune system, 28
Strupp, Hans H., 68
Styles
    conventional, summary of, 55–57
    interpersonal, difficult to alter, 68
    toxic, 88–89, 91
Subcultures, embracing of different, 9
Submerging, toxic strategy of, 88–92
Substrategy, interpersonal, definition of,
    56
Suffering
    Avoiders and, 237
    Christ and, 144
    in the Christian life, 8, 13
    Controllers and, 112
    Humiliators and, 178, 181–182
    inevitable in life, 16
    for the Kingdom of God, 221
    from mental disorders, 21, 25
    not necessarily noble, 19, 261
    putting in perspective, 12
    resentment and the infliction of,
        184
    Scurriers and, 105, 183, 191, 194,
        197–200, 202–203, 206
    side-effects of avoidance and, 257
    theological implications of needing to,
        183, 202, 204
    Victimizers and, 210, 213, 215, 218,
        223
Suggestions, interpersonal, 48–49
Suicide. See Self-destruction
Sullivan, Harry Stack, 37, 39, 53, 238
Supercilious, etymology of, 177–178

T

Tactics
    eight conventional styles and
        associated, 60–61
    toxic, 88, 90–91
Taking risks. See Risk taking
Task saturation, 259

Taxonomy of relationships, foundational, 35–36, 38
Technology, 14, 176
Theology of relationships, 3–31
Think, moral duty to, 35
Thinking relationally, training yourself to, 40–41
Thought-forms of the world system, 5
Tough love, 1
Toxic
  modes of relating, 85–88, 91–92. *See also* Chapters 7–14
  strategies, 88–89, 91. *See also* Chapters 7–14
  styles of relating, 88–92, 97. *See also* Chapters 7–14
  tactics of relating, 88, 90–91, 93. *See also* Chapters 7–14
  versus wholesome relationships, 18–19
Toxic and conventional styles, comparison of, 95–96
Toxic modes of relating, 85–88
Toxic strategies, 88–89, 91
Toxic styles, 88–89, 91
Toxic tactics, 88, 90–91
Toxicity
  anxiety resulting from, 19
  basic nature of interpersonal, 18–19, 84
  extreme behavior and, 39, 63
  intensity and, 88, 96, 81
  interpersonal, nature of, 84
  modes of, 85–88, 91–92
  occasional duty to endure, 19
  relational, general nature of, 18–19
  resentment and, 260
  rigidity and, 31, 63, 84, 96
  strategies of, 88–89, 97
  styles of, 88–92, 97
  tactics of, 88, 90–91, 93
  wholesomeness versus, 18–19
Training, interpersonal, occurs continually and automatically, 69–72
Training yourself to think relationally, 40–41
Trap of isolation and loneliness, 29–30
Trusting and supporting, conventional tactics of, 61, 64–65, 79, 88
Truthfulness and Christianity, 209
Twilight Zone, 61

U

Uncertainty
  anxiety resulting from, 19
  Controllers as reducing, 103, 111
  Drifters and, 120, 128
  motive to reduce, powerful, 57
  Victimizers as increasing, 210
Unconscious process
  Avoiders and, 225
  compatibility quests and, 80–81
  conscious versus, 58
  Controllers and, 108
  defensiveness and, 256
  Drifters and, 129
  Humiliators and, 182–183
  insight and, 249
  Intruders and, 141–142
  Scurriers and, 196–198
  sin and, 22
  striving for predictability and, 259
  Victimizers and, 219
Unconscious versus conscious motivation, 58
Unhappiness
  Avoiders and, 232
  Freeloaders and, 161
  nature of, 72
  Scurriers and, 198–199
Utopianism, 14, 249

V

Victimizers
  antidotes to adopting the style of, 222–223
  arrangement sought by, 216–217
  in the Bible, 215–216
  cases illustrative of, 209–213
  countermeasures to the maneuvers of, 223–224
  defense mechanisms of, 212, 214–215
  intimacy in the lives of, 220
  life script of, 209–211
  payoffs for, 217
  profile of, 210
  psychology of, 213–215
  responses induced in others by, 210, 218–219
  self-presentation and characteristics of, 210
  spiritual and moral choices relating to, 220–221
  typical life history of, 219–220

Victimizers, *continued*
    what, tend most to avoid, 217–218
    when the arrangement breaks down
        with, 219
Victimizing
    justifications offered for, 212
    potential benefits of, in mild form,
        210–212
    self-assessment for, 221
Victory, 197

W

Warm Assertion, conventional mode of, 34,
    53–55, 59, 63–65, 73, 77, 85
Warm Subordination, conventional
    mode of, 34, 53–56, 64–65, 73, 77,
    86
Wealth
    dominance and, 107
    Humiliators and, 176–177, 179–180,
        183, 185
    narcissism and, 180
    redistribution of, 14

rich young ruler and, 83
    using lack of, as an excuse, 252
Weeds, interpersonal, 260–261
Whining and appeasing, toxic tactics of,
    90–91, 93, 123. *See also* Chapter 12
Wholesome (nourishing) versus toxic
    relationships, 18–19
Willpower, usually insufficient for change,
    247–248
Winners, fail more than losers, 254
Withdrawing and rebelling, toxic tactics of,
    90–91, 93, 95. *See also* Chapter 14
Words, number of, describing human
    behavior, 38
World system
    misguidedly loving the, 132
    thought-forms of the, 5
World, fallen, 15, 28, 66

Y

Yertle the Turtle, 112
Yielding, conventional style of, 56–59,
    61–62, 64–65, 77–78, 96, 192